Early Praise for

JASMINE *and* FIRE

A *Food & Wine* Reading List Pick
An *Afar* Magazine Summer Reading Pick

"*Jasmine and Fire* takes readers on an unforgettable journey to home, family, and identity. Along the way we're also treated to glorious meals, political analysis, and some stirring reflections on the nature of becoming a global citizen. Salma Abdelnour is a wonderful host to a region that so many readers long to understand and connect with on a newer, more profoundly meaningful level."

—DIANA ABU-JABER, author of
Birds of Paradise and *The Language of Baklava*

"Salma Abdelnour captures the flavors of Beirut—the familiar mixed with the exotic—in her yearlong search to rediscover her culture, with recipes that will let you experience the sublime flavors of Lebanese cooking . . . no matter where you are."

—DAVID LEBOVITZ, author of *The Sweet Life in Paris*

"This is a sweet, heartfelt book by a writer who finds herself both insider and outsider at the same time. Salma Abdelnour beautifully evokes the mood of the city she left as a child and the memories brought back by its wonderful food. A delicious read!"

—MOIRA HODGSON, author of
It Seemed Like a Good Idea at the Time

JASMINE

 *and*

FIRE

A Bittersweet Year in Beirut

SALMA ABDELNOUR

BROADWAY PAPERBACKS
NEW YORK

BROADWAY

A few names and identifying details in this book have been changed to
protect people's privacy, and various episodes have been edited down
for brevity or clarity.

Copyright © 2012 by Salma Abdelnour

Published in the United States by Broadway Paperbacks,
an imprint of the Crown Publishing Group,
a division of Random House, Inc., New York.
www.crownpublishing.com

Broadway Paperbacks and its logo, a letter B bisected on the diagonal,
are trademarks of Random House, Inc.

Library of Congress Cataloging-in-Publication Data
Abdelnour, Salma.
    Jasmine and fire : a bittersweet year in Beirut /
Salma Abdelnour. — 1st ed.
        p. cm.
    1. Abdelnour, Salma. 2. Abdelnour, Salma—Homes and
haunts—Lebanon—Beirut. 3. Lebanese Americans—Lebanon—
Beirut—Biography. 4. Beirut (Lebanon)—Biography. 5. Beirut
(Lebanon)—Description and travel. 6. Beirut (Lebanon)—Social
life and customs. 7. Lebanese Americans—New York (State)—
New York—Biography. 8. Moving, Household. 9. Transnationalism.
10. New York (N.Y.)—Biography. I. Title.
    DS89.B4A23   2011
    956.92'50453092—dc23
    [B]   2011050266

ISBN 978-0-307-88594-4
eISBN 978-0-307-88595-1

Printed in the United States of America

COVER DESIGN BY LAURA KLYNSTRA
COVER PHOTOGRAPH BY ZUBIN SHROFF

10 9 8 7 6 5 4 3 2 1

First Edition

To Jamal, Mariana, and Samir

❂

INTRODUCTION

You can't go back home to your family, back home to your childhood . . . back home to places in the country, back home to the old forms and systems of things which once seemed everlasting but which are changing all the time—back home to the escapes of Time and Memory.

—Thomas Wolfe, *You Can't Go Home Again*

Yes you can.

Or anyway, I did.

Just as everything in my New York life was miraculously clicking all at once, and for the first time ever—work I loved, an apartment I adored, friends I cherished, a romance I'd rekindled—I decided to move back to Beirut. Messed-up, bombed-out, dysfunctional, infuriating, bewitching, baffling, beautiful Beirut. My home. The city I loved deeply, madly, more than any other, and could never manage to shake from my mind.

I'd been longing for Beirut, in a profound and nagging

way, ever since my family escaped when I was in elementary school, in 1981, at the height of the Lebanese civil war. In those years, bombs were ripping through the city day and night, wrecking buildings in our neighborhood, drastically disrupting and destroying lives all around. I'd been living with my parents and little brother in an apartment in Beirut's bohemian Hamra neighborhood, a tangle of lively streets packed with coffee shops, bakeries, bars, eclectic stores, and every kind of restaurant imaginable—sprawling Lebanese cafés, take-out *shawarma* stands, French bistros, Italian pizzerias, American burger joints, even a Swiss fondue place. Our condo building, full of aunts, uncles, and cousins who lived upstairs and downstairs and popped in regularly for spontaneous visits, was a short walk uphill from the beach and steps from a beautifully landscaped university campus. Just down the street was the private elementary school my brother, Samir, and I went to, the International College, a rigorous but relatively liberal establishment where many of our family friends, as well as expat families from around the world, also sent their kids.

I'd been happy at school at the time and had a close crew of coed classmates I looked forward to seeing every day. But like all other schools in Beirut in those years, mine was constantly suspending classes for weeks in a row whenever the bombs fell too close by. On one day I'll never forget, violent skirmishes exploded right outside the school building, and everyone in the classrooms had to run to the hallways to crouch down, away from the windows, until we could be safely evacuated that evening. In those years, the night was usually scarier than the daytime; that's when opposing militias would shell each other from rooftops around the city and often dangerously close to our building. I'd run and hide under my bed, terrified we were going to get blown up, too. "No, no, don't worry," my parents would always say, although I realize now they were just as afraid as I was.

But despite the horrors of life in Lebanon during the war, I remember feeling mostly content, in the way children can be when they don't understand much, and when they're surrounded by friends and family and all kinds of simple pleasures: a slumber party with cousins, a day at the beach during a cease-fire, a pistachio ice cream cone, a weekend playdate with a favorite classmate. The only evidence I have now that the good parts outweighed the bad, to my young mind anyway, is that I refused to leave Lebanon when my parents decided it was time to flee. At least I tried, as best I could, to say, "Nope, we're staying put."

"We're only moving to America for one year," my parents had promised my brother and me—and they believed it at the time, or wanted to.

But we didn't return to Beirut after a year—in fact, we never moved back at all. For a long time after we left, as we made our new home in Texas, I could never quite shake the sense that I'd been torn away against my will. A "Beirut is still home" refrain kept on humming in the back of my head. Year after year after year, there was no off switch in sight.

As time went by, my yearning for Beirut morphed into new shapes. At the beginning it was an aching sense of missing friends and relatives and the city itself, the sights and smells and sounds—the Mediterranean Sea nearby that I could glimpse from my aunt's apartment upstairs, the smell of juicy crisp-skinned chickens grilling on outdoor rotisserie stands in our neighborhood, even the angry Arabic slurs taxi drivers would yell out in traffic jams. Eventually I started sensing that my hunger for the city ran deeper than just the familiar people and sensations I missed. When the political situation started calming down every now and then, by the time I reached middle school and high school, I'd pay occasional summer visits to Beirut, usually with my family, and get to bask in all the sensory pleasures. But those short trips were never enough. They only seemed to reinforce a longing I could no longer quite name.

In the States, as one school year gave way to another and we stayed in Houston, part of me still felt unmoored. I was vexed by how much more self-conscious and shy I felt in my new life than I remembered ever being in Beirut. Bit by bit I overcame some of my shyness, and years later I found myself with a happy and successful journalism career and a thriving social life in New York. But even more than two decades after leaving Lebanon, I couldn't get rid of the quietly nagging sense that I was still the newcomer, a little late to the party—as ridiculous as that seemed after all this time. The feeling would bubble up in small ways. A perceived social slight, or a malicious look from a stranger on the street, or a sense of feeling tongue-tied around new people I'd just met, could take on more meaning than it deserved, reinforcing my insecurity that I was still ultimately an outsider.

I wondered if I was constantly giving off cues that I'm not "one of us," whatever "us" even means in immigrant America. As I hit my twenties and then my thirties, I was surprised to find myself still escaping to Beirut, in my mind, as a safe haven, whenever some outsider anxiety would ripple to the surface again. It was as if Beirut, my own personal Beirut, still waited, ready at any moment to spring up and rescue me, soothe all the persistent insecurities I should have shed by now. After all those years, it was still the only place I could instinctively call my true home.

Beirut wasn't actually my first home. My very first? A hospital in Urbana, Illinois—where, while I was barely a few minutes old on a freezing March night in the Midwest, my parents decided to call me Salma. They named me after my great-aunt Salma, who was one of the most serene people in our angst-ridden family, beloved by everyone for her easygoing approach to life, for warmly welcoming everyone into her world no matter their religion, race, gender, sexual orientation, or political views, and for her live-and-let-live philosophy, not a hugely common or even comprehensible one in 1970s Lebanon. She also chose to never get married, a daring decision, both then and now, in many cultures around the world—and most certainly in Lebanon.

We moved to Beirut shortly after I turned two. My parents, who were both born and raised in Lebanon, had gone to Illinois together for graduate school, and had me, and then managed to time our return to Beirut for the summer of 1974, only months before the start of a civil war that would last fifteen years.

I was barely two years old, and my name, Salma—"peaceful" in Arabic—already sounded like an ironic joke. My last name, Abdelnour, didn't quite hit the nail on the head either. It means "worshipper of the light." The light stands for god. In many Arab names starting with Abdel (worshipper of), the word that comes after it is one of the numerous Arabic synonyms for god: for instance, Karim (generous), Latif (kind), Malik (king). In Lebanon, those names can be Christian or Muslim. My family is mostly Christian—Greek Orthodox on my dad's side, Presbyterian on my mom's—although many of us consider ourselves secular, as

I started to also, as soon as I was old enough to understand what that meant.

My feelings about religion, that it's best enjoyed quietly or ignored completely, are not widely shared in Lebanon and never have been. In the mid-1970s, after we moved from Illinois to Beirut, I was soon enrolled in my school, on a campus that sloped downhill to the Mediterranean coast—its lawns thick with clover and yellow buttercups, or *houmayda* as we called them, edible lemony flowers that my schoolmates and I would munch on while sprawled on the grass at recess, Beirut's downtown skyline in the distance. I started noticing that for many people at school, it seemed to matter a lot whether your family was Christian or Muslim. Kids who were barely old enough to know what religion even was began asking each other "Are you Christian or Muslim?" At the time, I didn't understand why some of my classmates were interrogating one another about this. *Who cares? Can't we just climb the jungle gym and race to the bottom of the hill, all the way down to the edge of the sea?*

I didn't realize it at the time, but my family was ensconced in a utopian little bubble, feeling very much in our element in the religiously mixed sector of Beirut called Ras Beirut. That part of the city, which includes our Hamra neighborhood and a few adjacent districts, is known for its historic commitment to peaceful coexistence among the sects—one of the very few areas in all of Lebanon, as I'd later learn, that had so far managed (and still mostly does) to pull this off.

As the Christian-Muslim tensions started to escalate all over Lebanon in the mid-1970s, my family's and Ras Beirut's ideals came to involve a willful oblivion to the reality that was about to rip our country apart. Our close friends, my parents' and mine, were a mixed group of Protestants and Greek Orthodox and Maronite Catholics and Sunni and Shiite Muslims and Druze, pretty much all of Lebanon's major and minor religious groups— by this point Lebanon had unfortunately lost most of its Jewish population to emigration—and none of us considered our religious identities primary. It was like having brown or blond or red hair. You were born with it, and once you were old enough to care, you could embrace or change or ignore it.

For my parents and our like-minded relatives and family friends, a world in which religious identity was primary and the source of all political and social power was too disturbing to imagine. But that was the world we did in fact live in. And that world was blowing up into a billion blood-drenched shards.

So in the summer before my fourth-grade year, we—my parents and brother and myself—packed up to leave the country. That was by then the sixth year of the conflict, which had started with two explosive incidents among Christians and Muslims in the Beirut suburbs in April 1975 and hemorrhaged into a full-on civil war that killed 150,000 civilians by the time it ended a decade and a half later. But even from the start of the war, Lebanese Christians and Muslims were divided among themselves, too, each sect splintered off into dozens of factions, and each faction with its own armed militia and ideas about how to run Lebanon, as well as its own position on what to do about the Israeli-Palestinian issue that was now Lebanon's problem, too. The Palestinian Liberation Organization, created in the wake of the establishment of Israel in 1948 and the exile of Palestinians into neighboring Arab countries, was by then operating mainly out of Beirut and launching attacks on Israel from Lebanese soil, attacks that were met with extensive military counterattacks from Israel. Syria and the

United States and various Western and Arab powers also had their hands in the mess and were trying either to resolve or to profit from, usually both, the chaos in Lebanon.

Being Abdelnours, aka worshippers of the light, we packed up to flee sunny Beirut for sunny Houston, Texas, another land of hot sweaty summers and piercing sunlight. My father had easily found a job there through his brother, my uncle Kamal, who'd left Lebanon with his wife and kids years before we did and was able to get Dad's work visa and our green cards sorted out quickly. This was well before 9/11. There wasn't as much fuss about Arab immigration in the United States back then.

As I launched into a series of fearsome tantrums in the weeks leading up to our departure, I was too busy sulking about our move to admit to my parents that I was intrigued by the idea, planted in my head by a few of my more pop-culture-savvy Beirut classmates, that in Texas I could maybe discover who shot J.R.—a question that then preoccupied the international audience of the popular TV show *Dallas*. But mostly I felt sorry for myself, having to leave my school friends and cousins and everything I knew behind, even if my parents kept saying it would only be for one year.

Although my family got out of Lebanon in the nick of time, before the situation got even more vicious in the following months and years, a great many families had it much worse than we did: they stayed through the war longer, suffered deaths or terrible injuries or severe depressions or suicides. Our family left Beirut intact and plopped ourselves down in the middle of green suburban Houston to attempt to pick up where we'd left off. My brother, Samir, six at the time and already a dedicated sports lover, transferred his hobby to Houston and became addicted to baseball and

American football; my mother, Mariana, who had left her job at the UN to raise Samir and me, continued for the time being as a stay-at-home mom in Houston; and my father, Jamal, constitutionally mellow—a trait in short supply back in Beirut and among most of our relatives—had been a civil engineer in Lebanon but, in his new incarnation, became a vice president at the Houston branch of an international real estate development firm, working alongside my uncle Kamal.

As for me? Well, the Beirut me that I'd known so far—gregarious around my inseparable group of school friends, and deeply attached to a slew of cousins my age—instantly gave way to the new Houston me: an awkward, out-of-place kid. In Houston I tried, unsuccessfully I imagine, to pass as a normal suburban Texas girl playing kickball in the yard. But I was frustrated by my poor acting skills and subsequent sense of bumbling foreignness. Still, that was as bad as things got for a while.

It took some years before I realized that, no matter how much time kept going by, I could never quite shake the sense that something was off inside. And that, despite my best efforts, I couldn't figure out how to feel at home again anywhere.

But what did *home* mean anyway? What was I looking for, especially as time went on and my life in Beirut disappeared deeper into the past? Was it a less uneasy fit with the world around me? Or some other nebulous feeling I craved but still couldn't name?

Whatever it was, I had a hunch that at "home," I wouldn't always need to explain myself, my name, my culture, my past—even if the questions were often friendly. Or even if no one was asking me to explain anything, I wouldn't be wondering quietly if they looked at me a little differently or suspiciously. I wouldn't always be the one with the mysterious, interesting background.

Interesting could get oppressive, especially when the part of the world I came from remained endlessly complicated and messy, and its people, let's be honest, not always so well loved worldwide.

But another question nagged at me, too: Was I just being a wimp about this outsider business? After all, millions of people on earth have left home, kept a foot in two different cultures, and managed to live their lives well enough, balancing the two halves of their world. No such level-headed solutions for me, apparently. As the years have gone by, I've had trouble switching off a certain split-screen vision: If the United States and Lebanon are two parallel universes, two possible and potentially viable places for me to call home and play out my life in, was I choosing and living in the right one? Even though I'd come a long way by now from the shy new foreign girl hiding in the outfield during kickball games, and had built a compelling life in New York, I couldn't stop wrestling with the questions: Should I stay, or should I try once more to live out my life in Lebanon? Could I, after so many years, ever really go back, ever find "home" there again?

I could name plenty of reasons not to move back. Despite my fond memories, the place I once called home had come to feel increasingly distant over the years, foreign even. I wondered if, since we left, Lebanon had gone through profound changes that I couldn't tap in to just by passing through on my occasional visits. Surely it couldn't be the same place, after the long and punishing war, and after millions of Lebanese had escaped to safer havens all over the world, many thousands returning years later with new ideas and ventures. Obviously I, too, had changed and grown in the decades since I left. And now that I had built momentum in my journalism career in New York, I wasn't sure packing up and leaving was a brilliant idea. Not to mention that Lebanon's political situation had never fully stabilized after the war and was once again looking shaky.

And then there was the small matter of my love life. I'd recently restarted a romance in New York with a guy named Richard, an on-again off-again flame. I couldn't tell if the relationship was going anywhere this time, but I did know I liked him a lot. We'd first met a few summers ago through mutual friends, and I was attracted to him from the start—his warmth and quick wit, his dark blue eyes and floppy brown hair, his hilarious impersonations. He'd pursued me hard when we initially met that summer, then gotten cold feet a few months later. We soon got back together, but I broke things off myself weeks later, convinced he was still just playing around. Fast-forward a few years, and we'd found our way back to dating again, somewhat casually, over the past months, just as my Beirut plans were beginning to take shape. By that point I had already promised myself I'd commit to one exploratory year in Beirut, for starters, and had begun putting the word out for a subletter for my Manhattan apartment.

At one point, I did ponder canceling my Beirut move altogether. The summer weeks before I left New York were turning out to be hauntingly romantic, with lots of beach weekends with Richard, and nights cooking and watching movies, opting to stay in, just the two of us, instead of going out. But conversations about our future would invariably go in circles. Richard seemed sad that I was leaving, but when I'd ask whether he thought our relationship had a shot at surviving, he'd sound confused or defensive. "How should I know! You're the one who's leaving! I don't want you to leave!" A couple of weeks before my move, I asked him, "Should we make a point to stay together when I leave, or just see what happens?" He didn't know. Neither did I, truth be told; our history so far didn't necessarily inspire much confidence. Our relationship would either make it through my Beirut year or it wouldn't. But I did know this at least: my "home" question wasn't going anywhere.

However the Beirut move turned out, I knew I'd miss my New York life, at least at first. The city felt more right to me than anywhere I'd lived or visited since Beirut. I had a solid group of friends there, and I had plans nearly every night of the week. I was always meeting fascinating new people in my work and through friends, and I loved traveling for assignments or working on my freelance writing and editing projects at cafés and libraries all over town. New York's pulsing street life kept me alert, and I never got bored.

But even there, that old feeling of being an outsider would creep in again, sometimes in subtle ways or for trivial-seeming reasons. I sometimes suspected my persistent misfit anxieties were more about being human than about being far from home, whatever home even meant at this point. Still, I couldn't begin to know until I'd tried to answer my own questions. Would Beirut feel easier somehow, more right? In Lebanon, would my anxieties about never being fully an insider, about seeming out of my element, finally vanish, and I'd slide into my surroundings the way a river flows into the ocean? Naturally, fluidly—unquestioned and unquestioning.

"WOW, it's so neat that you're doing this now," an acquaintance I ran into at a party in New York said to me the week before I left. "People usually try moving abroad in their twenties."

"Er, thanks?"

I guess she meant well, but I felt patronized. I inched away from her, but later that night the subject came up again. This time a friend's date drunkenly confessed to me that she still cries over the house in Maine where she spent childhood summers with her grandparents, who'd sold the place years ago.

"That was the only place that ever really felt like home to me. I wanted to be there all the time. Now it's gone."

At other parties that summer, whenever my Beirut plan came up in conversation, people would chime in with stories about a long-abandoned city they still longed for, or a beloved house they'd lost, or a onetime vacation to a place that had unexpectedly felt like home in a way that caught them by surprise.

As I got ready to leave for Beirut, I tried to prepare myself to be sorely disappointed. I kept thinking about how the late Palestinian intellectual and Columbia University literature professor Edward Said, who was married to my mom's first cousin Mariam Cortas—and whose work I profoundly respect—had resigned himself to always feeling exiled. He'd grown up with Palestinian parents who'd lost their home in Jerusalem and had shuttled the family between Egypt and Lebanon, before sending the young Edward to boarding school in the States. Before Said passed away in 2003, he published a memoir, *Out of Place*, where he concluded, "I'm so resolutely against having this tremendous sense of where you belong. It's overrated."

That may be so, but it sounded to me, with all due respect, like sour grapes; since you don't quite know where you belong, you decide belonging is overrated. I wasn't ready to trash the whole concept yet. Or before I could reject the idea of belonging, which sounded to me like another way of saying "home," I needed to see if I could find home again, and feel at peace—see if I could finally, you might say, live up to my name.

Of course, it would be ironic if it turned out my true home was still Beirut—arguably the least peaceful place on earth.

AUGUST

I'm sitting on my suitcase, trying to force it shut so I can zip it; I leave for Beirut later today, and right now I'm grateful for these distracting last-minute tasks. If I keep dwelling on my decision too much, I'm afraid I'll chicken out and call off the car service to the airport. But as drastic as the big move feels to me right now, in my last hours in New York, I'm reminding myself that it's not such a crazy idea, at least from a logistical standpoint. It shouldn't really affect my work too much: I've been a freelance writer and editor for a couple of years now, having decided to quit corporate magazine life after nearly a decade and a half in the industry, to make time for well-paying freelance projects I'd been offered, and to be able to travel for long stretches without giving up a paycheck.

I could do the vast majority of assignments from Beirut just as easily as from New York. And at least I don't have to worry about
finding a place to live, since my parents have held on to our Beirut
apartment all these years, although they've continued living most
of the year in Houston.

Though two of the normally pain-in-the-butt logistics of
a move—the job, the house—are thankfully not an issue, the
should-I-shouldn't-I's are still running through my head, even
now at the last minute. For weeks I've been rehearsing every scenario that might play out in Beirut, knowing I'm probably leaving
out all the actual, unpredictable scenarios that will in fact unfold.
I've been lying in bed for hours night after night, rocked by waves
of insomnia and sadness and excitement and fear.

But there's no more time to fret. The subletter for my New
York apartment moves in tonight, and I still need to finish packing
and speed out the door. It's early morning, and Richard has just
woken up; he stayed over last night to say goodbye. But something ominous is already happening on my last day in New York:
right now there's no running water in my apartment or, it turns
out, in the entire building. Richard and I both need to shower, but
all the faucets in my apartment are bone dry.

Having the water in my modern downtown Manhattan.build-
ing vanish is just too fitting for a morning when I'm leaving for
Beirut, land of constant electrical and water-pipe breakdowns.
This must be a giant cosmic joke, or maybe someone-up-there is
gently easing me into Beirut life before I even arrive. But humor
aside, this sucks. I can't go on two back-to-back international
flights, a twenty-hour journey in total, without a shower. I go into
the bathroom to try again, and water does start to trickle out this
time—a freezing, arctic drizzle. Still not a drop of hot water.

No way can I walk into an ice-cold shower on a morning when I'm already a fragile mess. Last night Richard and I had both cried, held each other tight, fretted, and said I love you for only the second time; the first time was last weekend, when he'd whispered it to me as we lay side by side in the guest room of a friend's beach house, realizing we only had one more week together. Before finally falling asleep last night, we decided to try to make this morning like any other, just so we could get through it. We agreed to stay in close touch when I got to Beirut, and then see what happened as the months went by. We'd try to make the best of the situation and see where life led us as the year unfolded. Not the most comforting thought perhaps, but at least not apocalyptic.

Of course, pretending this is just a normal morning—him heading to his teaching job, me to the airport as if I were only off on a short travel-story assignment—was a preposterous idea to begin with. The only way for me to make it through the morning and get myself off to the airport without dissolving again is to remember that I'm planning to come back for a week sometime this fall, to pack another suitcase or two with my winter clothes and boots and various things I couldn't fit, thanks to my airline's luggage limit; to make sure my subletter isn't wrecking my apartment; and, if our spastic relationship survives until then, to see Richard. I'm wondering if he'll still want to see me. But the minutes are ticking by now, and I need to keep my focus on two things: getting ready, and making my flight.

I turn on the faucet again, daring to hope, but no; I flinch at the freezing splash, and . . . we both start laughing. Absurdity, slapstick, a dose of silliness. I need this right now.

Richard clenches his teeth and braves a cold shower, then gets dressed, and we say goodbye, both of us still giggling about the water, kissing, hugging quickly but trying not to linger.

How can I possibly leave? And how can I not leave now, after I've told everyone I'm going? Maybe I just want to hold Richard for hours and order pizza and stay here, with him, and with my New York life just the way it is, forever. Or maybe I'm ready to take on this adventure at last. I guess if Richard and I are meant to make it through it all, we will. I'm all over the place, everywhere. Excited, wrecked. Time to finish getting ready, zip up the bags, lock my apartment, and go.

In the cab to the airport, I'm trying to stay as stoic as possible as I watch Manhattan's postcard skyline, only half visible on this foggy morning, disappear behind me and Brooklyn's tenements and rows of ethnic grocers and delis flick by on the Williamsburg Bridge. These workaday scenes, so banal I rarely even register them anymore, suddenly seem poignant as the taxi speeds me away, the colors of store awnings and sanitation workers' uniforms and street vendor trucks standing out sharply now against the gray sky.

Soon I'm waiting at the departure gate at JFK, leafing through a celebrity gossip magazine I find on a chair and trying to think fluffy thoughts: Is Jennifer Aniston pregnant, for real this time? Didn't I see this same headline splashed on every gossip magazine a year ago, two years ago? Seems like yesterday. So a year is nothing, then! Right? . . .

I board my flight, spilling coffee on myself as I try to jam my carry-on into the overhead compartment while juggling a nonfat latte in the other hand. The effects of the gossip mag are wearing off quickly. No, a year is definitely not nothing.

I decide to let myself cry the whole flight long if I need to. Or ideally, I'll be tough and stone-cold determined if I can manage it. Or I'll slip into one of my Zen, play-it-as-it-lays modes, the emotional holy grail, available to me only in rare flashes throughout my life. All through the first eight-hour flight, and the two-hour layover in Rome, and the connecting five-hour flight to Beirut, I shuffle clumsily between the three states. I can't fall asleep even though, incredibly, there's no screaming baby and no turbulence on either flight.

All in all, my trip, including the connection in the normally maddening Rome airport, is one of the smoothest journeys I've ever had, objectively speaking. My luggage makes the transfer from Rome to Beirut despite the tight layover: unbelievable. Even the customs and immigration lines at the Beirut airport go fast. I notice for the first time, as I walk through that legendary airport—wrecked by bombs again and again before, during, and after the civil war—that it's been spiffed up recently into a gleaming twenty-first-century international hub and now seems to run more smoothly than JFK; not saying much, but impressive for a war-ravaged country with a less-than-stellar record for bureaucratic efficiency.

My luggage, despite the uneventful journey, arrives in better shape than I do. By the time I step off the plane, I'm zonked from all the emotional turbulence, and just dead tired. My cousin Josette and aunt Marcelle are picking me up at the airport on this hot August afternoon to take me to my family's old apartment.

As I walk out of the airport terminal onto the sidewalk, breaking a sweat in the late-afternoon heat, my cousin Josette, a stunning and trim brunette in her forties, sees me and calls out my name. She's always been one of my favorite relatives, warm but bitingly witty, a creative and successful interior designer who never married. I've often thought of her as exhibit A in the "see, it's okay not to marry" campaign I'm forever waging silently against my relatives and against an imaginary Lebanese chorus, or maybe just against myself. My paternal aunt Marcelle, Josette's mom, shy and soft-spoken, widowed when her husband died young of a heart attack during the war, is here, too, her chin-length dark hair neatly groomed, her dark purple skirt suit giving her olive skin a warm glow. We pile my bags into Josette's trunk and drive off to my old family apartment in Hamra, part of the hilly Ras Beirut area—the name means "head of Beirut"—on the city's west side.

Yesterday I was walking around Nolita, the trendy Manhattan neighborhood next to Little Italy where I moved in the late 1990s while it was still a little rough around the edges. I'd spent the afternoon gazing long and hard at the sights I've passed daily for years with barely a glance, the tiny but adventurously stylish clothing and shoe boutiques, the crowded bistros and umbrella-terraced cafés, the elderly Italian men in their white T-shirts sitting on the creaky fire-escape balconies of old brick buildings, the clumps of hipsters and curious tourists milling around Café Habana on a busy corner of Elizabeth Street, the slow-strolling pedestrians on their cell phones, the old Italian meat and cheese delis—taking in all the details, a zoomed-in snapshot uploaded straight to my brain, to flash back to in moments of deep New York nostalgia if they hit me hard in Beirut.

Today, a Monday afternoon in August, here I am arriving in Beirut on a humid hundred-degree day. The streets from the airport to Hamra are as chaotic as ever, cars and motorbikes going any which way: zooming in the wrong direction down one-way streets, cutting corners on the sidewalks, U-turning in the middle of traffic. In some ways, the city never seems to change, even as it's constantly changing: a schizo mix of glossy new high-rise condo towers, side by side with nineteenth-century arch-windowed stone houses with graceful balconies draped in geraniums and fragrant jasmine and gardenia, and bombed-out shells of old houses and hotels destroyed in the war, all lined up along the narrow winding streets flanked by pink bougainvillea bushes and bright green Sukleen dumpsters, the neighborhoods ringed by multilane autostradas wrapping around and through the city, and everywhere brand-new Ferraris and SUVs, and beat-up 1970s Mercedes and Peugeots, and street vendors pushing wheelbarrows through the traffic, and young messenger boys on mopeds riding up on the sidewalks. Honking and yelling from car windows everywhere, the mournful and sweet ballads of the singer Fairuz, the iconic voice of Lebanon, competing with Method Man thumping out heavy hip-hop jams from the next car over. Running alongside all this daily mayhem, and curving around the Beirut coastline on the city's north and west sides: the glittering bright blue Mediterranean.

The Corniche, the wide and busy promenade along the waterfront, looks out onto the magical sea. Now, in August, women in string bikinis are lounging at luxurious beach clubs just steps below the Corniche, while others wear full head-to-toe *hijabs* and stroll along the sidewalk, jockeying for space with hell-on-wheels skater dudes and spandex-wearing cyclists and miniskirted young women and elderly street vendors selling sesame bread and fresh-squeezed pomegranate juice while, down on the rocky shore, the Mediterranean waves roll and splash.

That sea has, for centuries, brought so much destruction to Beirut, from the ships bearing invaders and their weapons—the

Romans, the Egyptians, the Turks—centuries and millennia ago, to the A.D.-sixth-century tidal wave that wrecked the city, all the way up to the Israeli invasions of recent decades. And through it all, those salty blue waters and sun-drenched beaches have also brought so much pleasure and washed away so much pain.

Beirut is rushing back fast and strong now, as it always has when I've come back to visit. On its ruthless streets, now as ever before, drivers deal with the inadequate traffic lights by cutting each other off, and anyone operating any kind of vehicle needs to be instantly decisive and aggressive and defensive, all at the same time. There's no time to think and wonder when or if to turn. You have to make a quick decision and run with it, or end up waiting at the same intersection for six hours, maybe six weeks. On the way to the apartment, my dear cousin Josette plows through traffic alertly and carefully but with a fierce determination and flips the facial equivalent of the finger to any driver who assumes she'll play doormat. Along the way she tells me about the ever-rising number of people killed in traffic accidents so far this summer, as she slams the brake and shakes her head at a swerving moron in the oncoming lane, her blond highlights and gold hoop earrings catching the last rays of sunlight.

We're approaching my old neighborhood now, and minutes later we pull into Hamra Street, one of the main arteries of west Beirut, with all its retail and pedestrian hustle-bustle. As we line up in the bumper-to-bumper traffic, I look out at the strings of shops, the brand-new H&M alongside a few faded clothing boutiques displaying merchandise surely hanging there since the early 1980s, and the two-story Starbucks, and near it a couple of juice stands I remember from my childhood, and then a few feet away the wonderfully well-stocked Antoine bookstore, happily still there. Finally we hang a right onto Jeanne D'Arc, my street, my home way back in 1981, and again now.

The street runs, tight and car-jammed, past a flower shop and a few grocery and stationery stores to the edge of the lush green American University of Beirut campus, a few short blocks down a gently sloping hill. We circle around the block five times looking for parking and finally find a spot near the apartment, which is on the fourth floor of a white-stucco, eight-story building that my great-uncle Bahij Makdisi, a prominent Beirut engineer, built in the 1950s.

My aunt Marcelle keeps a set of keys that my parents gave her to our Beirut apartment, and when no one is here, she pops in and checks on it every month or so. It's not a huge place: just a narrow entryway as you walk in, opening out into a dining room and two adjoining living rooms forming an L-shape, with a baby grand piano in the corner and a balcony flanking each of the living rooms; in the back of the apartment are three bedrooms, and down a short corridor leading off the dining room is a sunny kitchen. It's a comfortable, modestly proportioned apartment for a family of four. But Marcelle and Josette, who live a half-hour drive away in east Beirut, supervise the place the way diligent, wary caretakers would look out for a sprawling estate— even though other relatives live in the building and there's a concierge on-site. Today Marcelle has stocked the kitchen with tons of food for me, lest I starve to death immediately on arriving in Beirut.

"Auntie, what's all this?" I ask her in Arabic, glad at the chance to practice my language skills. I'm still fluent but a little creaky, and although my aunt understands English, I want to get into an Arabic habit from the get-go.

"I thought you might like to have some chicken and rice after your long trip," she begins, in an accent that mixes Beiruti Arabic with twinges of the mountain accent of Aley, the town where she and my dad, her brother, grew up. "There's some tabbouleh, too. And just a few different kinds of cheese. I threw in some fruits and vegetables also. Some bags of fresh bread. I think I put some yogurt and mortadella in there, too. Cookies also. Just a few things you might like to snack on."

Her worries are, particularly in Beirut, absurd. The apartment is in the middle of the thumping Hamra district, packed as ever with countless restaurants, cafés, and late-night street food stops. You could easily fill up, at any hour of the day or night here, on just a dollar or two, even if the chicest clothes and shoes and hotels and restaurants in Beirut will cost you more than they do in New York. But I'm not complaining about finding shelves and shelves of food in my fridge and pantry tonight. Fantastic luck to have such sweet, perpetually worried relatives.

Along with the flashing images that make up my mental representation of Beirut, as it looked in the 1970s and early 1980s and as it looks in many ways even now—the wide and crowded Corniche overlooking the Mediterranean, the crumbling war ruins all over the city, the shiny high-rises, the tangled intersections, and everywhere the jasmine bushes and dark pink bougainvilleas—my favorite Lebanese foods also rush like flashcards through my brain. The first thing I've always done, just before a visit to Beirut in summers past, or a visit to any city for that matter, is to list all the foods I'm determined to eat while I'm there, even if it means doubling up on lunches or dinners when time is tight. Now that I've managed to parlay this lifelong pathology into a career as a food and travel writer, my whims have taken on the urgency of deadline assignments, even if they're really just self-indulgent missions I've dreamed up for myself—partly for sheer pleasure, partly for education, and partly as an excuse to disappear for hours on rambling adventures.

But my fridge is so full right now, there's no room even for the big bottle of water I've been dragging with me since Rome, let alone for any immediate food-gathering I might do on my own tonight. I spot the classic Lebanese dish of *rizz w'djej*—strips of tender chicken over rice studded with golden raisins and pine nuts—along with the creamy and thick yogurt cheese known as *labneh,* plus a plate of dandelion greens called *hindbeh* sautéed with garlic and topped with thin strips of sweet fried onion, and a basket of fresh Arabic bread, and a bowl of bright-green lemony tabbouleh garnished with small lettuce leaves—all foods I love, and enough to feed me for days. Since it's nearly dinnertime now, I convince Josette and Marcelle to stay and eat with me, and we take out the chicken and rice to heat on the stove, as well as the tabbouleh and bread. I'm too wiped out and emotionally shell-shocked to make much conversation, but they tell me how happy they are that I'm here, and this time not just for a quick flyby vacation. We exchange family gossip and tsk-tsk about the once-again-grim political situation.

"War is like salt and pepper here," Josette says to me, shaking her head and scooping up a mouthful of tabbouleh with a lettuce leaf.

At the moment, the perpetual standoff between the Hezbollah party and Lebanon's southern neighbor, Israel, is heating up again, in part over a UN special tribunal investigating the assassination

of former Lebanese prime minister Rafik Hariri and other prominent politicians and journalists in 2005. The tribunal is rumored
to be about to implicate members of Hezbollah in the killings, and
Hezbollah is blaming Israel for collusion. In the past few weeks
there have been skirmishes between Hezbollah and the Israeli military along Lebanon's southern border. Other long-running political tensions are brewing around Beirut. Last week a fight over a
parking space among a group of Sunni and Shiite men in a Beirut
suburb led to a shoot-out that left several civilians dead. In Beirut,
seemingly small-scale scuffles like this have, in tense times, triggered longer outbreaks of violence and even war. Some are saying
this parking space incident is an omen of a bigger sectarian war, yet
another one, to come.

In a way, these worries are like warnings about The Big One,
the huge earthquake that will allegedly hit California this century.
It will happen, seismologists keep saying. The question is when.
Now? Maybe. Maybe not for a long while. But it's bound to happen eventually.

After Josette and Marcelle leave, I discover there's no wi-fi
signal in the apartment tonight, so I walk around the corner to a
smoky Internet café to send Richard an e-mail, letting him know
I've arrived safely. There's an e-mail from him waiting in my inbox,
saying how much he already misses me. Reading his note makes
me swallow my stomach and tighten the small muscles around my
mouth. I can't cry in here, not within sight of the chain-smoking
cashier and the teenagers playing video games at terminals next to
me. I e-mail him back—*I'm so tired, I miss you so much, more news
tomorrow*—and I head back to an empty apartment. Unlocking the
door and walking into the dark, quiet space, this time without family around, is hard. Not just hard: it's been a long time since I've felt

this disoriented and down. My head is pounding from jet lag, and everything in me aches, from my feet to my neck to my heart to the inside of my brain.

I allow just one *what the fuck am I doing here?* self-laceration tonight, as I'm opening my suitcase and taking out a nightshirt to sleep in.

The regrets come crashing in: *What am I doing? I'm leaving behind my close friends, and a New York life I love, and a relationship that might have a future, and I'm turning my entire reality upside down for—what? To relive my childhood, to recapture a life that was interrupted so long ago? Shouldn't my childhood be over already, damn it? Beirut was just an early, long-gone chapter of my life. The New York life I've worked so hard to build is the now, the present, the reality. Isn't it?*

But if that's true, then why is my relationship with Beirut, which sometimes feels like yet another one of the volatile on-again off-again romances in my life, still unresolved? Why do I crave a final reckoning with this place?

I need to do this, I remind myself, and I need to do it now. Before I make any firmer commitments in New York, or to Richard if we make it that far, and before I potentially have kids (I'm thirty-eight, so I'm not breaking any speed records on that front), I need to make sure I'm living in the right place and that my head, on this one issue anyway, is straight.

Despite my smooth journey from New York, and a loving cousin and aunt who filled my fridge and drove me home from the airport and kept me company over dinner, my first night in Beirut sucks. I wake up at five o'clock to the sound of water crashing down on my dresser. It's cold water from the air-conditioning system backing up through the pipes into my bedroom—a problem my mother had warned me about. Before I went to bed, I was supposed to check on a pipe on the balcony and make sure it wasn't dislodged, so I'd avoid a middle-of-the-night leak. But I'd forgotten.

I'd also forgotten that in this building, as in pretty much every building in Beirut that I know of, the basic utilities are always breaking down. When I'd had no water in my New York apartment the morning I left, that was a fluke. Here? Just another day in Beirut. The electricity goes out for a few hours every single day across the city, early morning or midday or evening, depending on what neighborhood you're in. There's frequently no Internet signal, and often it's excruciatingly slow. On past visits to Beirut, the elevator in our building has broken down. Now the latest meltdown is happening just inches from my bed. My new digital video camera happens to be sitting directly under the leak from the air-conditioner—but is thankfully still in its case.

Lebanon has had a major drought this summer, but in my apartment there's water all right, too much water at the moment, and it's splashing cold and hard into my bedroom. A slapstick scene, an *I Love Lucy* episode, but I'm not in the mood to find it funny. After I go out onto the balcony to adjust the pipe, I can't fall back asleep. I'm exhausted and strung out on travel and on ninety-two different emotions, desperately missing New York and feeling my childhood memories rushing back here in my old bedroom. I'm hearing all the old familiar Beirut street noises, the car horns and motorcycle engines and the sidewalk chitchat at all hours, the middle-of-the-night muezzin's call to prayer from the mosque nearby, a baby crying in a building across the street. A rooster crows and reminds me of the one that used to live on a rooftop on our street during the war and would crow every morning at four. This rooster I'm hearing tonight is farther away, but not far enough. I sit in bed as the hour turns six, then seven, and listen to cars start their compulsive honking on the already trafficky streets below, and hear shopkeepers clanking open their aluminum shutters.

I'm hungry again, exhausted, sleepless, and sad, and I need serious comfort food. A little after seven, I walk out in search of the breakfast I'm craving, a *man'ouche*. I find it at a tiny old bakery around the corner from my building. This is the seminal Beirut breakfast: doughy flatbread smeared with olive oil and *zaatar*—a spice mix of sumac, thyme, and sesame seeds—and served hot, straight from the oven. I like mine slathered with labneh, the creamy yogurt cheese. My head is a mess, but my mouth, my eyes, my stomach, they're really enjoying this man'ouche, this warm, life-giving morning bread. I could eat this every single day, forever. No body-sculpting or health expert would ever advise such a thing, and I don't care—well, maybe just a little, but definitely not today.

After going back to bed until noon post-man'ouche, but failing to make up for the night's insomnia, I take a long hot shower and decide to spend my first day exploring a little bit instead of napping and crying alone in the apartment, a powerful temptation. I set out on a stroll around the Hamra neighborhood, to get my bearings again, and as I take tentative steps down forgotten blocks and get a little lost, I'm sure I look like a clueless tourist despite my Lebanese olive skin, dark-brown eyes, and long brown hair. I walk along a half-dozen of the crammed side streets shooting off from the main Hamra Street drag, poke into bookstores and record shops and clothing stores old and new, too zoned out to pay much attention to the merchandise as I spacily pick things up and put them back down, just to feel my body moving, feel myself somehow interacting with city life, even if I'll need at least a half-night's sleep, after all the travel, to function at a minimal level.

On my way back to the apartment, I reintroduce myself to the aging grocer and his wife who own the small, cluttered food shop on the ground floor of my building, and to the hunched man who has run the stationery store down the street since my mom was a teenager, and to the tall white-haired man, reportedly a star of Egyptian films in his youth, who opened a flower shop across the street some decades ago. I muster enough pep for a few sputterings of "Hi! I'm back to live here now. It's been so long, I know. How are things?" They're all surprised I'm back. Life in Lebanon is not easy; why would I leave America? But they all greet me warmly, give me a cheek kiss or an affectionate pat on the back. *"Ahla w' sahla!"* Welcome back!

Not much accomplished in one day, but I'm already sapped and it's only midafternoon. I return to the apartment and field some checking-in phone calls from Josette and from my aunt Nouhad upstairs. She passes by later in the day to sit with me a bit and welcome me back to Beirut and to the building, and smiles when she sees I look drained.

"We'll get together and catch up properly this week, whenever you like. And just come by or call anytime. So wonderful having you here." Nouhad hugs me, her pixie-short hair brushing my cheek.

The leftovers from last night are even more welcome right now, and after heating up some dinner, I climb into bed with a copy of Alain de Botton's tongue-in-cheek self-help book *How Proust Can Change Your Life*, based loosely on the life and writings of Marcel Proust. Each of the five times I've read the slim little volume, I've felt I'd stumbled into the best head-straightening drug.

I flip to the chapter titled "How to Suffer Successfully":

Sensitive to any disruption of routine or habit, Proust suffers from homesickness and fears that every journey will kill him. He explains that in the first few days in a new place, he is as unhappy as certain animals when night comes (it is not clear which animals he has in mind) . . . Proust preferred to spend most of his time in bed. He turned it into his desk and office. Did it provide a defense against the cruel world outside? "When one is sad, it is lovely to lie in the warmth of one's bed, and there, with all effort and struggle at an end, even perhaps with one's head under the blankets, surrender completely to wailing, like branches in an autumn wind."

But there's a helpful reminder lurking in all the self-pity. "Proust's suggestion," writes de Botton, "is that we become properly inquisitive only when distressed." Dubiously uplifting, but somehow enough to slide me into a deep sleep. Finally.

The following few days are spent walking along the Hamra streets again, lolling around in bookstores, browsing through Lebanese histories and novels, stocking up on groceries: soft and salty *halloum* cheese, paper-thin bread called *khibz markouk*, deliciously juicy lopsided tomatoes, sweet cucumberlike summer vegetables called *me'te*. I take naps, fight the blues, try to pull myself together by smiling for no reason—a trick I once read about in a newspaper mental health column—and answer more phone calls from aunts, uncles, cousins, and family friends. "So you're here! How's it going so far?" "It's so nice to have you in Beirut." "Will you come to lunch on Sunday?" "Are you free for dinner on Tuesday?" "Do you have everything you need at home?" "Will you promise to call anytime you need anything?"

Having so much family around, scores of relatives on both sides who either never left Lebanon or moved back after the war, makes me feel instantly embraced in a way I'd forgotten about. How strange to suddenly be surrounded by people who love you for no other reason than that you're Salma, their niece or cousin, or the daughter of their old friends. But at the moment, I'm too overwhelmed to sound upbeat on the phone, and I'm hoping they don't hear the sadness in my voice.

In my first couple of weeks, I'm also trying out different cafés every day, hoping to find the perfect environment where I can settle in for hours and work on the freelance editing and writing assignments I brought with me from the States. I have four long-term projects I'm working on right now, and the income from those, plus my free rent in Beirut, means I can get by well enough if not lavishly. This week I have to finish editing some content for a corporate website, and I have to turn in a column I write regularly for a travel magazine, where I interview chefs about their favorite restaurants around the world. As a freelancer, I can technically work from anywhere on the planet. In practice, it's a little trickier to find a spot where you can work efficiently, avoid procrastinating, and most of all: breathe. Every place I try so far is too smoky—Lebanon has been slow to see the charms of indoor-smoking laws—or else it's too sterile, too chainy, or too loud.

Socially, I'm off to an even slower start. Since I got here, I've been staring guiltily at a list of people I need to call: relatives I haven't talked to yet, a couple of old Beirut school friends I'm occasionally in touch with by e-mail, friends of friends who happen to be in Beirut right now, sources to meet for possible food or travel magazine assignments. But between my work deadlines and my general sense of listlessness—I'm lonely for my New York friends and for Richard, and I don't have much of a life or routine to speak of yet in Beirut—I haven't mustered the energy to pick up the phone much. A catch-22.

One blue afternoon—clear sky outside, stubborn blues in my head—my aunt Zelfa calls. She lives in London, but this week she's passing through Beirut with her husband, Randal, her father, Cecil, and her daughter and son, Soumaya and Skandar, the latter better known as Skandar Keynes, the teen heartthrob who played Edmund in the *Narnia* films.

I'm looking forward to seeing them, my witty and tirelessly well-traveled British relatives. It's been a few years since I last saw Skandar, when Zelfa invited me to hang out on the red carpet at the New York City premiere of *The Lion, the Witch, and the Wardrobe*. (I'd mostly gawked at Tilda Swinton and was, of course, utterly ignored by the photographers.) Skandar, a serious-minded university student back in England, is also the one person in our family to have somehow stumbled into Hollywood fame, and he's barely in his twenties.

For the most part, the rest of my clan has never been prone to the glamorous life or been exceptionally good at making money. But a few people in my family are prominent in their fields. Besides Edward Said and the Keynses—Randal, an author, is a descendant of both Charles Darwin and John Maynard Keynes—there's the late, renowned Oxford historian Albert Hourani, my mother's uncle. He was the author of a number of scholarly works including *History of the Arab Peoples*, a serendipitous bestseller since it happened to be released just as the first Iraq War kicked off in 1990. A handful of business-savvy, charismatic relatives, both here and abroad, run the international food-production companies Cortas and Clic, which may be where I got the food gene. And a number of uncles, aunts, and cousins lead low-key lives but are talented historians, political scientists, mathematicians, physicists, and doctors. Many are based in Europe or the States, although a few in my generation have returned to Beirut to raise their kids and pursue their careers in Lebanon.

As we chat on the phone, Zelfa asks me to drop by the apartment where she and her family are staying on their Beirut visit. I walk over to catch up with them over tea. They want to know how I'm holding up so far, and I tell them about my somewhat rocky first couple of weeks in Beirut. Skandar tells me about his stint filming another *Narnia* sequel on Australia's Gold Coast. An hour later his sister, Soumaya, restless with the whole parent-sibling scene, asks me to walk off with her to a café to play backgammon. I've only played backgammon, a staple of old-man village life in Lebanon, once in my life. She's dying for a game. I'm not sure why a recent Cambridge graduate with a posh British accent and a taste for trendy clothes is so addicted to backgammon, but I learn that her grandfather taught her to play. She ends up playing both her and my sides of the board, after we find one on a shelf at a café nearby. I haven't spent this much time with her since she was much younger, but I already love her sharp wit and glowing smile, peeking out from under a mass of curly brown hair. Alas, she's headed back to England in a few days.

Spending that time with Soumaya, even just a couple of hours fumbling through a backgammon game and taking a stroll afterward, has an unexpected effect on me. Soumaya spent the entire summer living in Beirut and studying Arabic, and she got to know some great little hangouts around Hamra. One is the café where we'd played backgammon, a cozy little spot with fragrant coffee and classic Arabic music on the sound system, and I'm eager to try it out as another of my home offices. Another is a well-stocked DVD shop she pointed to as we passed by. And one is a small takeout restaurant and butcher shop called Cheikha, where we'd stopped after backgammon to pick up shawarma sandwiches: warm, packed with freshly rotisseried strips of pink lamb, and oozing with tartar sauce. I have a feeling I'll be coming back to all of these places. As I fall asleep that night, stuffed with shawarma and feeling happy about the spontaneous hangout session with my relatives and especially Soumaya, I realize that I'd been feeling like a tourist here in these past weeks, but suddenly I feel a little less so. Bit by bit, I'm starting to acclimate, to feel out a rhythm and build a repertoire—crucial in any city if it's ever going to feel like home.

This is the hottest August in anyone's memory, and the city is a sweatbox. But I'm losing myself for hours at a time in air-conditioned cafés, in a fog of deadline work. In between I've been accepting more lunch and dinner invitations from my relatives, the only real social life I've mustered so far, but it's a start.

One Sunday afternoon, my dad's cousin Laure, a gossipy and affectionate woman who always looks put-together in her silk blouses and knee-length skirts, invites me to lunch at a new restaurant called Babel in the posh Christian suburb of Dbayeh. We try out some of the menu's weird but oddly compelling spins on Lebanese food: sushi-shaped pieces of *kibbeh nayyeh*—a Lebanese lamb tartare—here rolled in sesame seeds and topped with pine nuts. I'd rather eat straight-up kibbeh nayyeh, a mound of soft minced lamb topped with fruity olive oil and scooped up with fresh pita. But this tweaked version is admittedly tasty. As we eat, we watch a huge table of overdressed, Botoxed women and cigar-smoking men next to us throw a lavish baptism feast for their baby daughter. This particular slice of Beirut, aggressively cushy and willfully insular, disengaged from reality—if I may jump to conclusions about these total strangers here at the restaurant—has always made me feel I've landed on a low-oxygen planet far away. Laure whispers to me in Arabic about one woman's revealing, architecturally complicated dress.

"*Shoo labsi hay?*" What is she wearing?

"I'm not sure. A dress, I guess?"

"What's that strap that wraps around her back and her butt and makes her ass look like a strangled balloon?"

I nearly spit out my wine.

Even as I slowly ease into my new life here, my mornings are still mostly rough going: Almost daily I wake up at seven to the sound of power drills from a construction site down the street—there seems to be a construction site every ten feet in Beirut—and sometimes the sounds rip me out of an anxiety dream about losing everything I know in New York, or failing to make any friends or establish any real home in Beirut. My existence is ultimately lonely and unrooted. I don't belong anywhere. I will be forgotten. My dreams keep circling around these themes.

But one morning I wake up to a sunny August day, light spraying orange through my rust-striped curtains, and I'm instantly washed in nostalgia. It's pretty here this morning, peaceful and calm. It hits me how sweet it feels, bittersweet but serene, to be in Beirut right now. Maybe I did make the right decision coming back to live here.

Suddenly a wave of guilt—debris from a dream? long-repressed survivor's guilt?—busts through. Do I deserve to feel serene now, today, about waking up to a bright summer morning in Beirut? I skipped over most of the horrific 1980s in Lebanon, was ensconced safely in Houston—unhappy and awkward and culturally alienated, but safe from civil war as I romped around with Samir and the schoolkids in our neighborhood and fudged my way through perplexing new kickball and softball games. "Demented and sad, but social," to quote Judd Nelson's line from *The Breakfast Club*. Or maybe my slogan would've been "Hopelessly confused and foreign, but lucky to be thousands of miles from rabid armed militias."

It's a little too easy to ride out most of the war in America, then come back to Lebanon now and say, "Ah, I remember the old neighborhood. How utterly charming." Was six years of war too short, too easy? Should I have lived through hell for another nine years, like so many others in Lebanon, stuck here by circumstance or necessity or a perfectly reasonable fear of the unknown?

Is it fair that I'm coming back only now? I realize some of these questions are spurious. I wasn't the one who decided we should leave during the war. But Beirut is much easier to live in now, and my old neighborhood is not so hard to acclimate to, especially after a decade and a half in New York City: cool new bars and hipster cafés and boutiques and fragrant old bakeries just steps from my apartment here in Hamra. Of course, my new life hasn't exactly been easy so far. I'm struggling to adjust emotionally. Still, my physical surroundings feel oddly familiar. They're not just relics of my past; they also make for a fairly smooth transition from my New York life.

The cities remind me of each other in more ways, too. In New York, neighborhoods are constantly changing, forgotten one decade, trendy the next. That's true of Nolita, where my apartment is, and also of Hamra, the legendary, formerly hip, later war-ravaged, and now hip again albeit still rundown neighborhood in west Beirut. But from what I've seen, no city goes through cycles of rejuvenation and decay quite like Beirut. Even long after the war ended, Lebanon still lives through periods of conflict and renewal. Some Lebanese try to find patterns, or at least humor, in this grim routine. I've heard my relatives and friends quip that every time Beirut manages a few straight years of peace, and becomes chic again with the international jet set, and inevitably gets named one of the hottest destinations in the world by some glossy American travel magazine, that means only one thing: a horrific season of bombings, mayhem, and political catastrophe is surely on the way. The Beirut-based British journalist Robert Fisk once wrote about this place: "Some cities seem forever doomed."

Forever doomed, or forever rising phoenixlike: however you look at it, Beirut is not the same city now that it was three decades ago, or even five years ago. How could it be, after a fifteen-year civil war, multiple episodes of strife, and the beginning of a new century in an ever-changing, techno-mad global culture? But it is somehow, also, the same city. Any city worth a damn goes through changes but stays fundamentally itself, deep in its soul. If cities have souls.

To get past the bad dreams, the rough mornings, and the ruminations as I try to readjust to life here, I know what I need to find—besides mental peace: a cup of good strong coffee. I'm something of a caffeine addict, and one of the first things I did when I moved to New York was to figure out where in my neighborhood I could get decent coffee. I'd been spoiled by the excellent brew in Berkeley when I was in college, and I was surprised that in

New York it wasn't so easy to find at the time, although that's improved lately. Some mornings I like to make coffee at home, while other days I'm eager to get out the door first thing. On those days, I pick up coffee to go and cling to the warm cup like a security blanket, nursing it for as long as I can as I slide into the day.

So far in Beirut, my caffeine routine is still shaky. Sometimes at home I brew Arabic coffee—stirring spoonfuls of the ground dark-roast beans into a small iron kettle filled with boiling water and watching over the liquid as it boils again. Arabic coffee is meant for drinking in tiny porcelain cups though, black or slightly sweetened, and I prefer to have a shot or two as a postmeal digestive. In the mornings, I like my coffee milkier and in a bigger cup. But despite the recent influx of American-style takeout coffee spots in Beirut, I'm having a hard time finding a place that serves decent drip coffee or espresso drinks to go.

A few blocks from my apartment is a place called Café Younes, the flagship coffee shop of an old Beirut brand of coffee beans, and I adore it for its smells and its Beirutness and its history. On visits here in past summers, I've stopped in just to inhale the roasty smell. I love walking through the narrow Hamra streets to Younes, gazing at the antique coffee-making equipment inside, lounging at the outdoor tile tables under the big shade trees, smelling the aromas wafting out the door, and drinking small cups of Arabic coffee in the afternoon. In the past couple of weeks, I've experimented with their coffee-bean varieties and picked out a few that brew up beautifully in the French press at home. But I've found Younes's takeout coffee unfortunately mediocre, lukewarm, and flat-tasting on the days I've tried it.

So my search for good to-go coffee continues. Morning after morning I walk through the busy streets around my apartment.

The main Hamra Street drag was once the site of boisterous cafés that attracted intellectuals and artists from all over Beirut, Cairo, Alexandria, Baghdad, and Istanbul in the 1950s and 1960s, and was a beating heart of the era's artistic and literary and political movements. Since that street and the surrounding neighborhood near the apartment took a heavy drubbing during the civil war, many buildings are now dilapidated, the bombing damage still visible, or else they've been torn down to make way for condo towers and shiny retail chain stores. Now international coffee chains line the main street—Starbucks, Costa, Caribou—occupying the spaces where legendary Beirut cafés like Horseshoe and Modca used to sit. Funny enough, I've noticed that the new chains attract groups of elderly men who sit around all day, nursing cup after cup of Arabic coffee and debating politics, just as locals used to do in the old days. It's as if these lifelong Hamra habitués are willfully ignoring the sterile furniture and décor of the new chain cafés and thinking: *As long as there's a coffee shop on the corner where we can gather and drink coffee and talk all day, then good enough.*

On my coffee search, I've ducked into the Starbucks on Hamra Street now and then; unsurprisingly, a latte here tastes exactly like it does in SoHo or on the Upper West Side. But it feels a little shameful to get into the Starbucks habit in Beirut. I'm not crazy about the coffee at the British chain Costa, which tastes dull or burnt to me most days, but the coffee at Caribou I find I like quite a bit: it's strong, with the fresh-roasted smell I crave. The Minnesota-based chain, its Hamra branch furnished with leather club chairs and a faux fireplace, is a more recent arrival in the neighborhood, and it's just a three-minute walk from my apartment, so I've been succumbing. I feel weird buying American chain-store coffee in a city with such a historic coffee shop culture, but so it goes. As I feel my way toward a coffee routine—Younes some days, Caribou other days, and brewing at home on lazier mornings—at least I'm on my way to something like a life here.

Coffee has another crucial job to do as I navigate life in Beirut. It gets my brain cells in shape for the silent combat that goes on during my walks. In Beirut, everyone stares. At you. At him, at her, at everyone. Men whistle and hoot at women constantly. They can make you feel you're naked no matter what you're wearing. I dress here the way I dress in New York: in summer, a tank top usually, a skirt or light pants, sandals. So do at least half the women in Beirut. In most parts of the city, you'll typically see some women wearing skimpy fashions—miniskirts, sleeveless tops, and even more revealing strapless styles—while other women walk along inches away in head scarves or sometimes a full hijab.

But despite, or maybe because of, the long tradition of skin-baring styles in Beirut, men on the street often call out lewdly. In fact, they'll pretty much do that no matter what you're wearing. It doesn't take much for a woman to get stared at here. Be female, and be walking without a man or a full-body hijab—that's about it. Sometimes you'll be stared at no matter what you look like or even what gender you are. The unemployment rate in Lebanon is sky high, and business at neighborhood shops can be slow, so lots of store owners and their idle friends, usually all men, bring plastic chairs to street corners to sit around together, drinking coffee all day long, smoking cigarettes, and gossiping. And staring.

The glares feel intrusive, but if being ogled by strange men all day is the price to pay for Lebanon's relatively permissive lifestyle, I suppose I can live with that. Unfortunately, the freewheeling dress code is deceptive. Lebanon is not nearly as liberal as it seems on gender issues. Lebanese women can drive, work, and dress however they want, but they're still struggling for equal rights and a voice in government. And as an adult woman here, if you're not married—or if you're married but don't have kids—you'll be made well aware that you're living an alternative lifestyle. In some conservative families and more traditional villages, unmarried or childless women are harassed and shamed. Premarital sex, though widely practiced here, is still secretive. As a single woman in my thirties, I wondered before I arrived whether my status would be considered risqué here, even in the twenty-first century—or whether there are more women here like me now, taking their time with big decisions and trying to make choices that feel authentic and meaningful, rather than caving in to social and family pressures. *Is my lifestyle going to fly in a place like Beirut?* I've wondered. Too early to tell.

Well, if nothing else, at least I've finally sorted out the coffee problem. Whatever nasty looks or interrogations come my way, I'll be caffeinated enough to have a fighting chance.

SEPTEMBER

As I sit at my laptop on this Saturday in early September, working away while my New York friends are undoubtedly off at Long Island beaches for Labor Day, I'm thinking back to a time when getting stared at by strange men didn't seem so unpleasant. In my early teen years in Houston, I longed for the fashionable bikinis I remembered coveting on the Beirut beaches, but I made do with a modest grape-colored two-piece, hoping it would earn me some stares, despite my flat-chested stick figure, from one of the tan blond lifeguards at our pool club. The first weekend of the fall season in Houston meant the annual Labor Day party at the community pool, and all our neighbors would be there, barbecuing and socializing and drinking homemade cocktails out of Thermoses while the kids splashed around and jumped off the high dive for the last time that summer. The neighborly gatherings were always upbeat, and even though my parents stood out as the slightly awkward foreigners, they were game to have a beer and a burger, and talk about the children and the schools and the weather, and so were heartily embraced.

At those Labor Day parties, Samir and I and the kids our age would stretch out our beach towels on the lawn, share red-and-white-striped cardboard tubs of salty nachos coated in sticky neon-orange cheese, suck Mr. Pibb out of sun-warmed cans, and do cannonball jumps into the pool, our bodies slathered in woefully inadequate SPF 6 under the piercing Texas rays. Meanwhile I'd be casting sidelong glances at the lifeguards as they walked by. One summer when I was thirteen, I saw one of that year's lifeguards, a tall, spiky-haired eighteen-year-old named Josh, turn my way. I could swear he winked from way up in his high chair, and my skin tingled from my cheeks down to my skinny sunburned knees.

Back on those languid September weekends in Houston, it hadn't registered yet that as much as I looked forward to the Labor Day parties at the pool—the balmy air that reminded me of summer in Beirut, and the exciting junky soft drinks and snacks, even if those fake-cheese nachos didn't quite measure up to the grilled halloum sandwiches of summers past—the days I'd cherished even more were over forever. No more afternoons at the sprawling Coral Beach club in Beirut, gazing at the glamorous women in bikini tops that clasped together with gold rings or slinky silver chains in the middle, jumping around with Samir and our cousins in the white-capped Mediterranean waves. We'd always get to stay out late on the lounge chairs with our parents and family friends and their kids, watching the grown-ups smoke cigarettes, drink cold beers in frosty mugs, and crack pumpkin seeds, their hands moving nervously back and forth, mouth to ashtray, talking about things I didn't understand: the Phalange and PLO militias, and Israel and America and Syria. Whether the cease-fire this week would last. Whether we'd all have to leave this place soon, and maybe for good.

Here on my balcony in Beirut, many long years after those Labor Day parties and Coral Beach days, I'm overhearing a vigorous debate between two men on the street below—but it's not about politics; they're arguing over a parking space, which is in fact a crumbling patch of sidewalk—as I try to finish my editing assignment for a local university's English-language alumni magazine. I'd lined up this regular gig two years ago after seeing a listing for it on a freelance editorial jobs site. The staff members in the university's U.S. office who had hired me were glad, I suppose, to have found an American-educated editor who also happened to be from Beirut. For the current issue, the editors had promised to start e-mailing me the articles to work on two weeks ago, but I didn't get most of them until last night, Friday at midnight, and the edits are due Monday.

It's just as well that the articles came in only now. I'm in a better work mode than I was a couple of weeks ago, when I was still feeling moody and shaken up by the move. It may be Labor Day weekend across the Atlantic, but I'm in Beirut, and it's not a holiday here. Anyway, freelancers' work patterns never coincide with the rest of the world's concept of a vacation, or a weekend, or bedtime. That's both the pro and the con of freelance life, as I discovered when I left the corporate world. Freelancers work almost all the time—well, if we're lucky. But also if we're lucky, we work whenever we want.

Right now I need the work—for the money, yes, but also for the sanity and the reality check. At some point in my adult life, I realized work is a drug that can blow me past emotional tornadoes. By work, I don't mean any old job (although sometimes just about any distraction will do). I mean the kind of work I love and always have: writing and editing.

Apparently I've always been fascinated by the alphabet and language. As a one-year-old in Urbana, Illinois, I'd point to the K on the K-mart sign when my parents drove me by it, and then I'd see the same shape on the Special K box and yell with excitement. Pleasures came so easily then, a box of cereal and a store sign bringing heaps of delight. I kept up my crush on English letters and words when we moved back to Lebanon, even though my parents enrolled me in a French-focused curriculum at my Beirut elementary school. But I picked up more English from TV and from relatives who mixed English and Arabic into their sentences, Beirut style. When we landed in Houston and I started fourth grade there, the principal insisted on putting me in the lowest-level English class in my tracked school, since I was transferring directly from Lebanon and, like my parents, I had a thick Arabic accent. But much to my parents' smug satisfaction—after they'd failed to convince the principal that I could handle a more challenging level—my English teacher called them a couple of weeks into the semester to say I was in the wrong class. Within weeks I'd moved through the intermediate levels and landed in the highest section. Still, I was desperately shy and felt myself a misfit, my accent heavy with Arabic lilts. My classmates were friendly to me but constantly pointed out my foreignness: "You talk funny. Where do you come from again?"

I was pretty good at grammar and spelling from the start, and I won the fourth- and fifth-grade spelling bees at school. But my accent needed work, a lot of it. All through the rest of elementary school and junior high, I listened carefully and tried to copy American pronunciations, though I stopped short of Texan ones: I insisted on saying "What time is it?" as I heard it on TV, instead of "What tam is it?" But some words passed me by, into my twenties and probably still now. I pronounced pizza *peedza* until I was twenty-seven, when a boyfriend in New York said, one day when he was annoyed with me about something else, "There's no d in that word. It's *peetza*, not *peedza*."

My journalistic attempts started around the time when I was still teaching myself to say *whurrever* instead of *whatt'ever*. Back in fifth grade, feeling an early urge to write and get something in print, I'd tried to enlist my brother to help start a newsletter for our Houston suburb, tackling such breaking-news topics as the history of the pencil, and why cicadas spin around on driveways and make that bulletlike *ratatatat* sound. But I ended up writing the whole newsletter myself, when neither Samir nor any of our neighborhood pals could be enticed to take on reporting assignments in exchange for a few pennies. I'd promised them all that we'd split the profits from our ten-cent cover price. But strangely, I had no takers. Journalism was clearly not for them. I seemed hopelessly drawn even from age ten to a life of writing and research, and thinking up ideas that would make interesting stories for myself or other writers, and editing stories to make them fit for print—and accepting pay that often barely tops zero. A perfect candidate for journalism, marching gleefully off to the slaughter.

The urge persisted, so I signed up for my high school newspaper staff, writing features and editing the op-ed section there. Then in college I joined UC Berkeley's student paper, *The Daily Californian,* my freshman year. I learned to report news stories covering the campus and the region. (The city of Berkeley didn't have its own newspaper at the time and relied, somewhat absurdly, on the *Daily Cal.*) I also reviewed film and music events and spent a year as co-editor of the arts section and another as opinion-page editor. It was my time at the *Daily Cal* that not only convinced me to pursue a career in journalism but also gave me my first real soaking in the ferocious political debates on the Middle East.

As *Daily Cal* op-ed editor, I dove right into the raging campus wars over Israel and the Palestinians. I received hate mail from members of the Jewish student organization Hillel when I published a student or faculty member's plea for Palestinian sovereignty and an end to the cruelties of the occupation, and hate mail from Arab students when I published another contributor's defense of an Israeli policy. I tried to give equal space to both sides, or thought I did, but most likely I didn't, since my sympathies, along with those of some of my lefty Jewish friends in college, bent toward Palestinian liberation and freedom from the tyrannies of the occupation. In the op-ed section, I was aiming to create a space for lively, even-keeled argument among students and faculty on all issues, but most of the submissions I got at the time seemed to center on the Middle East. I enjoyed the challenge of moderating a vigorous debate among those who criticized Israel and those who sympathized with its policies. Those discussions, or sometimes heated arguments, have continued into my adult life, whether with friends, boyfriends, co-workers, or relatives.

That college op-ed gig might have been, in its way, not just a crash course on Middle East politics but also an outlet for my very Lebanese argumentative tendencies—and an early preparation for my move back to Beirut. People here are by and large compulsive debaters—about politics, yes, and about everything else, too. In a taxi they might argue about which road the driver is taking, and in a restaurant about the dressing on the tabbouleh, and at a wedding about the bride's hairstyle. And at some point in any given day, they're going to argue about politics.

In the States, as gridlocked as Congress gets and as infuriating and slow as it can be to get badly needed policies passed, it's possible to get through a day without smacking head-on into the dysfunctions, small and large, of daily life. In Lebanon, not so possible. On an average day in a service taxi—aka a *serveece,* a cheap cab that acts like a bus and follows a predetermined route, picking up multiple passengers along the way—you're likely to hear something like this from your driver or a fellow rider:

"Kiss ikht hal dawleh." Goddamn this government. Actually the remark involves a slur about female anatomy, but it gets lost in translation—perhaps for the better.

The response might be *"Yikrhib beita,"* may its house get wrecked, a common Arabic yell of exasperation.

Sometimes the conversation heats up, as several people in the service taxi—or in the grocery store, or at the dry cleaner— agree on a topic and get more specific with the bashing: for instance "Can we just hear the results of the UN tribunal already, and be done with it?" Or "Who does Hezbollah think it is?" Other times there's an awkward silence, and it's clear that not everyone is on the same page; best to change the subject. But in a country that's still in many ways religiously divided, with lingering tensions between and among Christians and Muslims, Sunnis and Shiites, and with an ever-addled government that never seems to govern, it's rare for politics not to make at least a brief appearance in a conversation. Now and then I jump into the fray, and other times I just want to say *"Khalas, intawash'd!"* Enough—my ears are ringing!

As I'm plowing through my editing assignment, I can hear the Ramadan call to prayer echoing from a mosque nearby. This is the third week of the annual Muslim month of fasting, and the celebrations that mark the end of the fast will be starting soon. During the upcoming Eid al-Fitr holiday, families and friends close out Ramadan by getting together for festive dinners, which, like Christmas or Easter feasts, can run from the cozy and casual to the lavish and showy.

I'm more aware of Ramadan traditions now—the daily fasting schedule, the Eid al-Fitr dinners—than I was during my childhood in Beirut. Arguably I wasn't consciously aware of much, culturally speaking, back then, other than Tintin and Asterix books and *Grendizer,* a *Transformers*-like Japanese cartoon that Samir and I would watch on TV. But one of the effects of the civil war was that many Lebanese, Christians and Muslims, felt their religious identities embattled and so deepened them; now religious celebrations, even around my comparatively secular and diverse district of Ras Beirut, seem more prominent than they used to be.

The war also reaffirmed, in some cases more strictly than others, the distinct Christian and Muslim parts of town—the Muslim west, the Christian east. Even though our neighborhood remained mostly an exception, it's become increasingly Muslim in head count, with more Shiites migrating from the suburbs and joining the Sunni Muslims and Protestants and Greek Orthodox and other sects already there.

I'm glad I arrived in Beirut in time for Ramadan; I've been hoping to experience more of it this year than I've had a chance to in the past. During the fasting month, I've been noticing that the Corniche, the promenade that runs east–west along Beirut's Mediterranean coastline, gets even more crowded with pedestrians in the late evenings. It's a lively scene: at night, after breaking the fast with the daily *iftar* dinner, people of all ages stroll along the Corniche, some women wearing veils or hijabs and others not, and little kids stay up giddily way past their normal bedtime. Muslim families, and young men smoking *argilehs*—the local word for hookahs—and groups of women friends, and children and teenagers tagging along with parents and relatives, often socialize after dinner, then have another meal just before they go to bed, so they can better cope with the long fast the next day: no food or water is permitted from dawn until sundown during Ramadan.

My mother's friend Umayma, who looks in photos from her twenties and thirties eerily like the glamorous, gamine-chic Jean Seberg in the Godard film *Breathless,* calls me one day just before the end of Ramadan to invite me to a special iftar feast for Eid al-Fitr at her home in Ras Beirut. At these dinners, families and friends gather and eat a series of specific dishes served in a set order. My mother has been telling me that Umayma is a great cook, and I'm thrilled to be invited. Umayma and my mother have known each other their whole lives. They met in elementary school in Beirut in the 1950s, at the Ahliah, a then-groundbreaking school run by my mother's aunt Wadad Cortas. The school still exists on the same spot in Beirut's old Jewish quarter of Wadi Abu Jamil, and in its heyday, it brought together kids of all classes, religions, and countries from around the Arab world: Muslims, Christians, Jews, and other sects. Umayma, a Sunni, and my mom, a Presbyterian, became best friends when they were ten and have stayed close ever since. Umayma's brother Ziad was also my dad's college classmate, and my parents first met at the siblings' home.

I walk into Umayma and her husband Nasser's apartment on the night of the Eid iftar to find a roomful of people, some of them old friends of my parents, plus my mother's cousins Huda and Afaf, who've known Umayma since their school days—all in all a lively, mixed group of Muslims and Christians. I've known many of the dozen or so people in the room since my childhood though I haven't seen some in decades, and my initial shyness on walking in fades when they greet me enthusiastically, wanting to know how my Beirut life is going so far.

Umayma passes around a traditional Ramadan date-juice drink called *jellab* and glasses of an apricot nectar called *amareddin*. Then we gather at the table for dinner. First comes soup, which Umayma explains to me is always a first course at iftar meals since it warms the insides and preps the stomach for eating dinner after a full day of fasting. The soup is often lentil, but tonight it's creamy asparagus bisque, from a recipe that Umayma's sister-in-law and my parents' dear friend Bushra, also an exceptional cook, has improvised for the occasion from the in-season asparagus. Then comes *fattoush*, a minty bread salad that combines tomatoes, herbs, and bits of fried pita with a dressing spiked with the extra-tangy sumac spice that's popular in Lebanon and a favorite of mine; then the main course: *kibbeh arnabieh*, lamb meatballs stuffed with sweet caramelized onions and fried pine nuts, in a sauce made with tahini and the bitter-tart juice of local bou sfeir oranges. It's not a light dish by any stretch, but I've always loved its mix of sweet and sour flavors, crunchy and saucy textures. Along with the kibbeh, Umayma serves another dish I adore, *tiss'ye*, made of layers of warm chickpeas topped with garlic-spiked yogurt, sautéed pine nuts, and fried-pita croutons similar to the ones in fattoush salad. Bushra helped make the dish, and I remember how my mother once told me Bushra won the heart of her husband, Ziad, by making him an exquisite tiss'ye during their courtship.

For dessert, Umayma sets out a classic rice pudding called *mhalabieh* drizzled with a sugar syrup called *ater*, along with bowls of the ice cream I brought her from a local confectionery: the pistachio scoops are studded with bits of salty nuts and made with *sahlab*, an ingredient that comes from wild orchid roots and that creates an unusually elastic texture found almost exclusively in ice creams from the Middle East and Turkey.

At the table, after discussing—what else?—the current political situation, everyone chimes in with gossip about new restaurants about to open in the neighborhood, and decades-old shops about to close, and corrupt contractors at nearby construction sites, and news of what some old family friends are up to these days. Everyone wants to know how it feels to pick up and leave New York and move back to this unpredictable little country. Their reactions range from "Salma, you must be crazy!" to "It's so nice to see your generation wanting to return."

Besides all the exceptional food on the table, as a side effect of the dinner, I feel a little more launched into Beirut life, having reconnected with familiar faces at the iftar and updated everyone on my time here so far. Still, I'm facing the fact that, for the most part, my social life is decidedly unrollicking. In the evenings, I often read or watch a DVD or take a walk. My night strolls through

Hamra take me along sidewalks where tiny, hip-looking bars, so many new ones opening lately, start getting packed at nine P.M. and go until two A.M. or later. In recent years, it is mostly neighborhoods on the east side of Beirut, across downtown from the west side where I live, that have become famous for their nightlife, but the Hamra area is picking up steam again. This area hadn't been trendy since before the war, and it's nice now to see the side streets around my apartment come to life in the late evenings. I'm not feeling part of the scene yet, but my walks are motivating me to try to plug into it somehow: to make an effort to reconnect with a few childhood friends and try to lure some of my cousins away from their kids and out for drinks now and then. And maybe even to make some new friends here, if I can figure out how.

Living in Beirut, it's hard not to feel pressure, real or imagined, to be out socializing on a regular basis. This is, after all, one of the world's most hypersocial cities. There's a definite partying imperative here. No matter how old you are, you're expected to go out a lot, whether to dinners and lunches or, for the younger set (by which I mean anyone younger than fifty), to clubs and bars and all-night parties. I'm not sure exactly where this high-octane social life comes from, but here are some theories. First, plain old Mediterranean-style decadence, a love of eating and drinking and dancing and sitting around for hours talking, passions shared by our neighbors across the sea, the Italians and French and Spanish and Greeks—maybe it's something in the water. Also, as a port town, Beirut has for centuries been a hub for travelers from around the world, and its historically mixed population has meant a more liberal attitude toward alcohol and partying. The Lebanese addiction to socializing fills more specific local needs, too—like catharsis, not just during periods of violence and fear but also as a way to numb stress from the ongoing unemployment crisis and political instability. Even parents with kids can go out all the time if they want to, since most Lebanese families from the middle class on up hire live-in nannies, immigrants from Asia and Africa who work for very low wages. The nightlife here is undeniably tied into Beirut's self-image and into the way tourists from around the world perceive the city.

I definitely need a social life, not just to feel like a normal Lebanese with a pulse but also to avoid going stir-crazy or wallowing in loneliness and self-pity. Even though I've always liked spending time solo, succumbing to too much of that in Beirut seems pathological somehow. So far I've had some phone chats with my childhood friend Zeina, whom I've managed to keep up with over the years. She's married, has a four-year-old daughter, and lives a half hour away in an eastern suburb, but we've vowed to hit the town together soon. One Friday night in mid-September, I'm holding a DVD of *Spirited Away*, an animated film by the Japanese director Miyazaki—I bought it for a buck at one of the many pirated-disk shops nearby, easier to find than decent rental shops—and I'm wondering if I should go ahead with a night of Japanimation. But on this beautiful Friday evening in Beirut, sitting home alone with a video seems a little too poignant. I wonder if I should call or e-mail Richard or one of my friends in New York, or try to find some random strangers' party to crash.

The phone rings, interrupting my self-pity spiral. It's Zeina. She and her husband, Marwan, are going to meet a friend or two later tonight in the hopping Gemmayzeh area on the east side, and do I want to join them? Yes. My lonesome Japanimation evening turns, in an instant, into a classic Beirut night. I put on a

silky sleeveless blouse, slim-cut jeans, and heeled boots—trying
for a certain Beiruti summer look, stylish but faux nonchalant—
and grab a taxi for the fifteen-minute ride across downtown and
into Gemmayzeh. I'm heading to meet Zeina and Marwan at a
place called Joe Peña, a loud Spanish-cantina-style spot on Rue
Gouraud, Gemmayzeh's main drag. When my taxi arrives, traffic
is already backed up on Gouraud, so the driver drops me off at the
edge of the street and speeds off. I walk along Gouraud, strolling
past the rows of restaurants, bars, and nightclubs that occupy the
ground floors of the street's beautiful old townhouses, with their
arched windows and wrought-iron balconies. Some of those houses
survived the war, although signs of damage and age are showing
in the dozens that have yet to be renovated. But somehow their old
elegance shines through: in walls painted colors like eggshell blue
or apricot or lemon yellow, peeling but with plenty of charm, and in
the windows, typically three in a row across the upper facade, the
glass forming a half-moon at the top.

It's just past nine, and the hangouts up and down the street
are already starting to spill over with crowds, as groups of friends
stand lingering on the sidewalk or meandering into the narrow
street, dodging the cars that are trying to squeeze through as they
honk at the oblivious partyers. I walk into the bar and find my
friends. Zeina and Marwan lived in New York for a few years in
the late 1990s, and the three of us had hung out regularly around
Manhattan's East Village, where they were living at the time.
They're a striking pair: Zeina with her short reddish hair, model-
curvy eyebrows, and porcelain skin, slim and stylish in jeans
and an off-the-shoulder top; Marwan with rakishly curly hair and
metal-rimmed glasses.

I'm happy to be out, nursing a couple of ice-cold Lebanese

Almaza beers and watching the crowd at the bar, as more and more trendy-looking types pack into the room, glance around for people they know, and light cigarettes while attempting to get the bartenders' attention. A deejay spins electro-pop and hip-hop in a back corner. It's getting too crowded to move much, but dancing often doesn't happen until later in the night anyway, as I remember from past summer visits to Beirut: around three or four A.M., people will sometimes jump onto the chairs or tables, waving their cocktail glasses and cigarettes, and dance.

Zeina and Marwan introduce me to their friends: one guy around our age who owns some hipstery bars in town, and a former classmate with a big laugh who recently moved back to Beirut with his Spanish wife. We compare notes on New York versus Beirut—everyone in our little group has spent time in both cities—and about the social scenes in each: Beirutis tend to stay out later, is the consensus. But we agree that the bar scenes are fairly similar—boisterous, energetic, and overflowing on weekends—and at some clubs in both cities, it's not unusual for people to be sneaking drugs in the bathroom. But here, I've noticed, people make more of an effort to look stylish, as a rule. And they can still chain-smoke their way through the night, as New Yorkers once did before Mayor Bloomberg's smoking ban.

It's starting to get a little too smoky inside this bar actually, but right now I'm not minding much. It's a festive and fun night, and we stay out, drinking and shouting at each other over the loud music and the crowd, until just past midnight. That's bush league in Beirut, but everyone except me has kids or early-morning obligations the next day. Still, I'm glad Zeina called, happy I rallied to join them, and relieved I finally made my own tiny contribution to the city's party scene.

Socially, things continue to look up, bit by bit, as the month goes by. My college friend Jeff has e-mailed to tell me his old Berkeley housemate Curtis just moved to Beirut with his wife, Diana, to spend a year. Curtis is an American from southern California, and Diana is British. Both are graduate students at Harvard, and they're in Beirut this year to work on academic projects. I've never met Curtis even though we were both at Berkeley at the same time and had a friend in common. I e-mail them to introduce myself, and it turns out they're living in an apartment near me. They invite me to a dinner the next week. I wonder if we'll hit it off.

On the night of the dinner, I walk up the wide marble stairs of their echoey Ras Beirut building and into their third-floor apartment and am greeted by the tall curly-haired Curtis and Diana, also tall, with long, wispy blond locks. We click instantly—both of them are laid-back and have a dry wit I quickly take to—and they introduce me to their friend Nimco, a Somali-American who lives in Boston but is based this year in Sudan with her husband doing research. Nimco is in Beirut to visit Curtis and Diana, and she's cooked dinner tonight. Our group of a half-dozen gathers around the table to eat her Somali soup of lemony broth with lamb bones, from which, on her instructions, we suck out the buttery marrow as we laugh at our messy technique, and her fragrant lamb stew over rice, similar to a classic Lebanese stew I'm fond of called a *yakhne*. For dessert, I've brought *ashta* ice cream, ultra-rich scoops of cold sweet cream mixed with sahlab, the wild orchid ingredient that creates an elastic texture. When I brought a similar ice cream to Umayma's Ramadan dinner, everyone there had grown up with it and knew it well. But tonight no one at the dinner has had this style of ice cream before, and I enjoy watching them try to figure out what to make of it, the spoonfuls pulling away like stretchy strings of chewing gum. After a few puzzled bites: big smiles.

At the dinner party, I meet an American woman named Wendy, who teaches political science at Northwestern University in Chicago and is here researching Lebanese emigration patterns. After dinner she gives me her business card, and we exchange cell phone numbers, promising to hang out again before she moves back to the States next month. As I look at her full name on the card, I realize it sounds vaguely familiar, but I can't place it right away.

Several days after Curtis and Diana's dinner, I'm home on a Friday evening, and I hear loud booming sounds outside. Fireworks? I'm not sure. They sound like shelling, a visceral memory from the civil war. I wonder if the annual Hamra Street festival I've been seeing posters for around the neighborhood has just started, tonight, with a literal bang, an explosive fireworks display. That seems unlikely, though. I didn't notice any festival preparations on the street earlier, or any vendors setting up food or crafts stands, and I don't remember what day the fest is supposed to start. I'm slightly panicked by the noise but keeping myself calm—a skill I hope I'll muster if, god forbid, the political situation in Lebanon blows up again. The sounds go on and get louder, and now I'm even more worried that they're not fireworks. I rush into the windowless bathroom near my bedroom and crouch on the blue-tiled floor, away from any glass. That's what we used to do during the war when the nightly shelling raids would start. The sounds continue for another half-hour, me still on the floor in the bathroom, alternately panicking and wondering if I'm being silly. Suddenly everything goes quiet.

I listen for noise, a reaction, sirens, and don't hear anything.

No sounds of trauma or mayhem out on the streets. So those must have been just fireworks after all. I call my aunt Nouhad upstairs, and she confirms: fireworks for the Hamra festival, but she's angry because these were much louder and longer-lasting than usual.

"Isn't it amazing that we keep blasting these sounds, here in Beirut of all places?" she asks.

Yeah, I say. In what other country that lived through fifteen years of shelling and rocket grenades nearly every night is there still such an appetite for fireworks? Fireworks for every wedding, political speech, lavish birthday celebration, holiday, festival, you name it. Are we hopelessly addicted to the sound of things going boom?

Back in May 2008, when scuffles exploded among militiamen from opposing sects on various streets around Beirut, some of my relatives thought they were hearing fireworks—but quickly realized they were actually shells. They all ran for safety to the windowless hallways of their buildings, and some slept on those corridor floors all night until the shelling stopped. Some of their buildings were hit. None of my friends or relatives were hurt, thankfully. But you never know around here.

Wendy, the political scientist I'd met at Curtis and Diana's, is living in an apartment near mine during her Beirut stay, and I call her after the fireworks die down. I need a drink. Luckily she's on her way home from a dinner. We meet on the sidewalk near my apartment—I spot her blond hair and small-boned frame from down the block—and we take a walk around the neighborhood. I tell her about the fireworks incident and laugh off my paranoia (she hadn't heard the booms downtown where she was). And I silently wonder if I can live like this again, in fear that the world is about to blow up around me.

Over beers at a small, divey Hamra bar after our stroll, I ask Wendy a question I've been meaning to ask her since the dinner party, namely what it's like to be Jewish in Lebanon these days. I'm wondering what the climate is right now, especially given Lebanon's mutually hostile relationship with Israel. Has she encountered locals who were suspicious of her for being Jewish? I want to know, too, because I'd like Richard, who is Jewish, to visit me in Beirut and to feel comfortable here. Wendy tells me she's avoided bringing up the fact that she's Jewish in the months she's been living here, thinking there's no point and it could potentially be disruptive. Hiding an identity strikes me as unfortunate, but I can understand the impulse in regions as messed up as the Middle East. Thanks to Israel's repeated invasions of Lebanon and its occupations of parts of the country, Zionism is not a particularly welcome stance in Lebanon, and unfortunately locals don't always make the distinction between Zionism and Judaism. Many assume someone who is Jewish must also automatically support Israel's policies. I can see how even opening the subject could be exhausting and time-consuming, and how it could seem less cumbersome to avoid it most of the time.

Leaving the bar, Wendy and I stroll along Hamra Street, past the stands that are being set up now for the first night of the Hamra festival—some to sell labneh sandwiches or shawarma, others coffee or lemonade or Arabic pastries, or all kinds of jewelry and handicrafts. The scene reminds me of the ubiquitous New York street fairs that I've tended to avoid since they cause so much annoying pedestrian gridlock. But a local rock band is playing on a makeshift stage, there's an upbeat vibe in the air, and we're enjoying our stroll. As we chat and get to know each other, it comes up that, a few years ago, Wendy published a collection of essays by Palestinians living in the Occupied Territories. And suddenly it hits me: this Wendy is the Wendy Pearlman whose book, called *Occupied Voices*, has been on the shelf in my Manhattan apartment for a few years. I'd bought it once while browsing at the Barnes & Noble at Union Square—this book, by a Jewish author compiling essays on Palestinians' experiences under occupation, had caught my eye—and after she'd given me her card at the dinner party, I'd thought her name was familiar.

"Small world" is an even bigger cliché in Lebanon than everywhere else. The country is fairly compact—the population is roughly 4 million, about 1.5 million of that in Beirut—and social and family circles collide and overlap constantly. You can chat up the cashier at the grocery store, or the manager of your local bank, or your taxi driver, or your orthopedist, in Beirut and discover you know a few people in common or even that you're related. Happens all the time here. I'm stunned by the Wendy coincidence, but I have a feeling this won't be the last time something like that happens to me here.

Sure enough, it's not long before it does again. One night later in the month, I hear that a Lebanese singer named Ghada Ghanem is performing a free show in downtown Beirut. I'd randomly met Ghada last year in New York, at a party at the home of my Lebanese friend Ahmad, and she'd sung a few a cappella Arabic songs that night. I was enchanted by her voice. Now here she is again, a not-yet-famous singer but this time with a gig at an outdoor theater in the newly rebuilt shopping district downtown, and luckily I'm in Beirut to hear her sing in her hometown. I invite my aunt

Nouhad, a music lover, to come with me. The concert isn't until ten thirty, but the late-night start makes it all the more dramatic.

When Ghada comes out onstage, under the night sky, the crowd hushes, and it's instant magic. She performs a series of old Arabic songs, a genre called *tarab*, her voice soaring out over the darkened city. An older woman, a brave audience member, gets up by herself and does a Middle Eastern dance called the *dabke*, right in front of the stage. The audience is clapping, cheering, singing along, the older members maybe feeling this is a déjà vu of the prewar Beirut that's lost, or was lost and is now *"inshallah,"* hopefully, on its way back, but you can never be sure. Ghada has that iconic Lebanese voice: mournful and hopeful at once. When she sang at that party in New York last year, a guest had called out to her, "Your voice is more beautiful than Fairuz's."

At the end of the show, Ghada says she's glad to see Beirutis coming together over pleasure instead of suffering. She's referring to the meaning of tarab, a musical style that's mournful at times but ultimately about the pleasure and even the ecstasy of a profound musical experience. And she's also making a dig at the seemingly eternal Lebanese tendency to accentuate and fight over differences. My mind drifts to an old Fairuz song, melodramatic but stinging: "To Beirut . . . peace to Beirut . . . From the soul of her people she makes wine . . . From their sweat, she makes bread and jasmine. So how did it come to taste of smoke and fire?"

The political situation here is, by most accounts, looking dicey yet again. There's a sense that another civil war may be on the way. The long-anticipated results of the UN Special Tribunal investigating the killing of the former prime minister are looking more and more like they may set off another round of sectarian violence in the coming months—likely between Hezbollah and the opposing March 14 Party, launched by ex-premier Rafik Hariri's son, Saad Hariri; Israel and Syria and Iran, all with allegedly vested interests in the proceedings, could get dragged in, too. All parties are speaking ominously about what's to come if the various sides don't settle their conflicts over the tribunal and other matters with all due speed: possibly not just another civil war but the biggest regional war the Middle East has ever seen.

But for now it's a beautiful September night, and Beirut is sparkling, from the window lights in distant buildings, to the yellow lanterns glowing in the dark along the downtown streets, to the flickering lights from ships pulling out to sea, and Ghada's voice is gorgeous, and we're happy to be here and to be alive. We're caught up in the magic of the tarab and the haunting minor-key string music of the oud, and life is sweet. You hang on to that feeling when it hits, and you hang on to it with all your strength, especially in Lebanon. You never know how long it will last.

OCTOBER

On some days, New York feels like another planet in the distant past. Other days it's as if I just left minutes ago. I'll be heading to New York for a short visit later this month, but in the meantime I've decided to throw a belated Beirut housewarming dinner for myself. I've been making some progress in feeling comfortable and settled into my Beirut life, and I want to bring a few people into a room together to eat, drink, and make my life here feel more real, my presence more official somehow, and my apartment a little noisier for a night.

I decide to invite Curtis and Diana, along with a few cousins and their spouses who teach at the nearby American University of Beirut, figuring surely they'll all know people in common and might have lots to talk about. It'll just be a casual evening, a way to bring people into my home—a particularly key gesture in Lebanon and in traditional Arab culture. The Middle East balances its famous penchant for political disaster and war with a somewhat more flattering reputation for hospitality. Ever since most of the region was made up of nomadic tribes living in tents, it's been considered important to bring in guests, even total strangers, make them feel at home, and ply them with food and coffee, even if you have barely enough to feed your own family.

For my small gathering, I'm going to make fattoush salad and some meze dishes like baba ghanoush, hummus, and maybe another kind of salad, too, since the summer produce is still abundant in this unseasonably hot October. Usually after the summer heat starts burning off in September, the thermostat inches down to around sixty degrees Fahrenheit by October, heading south another twenty or so degrees in midwinter. But the temperature is still hovering around eighty. I'm hoping to find some fat red summery tomatoes at one of the produce stands along Makdisi Street, near my apartment and named after my mother's ancestors, the Makdisis, who settled in this part of the city in the early twentieth century and built homes on what were then grassy open fields. I'm also going to pick up some Lebanese-style grilled chicken, called *shish taouk*, from the butcher shop and restaurant Cheikha, where I'd had an excellent shawarma sandwich with my cousin Soumaya back in August; later I went back alone to try their shish taouk and became an addict. My oven isn't heating up so well—only the stovetop seems to work, and a small countertop convection oven my parents had bought last year—so I'm not in any position to compete with the neighborhood grilled-chicken specialists, who can do shish taouk better anyway.

For three days before the dinner, I run around doing party errands: I find some tall-stemmed, Japanese-looking flowers shaped like green balloons and buy two dozen. I pick up extra wineglasses since I notice I have only three uncracked ones, and I make a hip-hop and R&B playlist with lots of Outkast and Curtis Mayfield and Betty Davis, the powerfully soulful former wife of the late Miles Davis, which I have on a CD Richard made for me a while back. I hire an aunt's housekeeper to clean the apartment the day before the dinner party. I feel like a harried Lebanese version of Mrs. Dalloway, except I'm having only six people over.

On the day of the dinner, I pick up a tray of shish taouk, smelling lusciously of lemon and garlic, and also some small triangular pies called *fatayer*, stuffed with spinach and onion and spiced with sumac. I buy the juicy lamb meatballs called kibbeh from a little bakery called La Cigale around the corner from me, where the air always smells of hot butter, and where I used to beg my mom for the chocolate meringue pastries called *succès* when I was little and the shop had the more alluring name Candy. I make a big bowl of fattoush, mixing chunks of tomato and cucumber with fresh mint, parsley, scallions, and purslane—the slightly peppery herb found all over here—along with small pieces of pita bread that I fry on the stove, and I toss the salad in a dressing of lemon juice, olive oil, and sumac. To make baba ghanoush, I roast eggplants on the stovetop flame, peel off the skins, and mix the pulpy insides with tahini, garlic, and lemon juice, then I make some hummus—extra-lemony, my favorite style—and quickly throw together one of my favorite easy hors d'oeuvres: toothpick-size skewers of red grapes, basil leaves, and chunks of halloum cheese, a riff on a *caprese* salad. I've made this in New York before for friends' parties, using tiny mozzarella balls instead of halloum, but here all the flavors pop more, thanks to Lebanon's late-season juice-bomb grapes and the just-salty-enough white halloum cheese.

I want the dinner party to feel very relaxed, as if I threw it together effortlessly, no big deal, but of course even after spending a couple of days chasing down and preparing the food, wine, glassware, flowers, and music, in the two hours before my guests arrive, I'm still running around like mad. I have barely time to shower and get dressed, and I smash a wineglass or two frantically trying to get everything clean and ready before they all get here.

In New York, my apartment and kitchen are small and I don't own a dining table, so I don't throw full-on dinner parties. But sometimes a few old college friends who love to cook come over, and we all make dinner together in the tight space, or cobble up something like a potluck, since my downtown Manhattan apartment is the easiest one for our far-flung crew to reach and no one minds sitting on floor cushions, bohemian-style. And I have, oddly enough, always been pretty relaxed and Zen when people come over, never really the nervous hostess in the moment—probably because I obsess about the details ahead of time, no matter how small and casual the gathering, and partly because I lubricate myself with a glass of wine before anyone rings the bell. I'm not quite sure how this Beirut housewarming dinner party will go: if my frantic efforts to pull it all together will make it look as easy as instant Jell-O, or if my hi-I'm-new-here awkwardness will flash like a Broadway billboard.

On the fateful night, two couples coincidentally arrive at my building at the same time, and I open my door to find them standing there, holding flowers and chocolates. My cousin Karim and his wife, Hala, are already chatting with Curtis and Diana, having discovered they have some AUB-affiliated friends in common.

We sit around the living room snacking on the fatayer and kibbeh balls and grape-halloumi hors d'oeuvres, and the conversation— about life in Beirut, and the political scene, and what it's like raising kids here (they all have small children)—flows naturally and cheerfully. The other two guests I'd invited, my cousin Kamal and his wife, Nour, call at the last minute, apologetic; they're ensnared by their seven-year-old son's bad earache. With just five of us, it's still fun though, and we press on.

"What's your take on the political situation now?" Curtis asks Karim, a political scientist and Middle East specialist, as he sips an Almaza beer.

"It's pretty atrocious. I'm not optimistic at all."

I duck into the kitchen to refill the platters of kibbeh and fatayer and hear the two erupt in laughter about something— somehow grim political conversations in Beirut often lead to laughs. Gallows humor; what else can you do?

Meanwhile Diana, who has been traveling all over Lebanon to shoot documentaries about Palestinian refugees, asks Hala, who works at the university nearby, for emergency child-care advice. The two chat away, comparing notes on their childhoods in England. Hala is half Lebanese and grew up partly in London.

The white wine I've bought tastes too syrupy to me, but I manage to make a spaced-out gaffe and forget to pour any for my cousin after asking him what he'd like to drink. I get distracted by the conversation and notice half an hour later that he's still drinkless. He's busy breaking down the chances of Lebanon erupting in war again, and I'm curious to hear his take. When I finally pour him a glass, he takes only a few tiny sips, having immediately noticed, I'm sure, that it's crap. I offer to switch him to beer instead, and he protests, "No, no, this wine is very good"—hyperopinionated about politics, but ever the polite dinner guest.

We eventually make our way to the dinner table, and the shish taouk is a hit, extra juicy, robust with the flavors of the fresh lemon juice and garlic marinade. And thankfully my fattoush, hummus, and baba ghanoush seem to go over well, too, everyone helping themselves to seconds and thirds as we sit around the table, pouring more beer and terrible wine and chatting up a frenzy.

Dessert is another near-bungle: the ice cream I've taken out of the freezer, a pine-nut-studded apricot flavor I love from a tiny old ice cream shop called Hanna Mitri, almost melts into a giant puddle after I leave it out for too long, again distracted by the conversation. But I rescue it just barely in time and scoop it into bowls to pass around the table. As the hours fly by, we eventually make our way back to the living room to nibble on chocolates, drink Arabic coffee, and lounge some more, listening to music and talking.

Does throwing a dinner party make you a local? Not really— surely it takes more than that—but as of tonight, I do feel more like I live here. Despite my little wine and dessert snafus, the night is a success overall. I've pulled off my first dinner invitation. As of tonight, my house is officially warmed. I've had people over, and I've fed them and stayed up into the wee hours talking and laughing and listening to music with them. Everyone leaves at one thirty, chattering animatedly as I call the elevator and kiss them all goodnight, and collapse into bed.

A week later Curtis and Diana return the invite and have me over for another dinner party, with a group of expat friends of theirs who are all in Beirut this year working or doing research. A British friend of Diana's parents named Rosemary, a professor at AUB for the past few decades, is at the dinner party, too. I learn that Rosemary knows some of my relatives and knew my maternal grandmother. I never knew her myself; she'd died when my mother was a teenager. I'm delighted that, of all people to be mentioned at the dinner party, my *teta* Wadi'a's name came up. It's of course not the first time I've experienced this tiny-world phenomenon in Beirut, but tonight was an especially unlikely and happy surprise.

At the dinner, there's also an American visiting professor named James, who recently finished his Ph.D. in Philadelphia and seems to be eyeing me from the minute he walks in. He comes over to introduce himself and starts off with a typical Beirut question: Where do you live?

"Nearby," I answer. "Around the corner and up the block from Bliss Street."

"Wow, really?" He does a cartoonish head spin. "I live right near there, too."

"Where?"

"Just up from Hamra Street, in a white concrete seventies building above a toy store."

This time I'm the stunned one. My parents and Samir and I lived briefly in that building in the late 1970s while our current apartment was being renovated.

After we note the incredible coincidence, we segue into a conversation about the foibles of Beirut life. James has muddy water coming out of his taps for the first few minutes every morning, and daily he has to climb over a car that always parks on the sidewalk right in front of his building. I tell him how I have to remember to flip off the air-conditioning when I do laundry in my kitchen, so as not to short out the electricity in the whole apartment. I mention that I vividly remember the concierge's wife at that building he lives in, a woman named Samira, who sometimes brought us plates of the lentil and rice dish *moujaddra* and used to always wear a dish towel tucked into her ample waistband.

"Wait, I think Samira is still there. I'm pretty sure that's the concierge's wife's name. She introduced herself to me the other day."

I wonder if Fate is calling down to me: *Hello? Date this guy.*

He's cute, a little too tall for me maybe, but with warm light brown eyes and auburn hair that keeps tumbling into his face.

"Here, take my cell number," he says later that night as he's leaving the party. "Let's get a drink this week."

He doesn't ask for my number, which I would've felt weird giving him since I, ostensibly, have a boyfriend. Or a guy I'm seeing in New York, in any case, even if Richard and I haven't yet embraced the boyfriend/girlfriend tags. I can't exactly refuse to take James's number—and it's too awkward to blurt out "I have a boyfriend!" just as he's walking out the door—so I punch the digits into my phone. I'm feeling slightly off kilter, not sure whether I should interpret the weird coincidences in both of our lives as some kind of cosmic sign and call him up some day this week, or just let the whole thing drop, forget I ever met him.

Meanwhile I turn my attention to the other guests at the party, all of us nursing our after-dinner drinks and enjoying the midnight breeze through the open windows. There's Paul, an American Ph.D. student living in Beirut with his boyfriend this year and researching gay culture in Lebanon, and Monique, a young Tunisian historian here on a fellowship. They're talking about good jobs in academia and how hard they're becoming to find.

I drift off a little and think about what it's like to have your job determine your home, or at least where you're forced to live. Over the years, my friends in academia have gone where the best or only job they could find was, and they've either grown to enjoy their new city, or else haven't liked it but have resigned themselves to living there indefinitely. As for me, even though I've loved living in New York, I eventually figured out that a freelance work life—mostly independent of any specific place—is the most ideally suited for me, or maybe a job that would let me work from anywhere anytime, although those still seem all too rare. The idea of relocating for a job to a place you don't like has always struck me as a major downside of the academic life and of certain other careers, although maybe city surroundings don't affect everyone as acutely. For me, having to move long-term somewhere that feels wrong would be pretty much a deal breaker.

It's tempting to think of our increasingly splintered geographies—work in one city, family in another, friends far-flung all over—as a mutation of our ever more globalized world. But moving around in search of a better life is nothing new, of course. Since the earliest *Homo sapiens* days, fifty millennia ago and beyond, humans have roamed to look for fertile land and a decent living, or to escape natural disasters or war. I wonder if those early nomads had the time or luxury to ponder the existential "where is home" question while they fled danger and searched for food. I suspect not. But now, with more careers going mobile and families scattered all over the planet, and with more options for where to live, the question seems more real and ubiquitous, even if it seems to nag harder and more urgently at some people than at others. Without an ongoing, reliably thick network of family and friends in the cities where we're born and raised, and with educational and career opportunities more and more dispersed around the world, and parts of our lives (family, friends, jobs) spread out all over, theoretically any place is a potential home. We can go shopping for cities now, just like we can shop for vegetables or smartphones or love. But is the "where is home" dilemma a modern luxury or a curse?

I've always been hyperaware of my reactions to cities, my visceral sense when I arrive in a new place. Houston felt alien to me at first; ditto the Bay Area when I landed there for college. So did Washington, D.C., when I first went as a summer journalism intern. But New York always felt familiar somehow, even from the very first time I visited, over Christmas with my family in junior high. I always sensed I wanted to come back someday and stay for a while, maybe try to make a life there. Needless to say, New York doesn't inspire this feeling in everyone. I've known lots of people—friends, acquaintances, former co-workers, relatives— who tried living in New York but left after a few months or even weeks, hating and cursing it. My instinct about the city kicked in again right after college when I moved there knowing hardly anyone. I felt a sense of relief, of "at last," wash over me as soon as I landed at LaGuardia. And that feeling never left, year after year after year, even as part of me always still pined for Beirut.

Now as the weeks go by, I keep pitting New York and Beirut in my head as potential permanent homes. What do I need to feel to know I'm home? Beirut has almost all the key ingredients of any recognizable definition of home. I have lots of relatives here and warm relationships with most of them. My neighborhood still has many of the same buildings and shops and people as it always did, even though it's changed too over the years. The noise and crowdedness and chaos of Beirut feel deeply familiar—that's one of the things I've remembered most about it—and that din can be comforting in ways. Maybe those aspects of New York, so reminiscent of Beirut, are what have always drawn me to it.

But do I need to be surrounded by family or friends to feel at home? In New York, I had to carve out my own social life mostly from scratch at the beginning. The city wasn't home because I had friends or family there. I sensed it had home potential as soon as I arrived, knowing hardly anyone—and well before a few college friends from California eventually moved there, too. Maybe the city's elusive mix of the stimulating and the soulful was what resonated with me instantly, long before I'd noticed any echoes with my former hometown.

I'm missing New York achingly now. But what I'm missing most isn't just New York as a city. Beirut can still match it in many ways, in its constant energy and mystique and surprise—the bustling city streets, the diverse mix of people, the vigorous nightlife, the dizzying churn of cafés, bars, shops, and restaurants, and all the alluring ingredients and dishes to rediscover and explore. What I'm missing in Beirut is the sense of ownership, that feeling of "this city is mine." In Beirut I still feel like a visitor much of the time, even as I'm making some progress in building a life. As the weeks go by, I sense that I'm not yet fully a part of this place, or not anymore, although I'm not ready to give up; it's way too early still. Maybe I'm not hypersocial enough to be comfortable as an adult in Beirut, and so far I've barely met any unmarried Lebanese women my age, living alone, too, so I feel like something of an outlier. In New York, none of that seemed to matter. The city is full of unmarried men and women, single by choice or circumstance, and living solo—a perfectly normal, unremarkable scenario in New York, a city that accommodates virtually every lifestyle imaginable. There I felt the city was mine even when I was sitting alone in my apartment night after night in those first weeks and months.

New York can certainly be a party city if you want it to be, but socializing all the time isn't a cultural mandate. Here in Beirut, I sense there are social butterfly expectations that I'll never live up to, but even so my calendar keeps filling up more as the weeks go by. A week or so after Curtis and Diana's party, Zeina and Marwan invite me out again to join them and a few of their friends at an Indian restaurant at the edge of downtown, a ten-minute taxi ride from my apartment. I walk into the ornate dining room, decorated in faux-Indian kitsch like so many in New York, and join the group of a half-dozen at the table. Sitting next to me is a former Beirut classmate of Zeina's named Randa, who also recently moved back here from the States, to work as an architect.

Randa is living with her parents and having a hard time adjusting to the loss of personal space—she had her own apartment for years in Los Angeles—but her parents are aging, and she wants to be in the same city and see how life here goes. She asks me about my own reasons for moving back to Beirut, and if I've made any new friends here yet. I say it's been slow going but I've met a few people, and I mention Curtis and Diana.

"Oh, I know them, too. I've met them once or twice through mutual friends at AUB," Randa replies. "So you probably met that guy James, too."

Incredible, the constant small-world swirl here.

"Actually I did," I answer. "I just met him at a dinner party at their place. How did you guess I'd know him?"

"He knows some of the same people at the university, and I think he hits on, like, every girl he meets," she says, laughing.

"He hit on me a couple of weeks ago. I told him I have a boyfriend in L.A., and he said, 'So? He's not here, is he?' "

So: James is a player then. A pro. I should've guessed. It was absolutely written all over his face, so obvious from his smooth, nonchalant style. I'm glad I decided not to call him.

That night at Curtis and Diana's dinner party, while I'd been making small talk with him, my mind had drifted to a scenario where we're dating and going on exciting adventures all over Lebanon. *Okay, hmm*, I'd started thinking: *I could meet a guy in Beirut.* A cute, witty guy I can have fun with and who knows some of my friends to boot. It's not like things with Richard are solidified. True that we've been e-mailing a lot and missing each other, but how can I know what he's really thinking until I see him next?

Then I'd smiled to myself as I remembered what a cousin who lived in Beirut for a while a few years ago told me, when she was feeling exasperated about the men she was going out with: "The guys I meet in Beirut want just one thing: to fuck me or to marry me."

An exaggeration no doubt, and a different scenario from mine. She was dating locals. James is an expat. Still, those words have come rushing back more than once since the party. I've been wondering if there wasn't some useful warning in there, even though I'm not exactly looking to meet men right now. I may not know quite where things stand with Richard—we haven't had any big "relationship" conversations since I've been here—but my feelings for him haven't changed, and I'm looking forward to seeing him in New York later this month.

Also, the more I think about it, the more I realize that I need to wrestle with how I feel about Beirut on my own terms, without my relationship to it hinging on a potentially volatile romance with a guy, whether it's Richard or someone I happen to meet here. In New York, my feelings about the city never had anything to do with a guy. Here in Beirut, I need to do my best to find out if the city is still my home before I can welcome someone else in, whoever that may turn out to be.

Even though I have a few friends here now, I'm reconnecting with family and with the old neighborhood, and my freelance work life is coming along, I keep waiting for that visceral "ah, I'm home" feeling to kick in. Maybe it comes in as a soft whisper now and then; mostly it's been palpably absent.

But walking always helps bind me to a place and clarify my feelings for it. So I'm taking as many long walks as I can. Nearly every day I'm wandering around Beirut, intentionally getting lost and forcing myself to find my way back to my apartment, to really drill the city streets into my brain. I'm trying to learn and relearn Beirut up through my soles and ankles and knees, anchor myself to it physically. I've always discovered and rediscovered New York this way, taking clusters of streets and alleyways and neighborhoods at a time.

One morning in early October, I walk around the corner from my apartment to noisy Hamra Street and all the way to the western edge of it. I pass a handmade jewelry shop I like, and the new Applebee's (*et tu,* Beirut?), scents of grilling hamburgers wafting out its door, and past a half-dozen condo construction sites, hearing the jackhammers and clanking sounds ring out over the car engines and honks and pedestrian chatter along Hamra. I reach a fork at the end of the block and turn downhill along a leafy, winding street to the Corniche. Walking downhill along this quiet path toward the waterfront, I stroll by a small scuba-diving shop and the cream-white Hotel Mozart with its lovely twirled-stone balconies, and past patchy empty lots overgrown with weeds, edging up against dirt-covered old apartment buildings ten stories high with laundry hanging from their balconies. I follow the street's downhill curve to the right, past a car dealership with a candy-red refurbished 1970s Datsun out front and a parking lot filled with late-model BMWs and Mercedes, past an old three-story abandoned apartment building with deep cracks running through its dirty stone walls, its crumbling rooms probably filled with squatters now. The sign over the entryway says TOKYO in faded red paint, the Y long since rubbed out by rain or age. The small wrought-iron gate out front is rusted, but a red hibiscus tree behind it blooms full and lush.

Emerging from the bottom end of that downhill street, I'm now facing the sea. I fight my way through six lanes of honking cars, none of them stopping at the traffic light, to cross over to the Corniche sidewalk. I spot the old Ferris wheel to my left. As a child, I used to beg my parents to let me ride that thing, but they didn't like the looks of it; too creaky, too rusted. I walk along. On my right, across the Corniche away from the water side, I see a faded pink three-story house, reputedly once belonging to a murdered dentist by the name of Dr. Dray. A tragic story, if it's true, but his name always makes me smile.

The Corniche is lined with palm trees. Ahead in the distance are downtown apartment towers and hotels of all heights, from five to two dozen stories tall, old or new or under construction. The city's landmark black-and-white-striped lighthouse sits on a hill, across the Corniche from the water's edge, and the newer, blander gray lighthouse rises up along the boulevard a short distance ahead of me. I walk past the Manara Palace Café, a longtime seaside hangout for smoking argileh water pipes and drinking Arabic coffee, and past the Riviera Beach Lounge, its white umbrellas hiding rows of tanned men and women sunning themselves on chaises longues on this warm October day. A few meters away, down on the rocks just below the Corniche, working-class families and women wearing veils have brought their kids to swim for free. I think back to something an aunt told me a while back, that when she was growing up and one of the trendy, high-ticket beach clubs in Beirut was called the Saint Simon, she and her friends would content themselves with sunning at the "Saint Balash," Arabic for "Saint Freebie."

I keep walking, dodging joggers and all the zooming mopeds and bicycles on the Corniche sidewalk, and look out at the Jet Skiers going wild in the water, wondering if one of these days two of them are going to crash into each other. In the near distance, in the hills to my right, across the Corniche, I spot the AUB's pink-brick College Hall clock tower, rebuilt after it was bombed in 1991 just after the civil war was technically over. Now the downtown skyline is coming more clearly into view, and I see the bombed-out Holiday Inn—a mid-1970s civil war relic—and a Starbucks on my right. Those two sights at once would make for a jarring view almost anywhere else, but in Beirut, where the decrepit and the brand new sidle up next to each other along nearly every street, no architectural pairing seems incongruous.

Slowly I'm approaching the old seaside district of Ain el Mreisseh, a web of small streets that rise up along a hill across the Corniche and are lined with lovely cottages. At the crumbling little fishing harbor that sits at the lower edge of Ain el Mreisseh, I see a group of straw-hatted men fishing along the rocks.

Just like the men who gather at Hamra's cafés daily—keeping up their habit even as the old coffee shops give way to shiny new chain establishments—these harbor regulars, or their fathers and grandfathers before them, have been coming down here to throw their fishing lines into the water year after year, decade after decade, as the city has imploded and rebuilt itself around them.

About a half hour after I first hit the Corniche, I'm nearing the edge of downtown. Still walking on the waterfront, I pass an elderly white-haired man selling fresh-squeezed orange juice from a wheelbarrow, his back leaning against the seaside railing, the Mediterranean waves rolling softly and breaking a few feet behind him down against the black and gray rocks. A few feet away on the Corniche, I pass a white Ottoman-style house with arched windows, a red-shingled roof, and a garden of purple hydrangea trees planted outside, and two groups of elderly men sitting at tables playing backgammon in the shade of the overhanging branches.

On one side of the house is a gated entrance that leads, past pink bougainvillea bushes, down to the glamorous La Plage beach club, where I spot a group of bleached-blond Lebanese women in bikinis and enormous sunglasses spread out on fluffy white beach towels. Past the Alfa Romeo dealership a few steps away is the expensive crafts shop Artisans du Liban et d'Orient, with its exquisite mother-of-pearl-inlaid tables, gold-threaded caftans, sea-blue blown-glass bottles, and hammered silver serving platters. The store's windows look out onto the water. I pass the famous Phoenicia Hotel, where visiting heads of state usually stay, and the new Four Seasons Hotel high-rise, with its curvy balconies and blue-glass windows overlooking the sea. Across from the hotel, rows of billboards with quotes from the international press scream out: "BEIRUT IS BACK . . . AND IT'S BEAUTIFUL."— THE GUARDIAN and "BEYROUTH REVIT SON AGE D'OR."—PARIS MATCH. The posters are interspersed with oversize vintage photos of women water-skiing in the Mediterranean near the adjacent Hôtel St.-Georges and Yacht Club, and photos of decadent society parties from Beirut's prewar heyday in the 1960s.

Now passing the iconic pink-stone Hôtel St.-Georges, scaffolded and in the middle of a prolonged renovation after it was wrecked in the war, and across from it a collapsed white building that was destroyed during the Hariri assassination car bomb, I notice that the hotel's Yacht Club, at least the outdoor terrace part, is open for business again, its long blue pool flanked by white umbrellas where members of the city's leisure class, and surely a few nostalgic souls, are sunning themselves under the piercing midday rays.

Time for a lunch break. I cross over from the Corniche, winding through the traffic toward downtown. I make a right after the Tom Ford boutique and go up a hill, past still more luxury-condo construction sites and into the new Beirut Souks shopping area at the edge of downtown. All the shaded benches in the Souks complex are full, shoppers with Carolina Herrera and Balenciaga and Zara and Stella McCartney and Jimmy Choo bags texting or drinking iced coffees out of the hot sun. Before the war, Beirut's downtown was a noisy, crowded area where people of all classes—coming from the posh Achrafieh district on the east side, or the mixed-class west, or the poorer suburbs, or the mountain villages—gathered to shop for produce or housewares or jewelry or knickknacks sold in small tightly clustered shops and at vendors' stands in the old, long-destroyed souk. But in the area's new postwar incarnation, it's an almost strictly upscale shopping district that looks more like a glam Western shopping mall, with rows and rows of shops along an indoor-outdoor arcade of herringbone-patterned stone buildings and arched tunnelways, designed by the Spanish celebrity architect Rafael Moneo and the Lebanese Samir Khairallah. The Souks are surrounded by expensive new real estate, construction sites shielded by billboards promising luxury residential and office buildings, and a swank new marina going up just across the Corniche on the waterfront.

There's no resemblance at all here to an old Arab souk, to the bustling, dusty market stalls that existed around downtown before they were flattened by war and reconstruction. Much of the construction of the new Souks was finished only this past year, and so far the district hasn't been attracting enough shoppers to create a din. On a weekday like today, I hear just a soft burble of voices, and heels click-clacking on the cobblestones. Bored security guards are standing around every few meters and staring idly, directing the usual once-over at passing pedestrians.

I follow the gentle hill that leads from the new Souks area into central downtown, then cross Weygand Street toward the twelfth-century Omari Mosque, near the edge of the business district, and into the star-shaped central square called the Najmeh, or L'Étoile; on one edge of it sits the ornate St. George's Orthodox Cathedral, built in 1767 and restored after the civil war. I walk inside the church, escaping the sun, and sit in one of the pews for a few minutes, staring up at the gilded frescoes along the walls. My mind drifts back to the Orthodox ceremonies I'd go to with my family and my grandparents when we used to visit them in the mountain town of Aley, when Samir and I were kids, and when it was safe to leave home for a weekend. I can still almost smell the warm, spicy incense and hear the priest's slow chants booming through the chapel: "Unto the ages of ages. . . ."

I grab an outdoor table at a Lebanese restaurant called Al Balad, in a yellow stone building near the newer of the two downtown clock towers, this one built during the French Mandate era in the late 1920s and early 1930s. Looking over the menu, I realize I want to try much more than I can eat all at once, but I'm not heading home right after lunch; it would be a waste to overorder since I can't take a doggie bag today. I finally decide on the eggplant *fatteh,* a dish I crave often and occasionally make in New York. It's similar to the chickpea dish called tiss'ye that I love and last had at Umayma's Ramadan dinner, but this one is made with roasted strips of eggplant instead of warm chickpeas. Like the tiss'ye, the eggplant fatteh is also a layered dish, with generous ladles of garlic-spiked yogurt, topped with fried pieces of Arabic bread and showered in pine nuts sautéed in butter. Al Balad makes an exceptional fatteh. I luxuriate in every bite, no need to share with anyone on this solo lunch.

As I eat, I watch pedestrians, mostly European and Gulf tourists on this sunny Tuesday afternoon in October, as they stroll along the stone lanes, stopping to gaze up at the buildings that line this part of the central downtown. Most of the buildings are just five or six stories high, in saffron and earth-toned stone with dark green or brown shutters, and were originally built during the Ottoman or French colonial period. Some of the buildings survived in part after the civil war, but most have been heavily reconstructed, in a few cases around walls that could still be salvaged.

I continue my walk past the center of downtown and up into the gently hilly Wadi Abu Jamil area, the city's old Jewish quarter, now a cobweb of construction sites, and I walk through the neighborhood along a black cobblestone sidewalk, past the old synagogue that's currently being renovated, and past my late great-aunt Wadad's Ahliah school. I emerge on the other side and make a right at the street that leads back down the hill toward the Corniche. There I make a left and walk back along the seaside for a while. Crossing back over, I pass the statue of the 1950s Egyptian and Arab nationalist leader Gamal Abdel Nasser and walk from there up the sloping street that leads back toward the AUB campus and Hamra, past a traffic jam of SUVs and mopeds and wheelbarrows piled high with onions for sale, then around the bend to Bliss Street, the campus's main drag, named after one of the Protestant missionaries who founded the university in 1866. Finally I'm making a left past the Dunkin' Donuts on Bliss and heading along a tight, car-crammed block toward my building.

All in all it's been a five-hour ramble, including my break for lunch. I'm sweating and my face is flushed—it's still hot here, not quite middle-of-summer heat but close—and although I'm tired, I feel I can keep doing this for hours, for days. I've never taken such a long walk around Beirut and never spent this much time just wandering around the city solo, trying to learn how the pieces all fit together—especially now, after so many of its parts have been rebuilt. On past summer visits, I've usually taken cars or taxis around the city, mostly tagging along with family. I needed this walk today—for the exercise, sure, but even more, for the sense that I'm reattaching myself, physically, literally, to Beirut, to its streets and its rhythms.

Ever since I can remember, I've planned food-related endpoints and landmarks for my journeys near and far. On that walk to downtown, I didn't know I'd end up eating eggplant fatteh for lunch, but I knew I wanted to find something delicious and Lebanese that I hadn't had in a while, and fatteh turned out to be just the thing. Another October morning I go on a more food-focused trek. I take a service taxi across downtown and into the Achrafieh neighborhood, on the east side of the city. I walk around the winding streets looking for a place called Sahyoun, which I've heard serves the city's best falafel. After I wrote a rant about falafel on my blog the other week, I'd heard from a bunch of readers instructing me to go to Sahyoun. I'm a falafel skeptic; it's not my favorite Middle Eastern culinary invention, but I'm willing to be converted after all these years. I stroll through the curvy uphill streets of Achrafieh, past the mustard-yellow brick Maronite church L'Église Notre Dame de l'Annonciation, with its serene tree-lined courtyard, into alleyways full of posh boutiques and old bakeries. A few cars pass by along the twisty streets, nothing like the perpetual traffic jams of Hamra. Here the buildings seem more orderly: either clusters of two- or three-story stone houses, their balconies draped with flowers, or condo buildings, mostly upscale but modest in height, no laundry visibly hanging from their rails.

Eventually I emerge on the southwestern side of the quiet residential area and reach the five-way intersection of Damascus Road, a wide avenue with an accurate name: the road does eventually lead to the Syrian capital. The intersection is flanked by parking lots and construction sites and has wide-open sightlines to the tall, bland condo buildings of southeast Beirut in the near distance, and to the crumbling-stone civil war ruins dotted among them. I find Sahyoun, actually two Sahyouns, which turn out to be side-by-side falafel stands owned by competing brothers who have both kept the same name; copyright laws are, one will quickly note in Beirut, very low on the list of enforcement priorities.

I order a falafel sandwich from the stand farther downhill, the one I've heard is better, and watch the cook take the hot falafel spheres off the revolving round fryer and wrap them in Arabic bread, topping them with dollops of tartar sauce, deep-red slices of tomato, and a sprig of mint. I take a bite: not bad, actually pretty good, fresh-tasting instead of too dry or too soggy, and not overly cluttered with ingredients. The mint leaves add an unexpected punch, brightening the creamy, fried sandwich filling. This is a much better falafel than I've had in recent memory, maybe anywhere. It even lives up to the hype. I won't crave one of these every week, but I'll be back.

Food pilgrimages, to me, aren't only about the food, or the trip. It's not just that I love to eat and to wander around. Even a relatively short, taxi-assisted trek to Sahyoun, and a winding stroll back, after having found the thing I was looking for—no matter whether I enjoyed the food itself or not—makes me feel recharged. Meandering through the city, taking in the sights and sounds, and reflecting on my day or my life or whatever other subject floats through, clears my head. It's a mobile meditation, with an edible reward at the end. Reminds me of one afternoon in Manhattan, before I landed my first food-writing job at *Time Out New York*, when I'd read about a certain kind of Portuguese cheese bread in the newspaper and had walked from Houston Street forty blocks uptown to Hell's Kitchen to look for the bakery that makes it. The roll itself wasn't such a thrill, and the cheese was too bland, at least the way this bakery made it. But I loved the search, the ramble, the mission fulfilled.

Another balmy Beirut morning in mid-October, I walk downtown again, stopping this time at the Virgin Megastore, housed in an old brick theater with slim dark red windows, to buy a CD from a now-defunct Lebanese trip-hop band called Soap Kills; then I pop into the downtown branch of the classic Amal Bohsali pastry shop to buy a piece of *knafeh*. Knafeh is one of my favorite breakfast-dessert hybrids, a cakelike confection made with a crumbly dough called *mafroukeh*, topped with a melted, oozingly stretchy mild local cheese called *akkawi*, and generous drizzles of hot sugar syrup. Bohsali serves an exceptional knafeh, and although it makes for heavy eating at any time of day, it takes me straight back to childhood and back to family dinners in Houston, when my parents would pick up knafeh from a Lebanese pastry shop there, or order it by FedEx from an Arabic confectionery in Michigan, to reheat at home.

I stroll back to Hamra through the short hills above the Wadi Abu Jamil district, taking a path I haven't gone on before. I navigate back to Hamra mostly on instinct, trying to sharpen a directional skill that's always felt sorely lacking. I walk along a paved pathway above the construction sites of Wadi Abu Jamil, past parking lots, trees, and renovated old houses, and reach the foot of a concrete stairway that leads up to the edge of the neighborhood, from which I'll cross an intersection and end up at the eastern edge of Hamra. Before I climb the concrete steps, I stop to look up at a butter-colored old townhouse with elaborately carved stone balconies and a lovely violet house next to it.

As I'm reaching the top of the stairs and about to cross over to Hamra, an armed guard stops me and asks where I'm going. Home, I say. He looks me up and down, waits two seconds, waves me by. One of the mansions owned by the family of former prime minister Hariri is nearby, so there are armed guards and chained-off sidewalks and tanks positioned on the street, as in so many other spots considered likely targets all over the city. Beirut still looks like a military zone in certain places, until you get used to it and almost stop noticing.

Despite the interruption, I'm finding this route through the hilly edge of downtown so pleasant today—it's quiet and traffic free and cuts a straight line through to Hamra. As I walk, I try to picture how Beirut looked in the nineteenth and early twentieth centuries, when it was all rangy gardens and agricultural fields and stretches of grass sprinkled with yellow *houmayda* wildflowers, with red-roofed stone houses dotted across a wide-open landscape reaching down to the Mediterranean. As a young girl, my mother would walk back and forth from Hamra to the Ahliah school in Wadi Abu Jamil every day, taking roughly the same path as I've taken today, but with no construction sites to snake through, no buildings blocking the view clear across town and down to the sea.

I'm conscious, as I take these long walks now, that my stride is firmer, more confident than it was in those early weeks in August and September. With my feet, I'm already starting to feel like I own the city again, at least in some small way. I'm memorizing it physically, learning the routes. Route/routine. It hits me that this is what a routine is—a kind of route. I need routines to feel at home. More and more they're taking shape, my routines, my routes.

I was thinking as I walked today about what a city can say to you if you listen. New York, to me, has always seemed to say: *Here you are. Stay. This is what you've been looking for, isn't it?* Beirut, as far as I can tell now, is saying something like *You can stay if you want, if you're up to it. But it's not going to be easy. Not in the least.*

Obviously what a city "says" to anyone is a projection. The question is, can that message be ignored, overruled? Time can potentially override it, and so can new friends and routines, but might the city still say what it always said, even if it says it in a slightly lower voice as the years go by? Can you fall in love with someone whom you knew early on you weren't in love with? Can you fall back in love with someone or something you once loved, after years of mystery and distance?

As I sip my coffee one morning, I scan through cultural listings on a local website and read about an event that night to celebrate the launch of a book called *At the Edge of the City*. It's a compilation of essays about the Horsh al-Sanawbar, an eighty-acre park in southeastern Beirut that's mostly closed to the public. The reasons it's closed are nebulous, and apparently some of the contributors to the book have tried to get official answers out of the government but gotten nowhere. The theory seems to be that the authorities are trying to keep the park, the 80 percent of it that's officially closed, pristine, so city elites who have a government *wasta*—a personal connection—can use it privately, without having to commune with the riff-raff. I go to the event that night, just a few blocks from my apartment, and walk in as the book's editor, Fadi Shayya, is talking about the history of the park and showing a nineteenth-century postcard of the Horsh as a snowy pine forest, with men riding through it on donkeys. The park had been created in the seventeenth century by the Druze ruler of Lebanon under the Ottoman Empire, Fakhreddine Maan, to protect Beirut from the southern winds. In the centuries since then, it's been alternately protected, neglected, and bombed, most heavily during the 1982 Israeli invasion of Lebanon. For the past decade, the Île de France municipality has been contracted to help maintain the park.

During the Q&A session after the presentation, I strike up a conversation with a friendly-looking woman named Joumana, one of the contributors to the book, who made some of the more fascinating comments about the park's history. She also looks slightly familiar. We quickly find out that, in typical Lebanese style, we know people in common: she's friends with the son of some old classmates of my parents, and it turns out Joumana and I met briefly at his wedding reception a few summers ago. Since then she's grown out her hair, but her delicate features and warm smile instantly come back to me. Joumana lives in Dubai now but is here visiting for a week, and she invites me to a related event the next night at a place called Sanayeh House, in a district not far from Hamra and adjacent to a public park called Sanayeh.

The next evening I spend the half hour before the event starts walking around that neighborhood, past rows of glass-balconied condo buildings, searching for the address Joumana gave me and peering at the map I printed out. I spot another woman who seems lost, too. She looks about my age and is wearing stylish low-slung pants and a slim-fitting purple sweater that sets off her shoulder-length chocolate hair, and she seems approachable despite her striking looks. We make eye contact, she introduces herself as Mirna, and we quickly learn we're searching for the same place and that Joumana invited her, too. We amble around together, lost.

We ask for directions several times and keep getting pointed to Zico House, a well-known events venue nearby. We eventually walk in, thinking Sanayeh House must be a nickname for Zico House, and go up the stairs, following the light and noise to a room where the door is cracked open. This has to be it. We push open the door and walk in. A group of people who seem to be in their twenties and thirties are talking animatedly, as someone with long black hair and a wool hat writes on the chalkboard. Sounds like a vigorous discussion, and Mirna and I stand briefly, waiting for an opening in the chatter so we can make sure we're in the right place and take our seats.

I silently clear my throat, then hear myself saying "Hi . . ."

Suddenly everyone in the room is quiet, staring at us. I eke out my question.

"No, this isn't Sanayeh House," a voice from the back of the room chimes in. More silence. No one else speaks up. I'm mortified that we've barged in and interrupted, although I'm not sure what we've just walked into.

We apologize clumsily and hurry out. Mirna tells me, when we reach the bottom of the stairs, that we must have crashed a transsexuals meeting. I later learn that Zico House, among its many functions, is a meeting place for a Lebanese organization that lobbies for gay, lesbian, and transsexual rights. No wonder people in the room looked anxious when they saw two unknowns standing in the doorway watching. Lebanon is less aggressive about persecuting gay and transgendered people, at least vis-à-vis other countries in the Middle East (which isn't saying much, I realize), but two strangers barging into your meeting is understandable cause for worry here.

By now the Sanayeh House event, wherever that is, must have started. Mirna and I both call Joumana's cell but don't reach her. We keep on looking, and a half hour later we give up. But we've hit it off nicely, Mirna and I, in our clueless wanderings. I've learned that she grew up here and has just moved back from Dubai for an urban-planning job. We're new Beirutis and old Beirutis, the two of us. We exchange numbers.

I e-mail Joumana the next day to apologize for getting lost and not showing up at her event. Later in the week, she invites me to lunch with Mirna and another friend of theirs. The group of them are easy to be around, and refreshingly, nothing feels forced about our conversation, even though I'm the newcomer to this crowd. The chitchat roams from Beirut-versus-Dubai (a favorite topic around here these days, with so many Lebanese emigrating to Dubai for work), to relationships, and to what we love and hate about this city.

It's a stroke of luck to have stumbled into Mirna and Joumana—hanging out with them feels oddly effortless. Joumana seems to have a sharp, creative mind but also a genuineness, a mellow vibe, an appealing expression. It reminds me a little of what first drew me to my New York friend Claire, a certain lighthearted openness and a quick intelligence coming through all at once in her eyes. Though Joumana is returning to Dubai soon and comes to Beirut only occasionally, perhaps Mirna and I will get together again. I still don't know many people my age in Beirut and could use a few more friends.

I'm about to have more company soon, too. My parents will land in Beirut in late October for their annual Lebanon homecoming trip, and I'll spend a few days with them here before I head to New York. I want to stock the fridge before they arrive. At the Co-op, a compact two-story supermarket a few blocks from the apartment, where my mother used to shop when we lived here, I pick up a few tubs of labneh and of tangy Lebanese yogurt, and some bags of Arabic bread, and a few kilos of the vegetables and greens my parents like having around: the finger-sized local cucumbers, tomatoes, radishes, and fresh zaatar leaves, a local variety of thyme, to fold up with bread, labneh, and olive oil at breakfast. I grab some carrots to slice into sticks and soak in water flavored with lemon juice and salt—a popular Beirut snack. I also can't resist buying a tube of Choco Prince cookies and a box of Picon cheese, for old times' sake. Choco Prince billboards and TV ads were ubiquitous when I was growing up here, and Picon commercials had a jingle that my school friends and I had endless fun with:

> *Jibnit Picon, jibne khira'iye. Min teez al' kalb . . .*
> Meaning: "Picon cheese, a shitty cheese, from a
>   dog's ass . . ."

The real words were something like "Jibnit Picon, a French cheese, from cow's milk," but the dirty version rhymed nicely in Arabic. When I get home from the store, I open a wedge of Picon and wrap it in a piece of Arabic bread. I haven't eaten it in so many years, and I'm curious if it will be remotely edible now. Hmm, not too bad: just salty creaminess, with a sticky, almost plasticky texture. It's processed cheese and tastes like it, but it's not horribly objectionable, I have to admit. The Choco Prince is sheer pleasure, just as I remember it. Buttery biscuits sandwiching a chocolate cream filling. All processed, nothing terribly original going on. But a very basic kind of comfort and joy. Two major culinary fixtures of my childhood, and here they still are.

The days before my parents arrive quickly fill up. I stop by a restaurant called Tawlet, specializing in Lebanese regional dishes, and catch up over lunch with its owner, Kamal Mouzawak. He opened Tawlet a few years ago after creating the Souk el Tayeb, billed as the first farmer's market in Beirut, although in some ways it's a revival of the prewar produce souks around downtown. I'd met Kamal in New York at a food event a couple of years ago, and I'd run into him here in Beirut while shopping at Souk el Tayeb a few weeks ago. The market is downtown on Saturday mornings, and I've tended to sleep through it most weekends, but when I've motivated myself to get up in time, I've always been glad I did. It's one of the most reliable places to find high-quality, organically grown fruits and vegetables—plus cheeses, honey, pastries, and cooked dishes made by the farmers' families.

While Kamal greets some Tawlet regulars, I flip through this week's issue of *Time Out Beirut* as I devour a plate of kibbeh nayyeh, the Lebanese lamb tartare, wrapping it up in fingerfuls of pita with a slice of white onion, a pinch of salt, and a drizzle of olive oil. Soon Kamal comes back to the table and tells me he wants to introduce me to another New York expat now living in Beirut. She and I look at each other for a long second, then both smile. It's a journalist named Kaelen, who had worked at *The Village Voice* at the same time I did, more than a decade ago. We never knew each other very well, but I'd heard she'd moved to Beirut about ten years ago to cover the art scene and ended up staying and marrying a Lebanese. She's on that list of people I've been meaning to contact in Beirut. I should've guessed, after all the other coincidental run-ins I've had so far, that I'd bump in to her sooner or later. We catch up for a few minutes, then she has to start her interview with Kamal for a profile she's doing for a magazine, but we vow to plan a proper drinks session.

An unexpected e-mail arrives that night. An acquaintance from a recent freelance project in New York tells me two of her friends from the States are visiting Beirut this week, on a whim, while en route to a Dubai fashion event, and asks me if I'd mind showing them around a little. I make plans to meet them the next night: Alison, a magazine editor in New York, and her friend Stacy, a TV writer in L.A. We meet for a drink at the glass-enclosed rooftop bar of the new Le Gray hotel downtown, where they're staying, then head to the dinner I've booked for us at Abdel Wahab, a Lebanese restaurant I like in Achrafieh.

It's a hot night—the temperatures still haven't dropped—so instead of walking, we take a taxi across the flat, open middle of downtown. We cross Martyrs' Square, with its bullet-ridden metal statue of gun-toting Lebanese revolutionaries who were hanged by the Ottomans in World War I, and drive past the luxurious new brick mansions of the Saifi Village neighborhood on the eastern edge of downtown. Our taxi then goes up a slow-sloping hill into Achrafieh. We walk into the restaurant, my companions admiring the ornate green and gold door that leads in and up to the leafy rooftop terrace. Over plates of eggplant fatteh, and shish taouk dipped into the creamy garlic sauce known as *toum*, and fresh sumac-spiced fattoush salad, and glasses of *arak*, the local anise liqueur, we chatter about the New York media world, people we know in common, and their impressions of Beirut.

"Such a beautiful and fascinating little city. I can't believe more Americans don't come here. Is there much tourism going on these days? Do people still think it's dangerous?"

"I guess so," I reply. "A lot of tourists want to feel it's a hundred percent safe before they visit. It's the Middle East, though. There's always something brewing. But I've been overhearing more American, European, African, and Asian tourists around Beirut lately. Not tons, but more than I'd noticed in the past."

After dinner I take them on a stroll through the cobblestoned Achrafieh streets down to the adjacent Gemmayzeh area, lit up as always, its bars buzzing but quieter than in midsummer, and we drink beers at a little dive bar called Godot before I drop them off by taxi at their hotel.

A happy side effect of this night is that I felt like the Beirut expert in the group. (Competition was not stiff, granted.) I'd made the plans and ordered the food and drinks, and after our nightcap I'd sent Alison and Stacy off with advice on where they should stroll and explore the next day, and on where to find original handmade Lebanese textiles and housewares to take home. As we walked to Godot, I also gave them a general overview of Lebanese politics, since they asked about the current situation. I don't think I would've felt this confident showing visitors around just a few short weeks ago. But more and more, I'm realizing now, this city is mine. I live here. More and more I know what to do, where to go—or I know enough for now, anyway. I haven't yet figured out the home question and likely won't for a while. But I'm feeling much less like a visitor.

At what point, then, does one definitively cross over from "visitor" to "local"? In my sixth or seventh year in New York, I would jokingly ask my native Manhattanite friends, "Am I a real New Yorker yet?"

The answers would usually range from "Yes, ever since you were born," to "No, in New York you have to give it another three years at least."

I've been thinking in these past weeks about how we negotiate spaces, how we take foreign environments—cities, neighborhoods, houses—and make them familiar, or how they gradually become familiar over time, whether or not we ultimately fall in love with them. Spaces that seem cold, new, and unfamiliar to our bodies and movements gradually take our shape, and we start to flow through them naturally, unthinkingly. We may feel love for some of those spaces, indifference to others, but still most of the spaces we move through start to mold themselves to our lives, to become easy and practically unconscious.

Maybe the where-is-home question is ultimately chicken and egg, whether it's about specific spaces or entire cities. Do we move to a city and then it becomes home? Or in these days, when we have more choices of where to live, do we choose to live somewhere long term mainly *because* it feels like home?

The German twentieth-century philosopher Martin Heidegger was preoccupied with physical spaces and our relationship to them. With apologies to the Heidegger scholars I studied with at Berkeley (and who gave me wondrous A-grades even though I remained mostly in the dark about his major work, *Being and Time*), this is what I took away, and what I still think about all the time. One of Heidegger's ideas was the notion of "worlding," or the way we come into contact with objects and spaces around us, and the way we construct and negotiate our world by unconsciously responding to and interpreting the spaces we move through. I notice how my bedroom here in Beirut felt alien when I first arrived in August, even though it's the same bedroom I slept in as a child and have stayed in on summer visits over the years. But compared to my New York bedroom, which I'd grown so used to in recent years, this space felt foreign when I walked into it in August, not yet molded to my movements and my life. The bedroom had been an unconscious part of my life before, a very long time ago, but no longer. Now, a couple of months later, I move through it naturally again, unthinkingly.

My living room in Beirut, too: I felt strange and uncomfortable and lonely moving around in it at first, trying to decide which part of the long navy-blue sofa to sit on, whether to put my feet on the thick-legged wooden coffee table, whether the vase-shaped antique table lamp was at the right height. I needed to forge my own pathways through that room, arrange my stacks of books and magazines and papers on the coffee table in a way that felt comforting and accessible to me. Now I move through that room, too, as if I've always inhabited this space, not minding or even noticing if the table lamp is too low or the coffee table a little too high to put my feet up on. I've gotten in the habit of automatically sitting on the right-hand side of the sofa, nearer the window. It's as if I'd been living here all along, during those civil war years away when this room, this apartment, became foreign and distant spaces in another world.

But sometimes familiarity with a place doesn't, despite all efforts, make it home. Once in Vienna I passed in front of the house that the twentieth-century Austrian philosopher Ludwig Wittgenstein spent years designing only to discover that it was unlivable. When the house was built, with Wittgenstein's precise specifications about the height of ceilings and the plainness of doors, windows, and other normally ornamental bits, hardly anyone in his family could live in it. It was too austere and too devoid, on principle, of any decorative touches. One of Wittgenstein's sisters publicly declared the house unlivable, and another lived in it only briefly. It now houses the Bulgarian embassy. On paper the house was a minimalist's dream. In real life it was chilling, lacking any of the small soothing details that bring comfort or a human touch, at least to those it was built to house.

Whether or not a city, or a house, is ultimately a viable, beloved home must have at least partly to do with how it feels wrapped around you—its spaces, the whole shape and tone of the place, whether it fits snugly or widely, whatever your taste. Or is it ultimately a moot point to wax philosophical about home? Isn't home just the place where you grew up, or if not that, then the place where you live now, work, have friends or family?

Still, I can't get around the idea that sometimes "home" doesn't feel like home—or home doesn't feel like "home"—and sometimes a place that isn't "home" feels like home. (Put the quote marks wherever you like.) Maybe home used to be, necessarily, the place where you were born or grew up or where you live and work. But now that "home" can be a choice, at least in theory, just like every other consumer or lifestyle option, I don't think there's any going back to a world where Home wasn't a concept as much up for grabs as Career or Hobby. Now that we can almost easily, in many cultures, switch houses, towns, jobs, spouses, and friends, will more of us do as the most adventurous expats have done for centuries—leave the home of our past, if it doesn't fit right, and look for our true home?

But for anyone who has the option, I wonder if it would be a net plus to be able to say: "This city where I grew up, or where I've moved for work or for a relationship, or where I'm living my adult life at the moment, isn't the city where I feel most comfortable, happiest, most optimistic. So let me find another one—after all, there are roughly 36,000 other cities in the world to choose from." Or would that just bring on eternal questioning and longing? Would it be simpler to say This City Here Is Home, thanks to family or work or other necessities, and be done with the whole thing?

On days when the blues creep in, I wish I'd never left all my familiar routines in New York, and my good-enough comfort there, to come back to Beirut. On clearer-headed days, I do know what I'm doing here—seeing whether it still fits, snugly, in the way I want home to fit, but also not too snugly.

My parents fly in from Houston today, and they call tonight, a Sunday in late October, to say they're en route to Hamra from the airport. The electricity has just gone out in our building, more severely than during the usual partial blackouts. We have a generator, but it's not kicking in right now for some reason. An electrician is here, on his night off, trying to figure out the problem, so the building concierge, a lanky thirty-year-old named Ali, helps haul my parents' luggage up four flights of stairs to the apartment.

I open the door to let them in, we hug, and my mother says cheerfully that it's so refreshing to walk into a lived-in apartment. Normally when they come to Beirut on their visits, the apartment has been empty for long stretches. I haven't seen Mom and Dad in a few months, since before I left the States, and I've missed them. Even though it's nearly midnight when they get here, just after they finish dropping their bags in the master bedroom, we sit down for a nightcap glass of wine and catch up a bit. They're obviously exhausted and ready to crash, but I hear myself dropping the million-dollar question: "Where is home for you guys? Is it still Beirut? Is it Houston?" My mother chuckles, says nothing for a few seconds, then tells me she needs to think about it when she's more awake. My father answers right away: Houston is more comfortable, he says, because as much as Beirut feels like home and they're planning to spend more time here now that he's just retired, the city gets claustrophobic after a while, and he craves the infrastructural comforts (reliable electricity and a building elevator that works, for instance) and more open spaces. But coming to Beirut feels like a battery recharge. Seeing friends and family makes him feel a connection and vitality he doesn't feel in the same way in Houston. He seems to have figured out what each city means to him, and how it fits into his life now. My mother still doesn't say anything; she just gazes out the window.

Friends and relatives drop by from morning to night the next day to welcome my parents back. My mom's cousin Mona, stirring sugar into a cup of Arabic coffee and leaning back in the wooden rocking chair in our living room, glances over and says to my mother, "I wonder if I know any nice men for Salma to meet." My great-aunt Nida stops by, too, that afternoon and, in between casual chitchat with my parents and me, looks over and says to my mom, "Salma is lovely. *Yikhreeb ʒouk al rjal.* Damn those men." Meaning *"It's crazy that a man didn't nab her"*?

So far I haven't heard the "Why aren't you married yet?" bit since I got here in August—although I'd heard it on past visits to Beirut—and getting a version of it now, twice in a row, catches me off guard. Auntie Nida in particular has always struck me as progressive and independent-minded, far more so than many others of her generation. Maybe I'd forgotten, perhaps willfully, how my ongoing singlehood might puzzle and distress my relatives. Nida then tells us a story about how her aunt Amineh gave up her shot at marriage when, asked to dance on board a ship going to Europe in the 1930s, she'd said to the suitor, "Dance? No thank you. I am a Protestant."

My mother whispers to me that Nida is full of stories from the old neighborhood in Beirut and is delighted by the company of her nieces and nephews. I make a mental note to stop by her apartment for coffee sometime. There's a half century between us, but I love her sparkling eyes, her warmth and wit, and her infectious desire to tell funny stories and be surrounded by family. I want to get to know her better. And I'll forgive the "damn those men" comment.

It's not just my parents who are in town from the States this week. Kareem, the thirty-something son of my parents' friends, is also passing through Beirut. I've known him since we were kids although I rarely get a chance to see him these days, and he's here now visiting from California with his wife, Dionne—a vivacious blonde from Mississippi who I liked from the minute I met her at their wedding reception. They call one night to ask me to join them at a bar called Ferdinand in Hamra with some of their friends. One of Kareem's former Beirut classmates, Naji, shows up that night, too; he's a tall, good-looking guy in his early thirties who is in a wheelchair after getting paralyzed from the waist down in a car accident in college. As we all gather around a table ringed with ottoman seats in a corner of the indie-rock-thumping room and order our drinks, the question of what I'm doing in Beirut comes up. Soon we're all talking about home—where it is, what it is, what we make of it. Everyone here tonight either emigrated with their parents during the civil war or has lived outside Lebanon at some point.

Naji takes a sip of his beer. "Drinking is home, isn't it?" We all laugh. Naji is a champion athlete in the local version of the Paralympics, and he works in a high-powered job for a local disability nonprofit. He's not an alcoholic, this guy. But he says what any of my New York friends might have quipped on any of our nights out drinking, catching up, blowing off steam.

Easygoing and likable, Naji wears his disability as lightly and gracefully as I've ever seen anyone do it, and he makes it comfortable to talk about the subject, without awkwardness. I've known Naji for only a couple of hours, and I can't venture to guess what the rest of his life is like. But meeting him is a reminder that accepting circumstances and forging ahead with humor and grace is the way—albeit not the easiest way, and certainly not the only way. If he can rework his reality so he's living gracefully in a wheelchair, my move to Beirut is nothing in comparison. I decide I'm going to try to face down the emotional, social, and logistical challenges of living here with grace and humor. At least for the next few hours, while I'm remembering my vow.

The truth is, I've been madly impatient for my brief break from Beirut to visit New York, and to fall asleep next to Richard, and to have New York back, and my New York life back, even just for a few days. After which I'll have to leave it all behind and come back to Beirut. And probably ask myself all over again why I'm doing this. I know why, but that doesn't make it any easier. I've only just started picking up momentum here and accepting that Beirut is no longer a city I'm passing through on vacation, with a get-out-of-jail-free pass in my pocket. I don't want to escape in a hurry this time.

I'm sitting at the Lufthansa departure gate at the Beirut airport for my three-thirty A.M. flight to Frankfurt, then to JFK, and I'm finishing Julia Child's memoir *My Life in France*. In their long and seemingly very happy life together, Julia and her husband, Paul, jumped around and lived in various cities, houses, and apartments, every time Paul's diplomatic job forced them to move. They busily tried to make a home wherever they landed. The two of them were like their own mobile home unit; they created a life, and seemed to have a grand old time, in every city, save maybe the drab-sounding Plittersdorf, Germany—but even there they thrived for a while. If you have a talent for making yourself feel at home no matter where life takes you, is there even a need for another, more permanent kind of "home"?

Last night as I fell asleep, I started wondering if Richard and I, the two of us, could ever be home. I'm excited and anxious about seeing him when I arrive in New York tonight. I just want to soak him in, feel missed. But why haven't I yet been able to form anything that feels like home with someone else? With guys who've hinted at the marriage path, I was always scared I'd feel trapped. With the more elusive ones, I'd let myself entertain the idea silently—the eternal cliché of the hard-to-get—but I'd eventually tire of the lack of intimacy and make a preemptive strike, or they'd pull the plug. In my late thirties, I'm wondering: *Am I now scared of not being trapped enough, of being too free to roam? Or what if I discover that, for me, roaming is home?*

The afternoon I arrive in New York, Richard finishes up work early, comes home to find me in his bedroom napping, and wakes me up with a kiss. We snuggle for a long while and keep looking at each other and giggling and kissing. We go grocery shopping, open a bottle of wine, and cook dinner together, talking and laughing nonstop. I've been keeping him posted on my Beirut adventures, but we have lots to catch up on, and our conversation as always crackles and goes on for hours on end, and underneath it all, there's an intense serenity and ease. Not at all like I've been away for two months. And surprisingly, not like we'd parted on fairly wobbly terms the last time we saw each other.

While he's at work the next day, I roam around downtown Brooklyn near his apartment, where I'm staying this week since I've given my subletter a one-year lease. I find a café to sit in and finish up an editing project, and the routine feels natural, as if I'd never left. It also, oddly and unexpectedly, feels like a nearly seamless extension of my life in Beirut. To some extent, I'm doing here just what I do there. And vice versa.

I talk about cities that night with Richard's roommate, Dan, as we all hang out in the kitchen making pasta. Dan, who has moved around various cities for work in the past few years, tells me he can only feel like a city is home if he decides from the beginning he's there to stay. That way, he believes, people take you more seriously, invest in you more.

Others have been saying the same thing to me, in Beirut, too: "You have to make a decision where you're going to live, and commit to it." Meaning, decide whether the place you're in is home, and act like it is from the get-go. My childhood friend Rana said this to me over pizza when we met up for lunch in Beirut the day before I left for New York. I hadn't seen Rana since elementary school, but we'd reconnected a few years ago over e-mail. Since I'd landed in Beirut this summer, Rana and I had talked on the phone a few times, but she'd been busy with her four-year-old and family obligations, so we hadn't caught up in person until the other day. Seeing her felt strangely normal, as if we'd still been hanging out every day since elementary school, when we used to take ballet classes together and I'd braid her hair, still the same silky-straight auburn strands I loved playing with. She has the same bright smile and easy laugh I remember, and we didn't need hours and hours of catch-up conversation to get back on track. Once we'd rushed to hug each other as soon as we met up outside the pizza place in Hamra—"You look exactly the same!" "No way. But you do, seriously!"—we were back in business.

After Rana said to me over lunch that it's better to decide

where home is going to be and stick with it, she paused, then added: Even though Beirut is home for her and her husband, and has been home for most of their lives, now they want to leave for good. A few bouts of street violence in recent years, and the ongoing instability since the war, finally made them decide, *Khalas. That's it. We need to get out of here if we can figure out how.*

"But isn't everyone in Beirut always talking about leaving, or at least thinking about it?" I ask her. That's true of New York, too. As much as die-hard New Yorkers are in love with their city, the cliché about life in New York is that most everyone is always planning to leave. Both cities are exhausting in their way, hence the constant escape fantasies. For those like me who can plausibly transport their career or life elsewhere, Beirut might feel more livable and appealing precisely when it's a potentially temporary place, not an eternal trap of looming war and chaos and dysfunction. If you're there for only a little while, in your mind anyway, it's easier to get through the roughest times.

My New York visit is only a week long, and the time spent catching up with friends, and staying with Richard, turns out to be magical. Somehow after being away and coming back, things feel closer and sweeter and better than ever between us. Mostly we make each other laugh, or we curl up and talk about our worlds—friends and family dramas and work stresses and the news and weird pop culture obsessions—and, an eternal favorite, the Middle East. And even if we argue about the region's politics, as we have in the past and do a couple of times on my visit, we end up joking or deciding to drop it for now: we don't have to solve the entire Middle Eastern crisis tonight. I've never been able to argue so vigorously with someone, over something personal or political or whatever, then laugh about it minutes later.

I'm headed back to Beirut tonight, flying via the Frankfurt airport. The New York trip went by so fast, and I struggled to fit in plans with my friends, and spend lots of time with Richard, and meet with a few editors, and check in on my subletter, and pack up my winter clothes to bring to Beirut. But despite the whirlwind schedule, the trip was relaxing in its way. I left New York feeling relieved about how no-big-deal it can be at times to adjust and readjust to new and old places, new and old lifestyles, new and old friends.

My parents are still in Beirut when I return and are heading back to Houston in a few days. Their college friends Ziad and Bushra have us over for brunch, and Bushra makes her special tiss'ye, the chickpea, yogurt, and fried-bread dish I love. After we eat, I sit in their garden on the porch swing with Dad and Ziad and watch a video of his and Bushra's 1970 wedding. Ziad had the family's old Super-8 films turned into digital videos. Bushra, a brunette beauty with her hair piled high Marie Antoinette–style, and Ziad, a dashing mustachioed twenty-something with dirty blond hair, look vibrantly happy in that video and much the same now. Happiness for them seems to come so naturally: marrying for love, having four dynamic kids, and forty years later here they are, and here we are with them, in their garden drinking mint tea in blue glass tumblers and talking about old times, and the present, and the future. A family trip to Yellowstone next summer, perhaps? All of us reunited after having traveled through America on vacation, Samir and me and all their kids in tow, back when I was seven years old and we still lived in Beirut.

As I've struggled over the years about whether I want to get married and have kids eventually, I've noticed that most of the married people I know don't seem happier than most of the singles, and many seem much unhappier. And I've wondered why, in these days when women in many parts of the world can make their own money and the traditional economic arrangement applies less and less, marriage is still considered the conventional path and all other choices are considered deviant. But watching the wedding video at Ziad and Bushra's makes me think, more than ever before: *This looks pretty good. I get it.*

I wonder, *Could I ever have a life like this with Richard? Could we ever pull it off?*

NOVEMBER

"You should break up soon because you are likely to break up over Thanksgiving, anyway."

This advice comes from one Rebecca Elliott, a Ph.D. student in sociology at UC Berkeley, in an op-ed published in the *New York Times*. It's aimed at high school students who are about to leave for college and are unsure what to do about their boyfriends and girlfriends back home.

She goes on:

"You'll give it an earnest try, but you'll start to resent each other for forming new attachments, for not really 'getting' what it's like at your respective schools, for being the reason you're both missing out on important experiences."

Sound advice. The same thing did happen to me in

college. My high school boyfriend and I stayed together our first fall semester at different schools, but then broke up right on schedule, during the holiday break, feeling too estranged after the first transformative new adventures of our lives.

I'm not exactly the target audience for that *Times* op-ed now, being two full decades past eighteen. Still, I've been wondering, ever since James tried to ask me out, whether I should be exploring new options if they open up here in Beirut—not with him necessarily, but just on principle.

Richard had brought this issue up over the summer, just before I left New York.

"It's going to be raining men in Beirut" was what he'd said to me back in August. During my October visit to New York, we'd conveniently dodged the subject of our relationship and its future, enjoying our time together but both feeling too sheepish, I suppose, to have any momentous talks yet.

It's hardly raining men in Beirut, but I also have my umbrella up right now. I'm dropping the word *boyfriend* into conversations that I'm sensing are about to take a "Can I have your number?" or "I have a guy for you to meet" turn. Is this a bad idea? Should I let the rain just pour on down, whip me right up into the storm, and see what happens?

But I'm reminding myself, again, that I'm not a college freshman. I'm in my thirties. I've dated plenty of guys since then, and I'd like to think I've learned one or two things about myself and about relationships over the years—even if a few teeny little issues, like the Where Is My Home question, are still working themselves out.

I've at least figured out that if home were to boil down just to where some guy happens to live, it may as well not even exist as a real question. I need to know if I can love Beirut, if I can come back home to it, for reasons deeper and sturdier than a romantic relationship. Whatever happens between Richard and me—our time together in October, however sweet, didn't shed much light on our future—I'm not sure putting myself on the market here would be a terrific idea at the moment.

I do know one thing, though: it's November, and it's coming up on Thanksgiving, and this year for the first time I'll be spending the holiday in Beirut. Of course, it's an American holiday and doesn't officially exist in Lebanon, and it may slink by without a sound this year. I'll miss it if it does. Ever since my family moved to the States, I've had a thing for Thanksgiving. It's not just the food—I'm not even that wild about turkey. It's the boisterous, generous mood of the day. That is, of course, if you're lucky enough to have a food-fixated family like mine who'd mostly rather gorge themselves than fight. This year I'll likely spend Thanksgiving solo, with a shish taouk sandwich (it's chicken; close enough) and a rom-com classic on DVD.

But I'm still hoping for a Thanksgiving invite. Wouldn't be such a far-fetched idea. Every Lebanese person I've ever met who has lived a stretch in the States is crazy about Thanksgiving, too, and the odds aren't so bad that one of them will re-create the holiday here this year. There are obvious theories I could float about the love affair between Lebanese émigrés and this ultra-American holiday: Thanksgiving is about eating piles of food, filling every inch of the table with overflowing platters, packing the house, and stuffing your guests until they collapse—all things the Lebanese have a special talent for even when there's no particular occasion to celebrate.

Of course, Thanksgiving is also about counting your blessings, and the Lebanese, religious or not, have a few compulsive year-round expressions for that, too: *Nishkur'allah!* Thank God! *Hamdulillah!* Praise God!

Getting together with relatives, for most of my American friends, is a prospect fraught with anxiety. For the Lebanese, it's just what you do. All the time. Sure, you may love some aunts and uncles and cousins more than others, and some may piss you off to no end, but they must all be kissed three times on the cheeks, welcomed, entertained, endured, and above all fed. Copiously, and often. The Lebanese are traditionally around their extended families almost daily, so big family dinners aren't quite the exotic, tension-fraught occasions they can be in America. On top of that, turkey, in no way a part of Lebanese cuisine, is considered an unusual and glamorous Western ingredient here in Beirut, and figuring out how to cook it expertly is the sign of a certain genius and cosmopolitan panache.

So I'd even argue that Thanksgiving is better suited for Lebanon than for America, even if the Puritans were just about the only foreigners never to invade the eastern Mediterranean.

Days after my mini—angst session, a promising e-mail subject line pops up in my inbox. I click open the message, and find— yes!—an invitation to a Thanksgiving dinner with my parents' friends Bushra and Ziad. They've never lived in the States, but three of their kids—all around my age—live on the East and West coasts. Bushra and Ziad are going to celebrate Thanksgiving on the exact day, the third Thursday of this month, which although not a holiday in Lebanon will now officially feel like one. *Nishkur'allah.*

Bushra is one of the best home cooks I've ever known. I'm eager to see what she does with the turkey. Mainly I'm glad to have something to look forward to this month, the first fall I've spent in Lebanon and the first cold (okay, cold-ish) season I've experienced here since I was nine. Up until now, it had been a long hot Indian summer ever since I landed in Beirut in August, and even though that's disastrous for agriculture and terrifying for the planet, the truth is I've always dreaded winter. So I guiltily thank the cold for creeping in so late this year. Right now it's hovering just over fifty degrees Fahrenheit; the temperature likely won't drop much lower than that as the winter goes on, but with the sun having vanished today, it feels chillier outside than it actually is.

The first couple of weeks of November bumble along slowly. On mornings when it's not raining—fall and winter are the rainy seasons in Lebanon—I sit at the colorful mosaic-tiled table on the balcony working on my laptop. When I'm distracted or need a break from my computer, I gaze out onto the corner flower shop below, run by a large Sunni family who've lived on this street ever since my mom's Protestant grandparents built their house on this block in the early twentieth century. On the rooftop across from mine, I watch as, midmorning every day, one of the middle-aged men of the flower shop family, his hair turning prematurely stark white on his head and along his bushy mustache, flies his flock of pigeons around and around in widening circles, like Forest Whitaker in *Ghost Dog*.

On rainless afternoons, I take walks. One day after turning in an editing assignment, I reward myself by heading off on an adventure on foot. I decide to explore downtown some more, and I bring with me a new book I've just bought called *Beyroutes*—a combination guidebook and critical treatise on the city. As I wait for my building elevator, I flip to a random page: in modern-day Beirut, writes one of the contributors, "a visitor can recognize a certain restlessness to reconstruct, to renew, or to realign the present in reference to a certain past."

I follow the book's walking tour around some monuments downtown: the ancient Roman road that runs at the seaside edge of Martyrs' Square, the part of downtown that before the war was a bustling area of shops and theaters and is now a flat open space dividing the city's east and west sides. The Roman road runs past a hole in the ground into which passersby can see Byzantine-era ruins from a caravanserai, a sort of roadside refreshment area for caravans traveling through Beirut around A.D. 400. The road is paved now, of course, just another trafficky artery through Beirut, but I'd never realized before that it had ancient roots. The walking tour takes me past the two mosques on the edge of downtown: the small and elegant, caramel-colored sixteenth-century Amir Assaf Mosque and the larger Omari Mosque, originally a Byzantine church; the enormous new sky-blue-domed mosque built by the late Rafik Hariri is visible just behind. I walk around one edge of the city center and up a set of stone stairs to a parklike area where pedestrians can look down at the ancient Roman baths that were excavated here and that now form part of a quiet garden set below street level, and then look up at the Grand Serail, the Ottoman-built parliament building, heavily guarded and still the seat of the Lebanese government.

Afterward I climb back down the stone stairs, wind through some streets, and stop in to see the huge, luxurious TSC supermarket in the Beirut Souks shopping center. The supermarket, tucked between the Souks' clothing and shoe boutiques, is like an art gallery of high-end food, its sleek black-and-white aisles and butterscotch tiled floors a shiny backdrop for rows of perfect produce and products: purple and white eggplants, trim bright yellow bananas from Somalia, boutique international teas, imported pastas, cured meats, beautifully packaged spices, a fastidiously arranged frozen-foods section, and areas where shoppers can perch at high stools and order sushi or freshly made salads or the elegantly plated Lebanese home-style specialties of the day. But browsing the aisles, I sense no sign of real life in the store, as I haven't in much of the new Souks area when I've passed through it on my October walks and again today. Just a few scattered rich people browsing, window shopping.

If only downtown Beirut could feel more *sha'bi* again, more "of the people," not just a stiff new monument to an aspirational life of riches and—Lebanon's depressed economy and shaky political situation being what they are—of amnesia and self-delusion.

In the months since I got here, I've been playing tourist in my own city, but at least now I know where certain streets and landmarks and shortcuts are, much better than I ever have before, and I'm feeling more legit as a Beiruti, even if true long-term Beirutis never bother to do this sort of thing. The same way many New Yorkers have never been to the Statue of Liberty, myself included.

I sit on one of the benches ringing the downtown and text my cousin Shireen to confirm directions to her friend's birthday get-together tonight. Shireen is a few years younger than me, a stunning Lebanese-Palestinian brunette with enormous thick-lashed eyes. She grew up in Washington, D.C., but moved to Beirut, just down the street from my building, after finishing her master's degree at Columbia last year. We'd rarely seen each other in the States—we're only distantly related—but a couple of weeks ago, after a lively catch-up session at a family dinner in Beirut, we'd decided to start hanging out. After I text her, I get up and continue walking around for a while, poking along the downtown streets, no particular destination in mind.

The sun starts dropping, and soon evening falls. A real shame, this early darkness, the end of daylight savings time. Such short days. I need to get an earlier start on my walks, take in more daylight, since when the sun starts to go down, especially here, I feel a shot of the blues. But the blues are getting lighter as the weeks and months pass, now that I've been settling in little by little.

One of my uncles invites me to lunch one Sunday at his house across town, along with a bunch of older relatives. I haven't seen some of them in years. It's a cheerful gathering, and over cups of Arabic coffee before lunch, there's juicy gossip about a married neighbor who ran off with a well known divorced singer. We dig into a meze of more than a dozen plates—tabbouleh, *baba ghanoush*, fatayer, kibbeh balls, labneh, more—and feast on baked eggplant stuffed with ground beef and rice, and an enormous platter of roast lamb. It's delicious home-cooked food, but it's like having three meals at once. The lunch goes on for six hours. By the fourth hour, as we're sipping *ahweh bayda*—"white coffee," hot water flavored with orange-blossom nectar—I'm restless and wanting to get back on my way. I feel rude leaving first, and if I make a motion to call a taxi, someone will insist on driving me. That's the way my relatives and the Lebanese in general tend to behave. Every minor inconvenience you intend to take on yourself, they want to take over for you—even if it's actually less convenient for you if they do it. They'll argue with you until they win. So I stay. I finally get home in the early evening, sapped, the day having vanished into that endless lunch. I'm feeling stagnant and grumpy, and my ears are ringing with the hours of loud family chitchat.

But I try to slam the brakes on. *Stop complaining*, I tell myself. *Your relatives care about you, and they invited you over, cooked for you, regaled you with stories. That's precious.* A thick web of family, to catch any one of us who falls. I need to strengthen that web for myself. This is part of why I'm here in Beirut. I'm picking up those strands that have frayed over the decades since we left the city. My big family can be overbearing at times, but I love them, and they're here for me unconditionally. For someone with my chronic social anxieties, that's nothing to take lightly.

Waking up with a slight emotional hangover from the long lunch yesterday, still feeling claustrophobic and restless, I feel an urge to bust loose again. The sun is bright this morning, so, wearing a sweater and a scarf—too warm today for extra layers—I decide to wander around the Sanayeh Garden, the only substantial public park left in overbuilt Beirut; unlike the Horsh al-Sanawbar, it has no closed-off sections. I look at a map to decide on my path there, not the straightest course but one that will loop me around past the eastern edge of Bliss Street, and the stone wall demarcating the edge of the AUB campus, then through the quiet residential Clemenceau neighborhood to Sanayeh. I walk past Clemenceau's posh women's and kids' boutiques, and its low pastel-colored apartment houses with wrought-iron balconies, to the cluster of red-roofed, ivy-covered stone buildings and flowering trees of Haigazian, a small private Armenian-founded university. I buy a labneh sandwich from a deli that sells dairy products from the farmlands of Chtaura in the Bekaa Valley. Too many tomatoes and olives in this sandwich; I like mine nearly plain, the way they serve it at the Bekaa dairies I've visited in years past, with a generous smear of labneh sprinkled with just olive oil, dried mint, and salt.

As I eat, I pull out my map again to double-check that I'm following the right side streets that will take me straight into Sanayeh. It seems strange that I've been to the neighborhood around the park but never strolled inside the garden itself—but going to parks isn't a big part of Beirut life, and it certainly wasn't when I was growing up here during the war. A man comes up to me and says in English, pointing to the building behind him and surely thinking I'm a tourist, "This is the Aresco Building. What are you looking for?" I reply, in Arabic, *"Wein al Sanayeh?"* Where's Sanayeh? He's probably never seen this before. A Lebanese with a map, looking for a park. Or maybe he has. Maybe this happens now in Beirut, a city that keeps slowly drawing homesick exiles back, in the thousands, then tens and hundreds of thousands, since the war ended, to rediscover a city they'd left mostly unexplored during the war. Maybe, like me, they come back with a visitor's eye, to see not just their old neighborhood but the rest of the city, too, and the parts that have been rebuilt or are unrecognizable now, or were never before traversed by routines, habits, necessities.

The park is nearly empty on this Monday morning. It's a rectangular garden bounded by four streets, and about the size of a soccer field. There's a round empty stone fountain in the middle, creaky wooden benches with peeling green paint, and everywhere patches of landscaping—olive trees, pines, geraniums, palm trees, pink and yellow lantana flowers. It's tropical and green yet rundown, with mounds of dry dirt all over. One condo building along the edge of the park is like a vertical garden, its balconies tumbling with jasmine bushes and moss-green plants that look like tiny weeping willows. The Sanayeh Garden reminds me of Washington Square Park in Manhattan, especially in its state of partial landscaping, partial neglect, and its old men playing backgammon or chess on the benches. A similar scene here. I sit and look out onto the expensive apartment buildings surrounding the park, adjacent to more down-at-the-heel buildings now occupied by poorer Shiite families who migrated to the neighborhood from southern Lebanon and Beirut's southern suburbs during the war and in the various periods of conflict or tension since then. A few veiled women push their baby strollers past me. A stray orange cat scurries along. I feel the sun on my face and zone out. It's nice here, though the weekday quiet is a little ominous. An hour later I'm retracing my steps home.

My mother's cousin Sami and his wife, Najwa, live on my street, and they invite me to lunch a few days later. They're both Quakers, and since childhood I've found them pleasantly laid back, soothing to be around. Their cook Fahimeh serves us a soup called *hrisseh*, made with slow-braised lamb so soft it shreds in tender threads into the soup, its broth thickened with ground wheat and generously flavored with garlic. Soul medicine. As we linger at the table, dipping pieces of pita bread into a bowl of *dibs kharoub*—sweet, thick carob molasses mixed with tahini and a fixture on many Beirut tables—I tell them about my visit to the Sanayeh Garden the other day. After lunch Sami opens the curtain in the dining room and shows me two baby birds nesting in a crevice in the rocky windowsill outside: "There are almost no trees left in Beirut. Look at what happens."

The birds get me thinking about nature as home. We all, people and animals, try to make do in our habitats. In a war-torn country like Lebanon, through the conflict, through the constantly shifting cityscape, through the decimation of nature, the people who've never left and the people who've come back try to make do. Those birds on Sami and Najwa's windowsill are doing what they can. They're typical Beirutis, making the best of a compromised situation.

In Beirut, the idea that both animals and people need healthy trees and fresh air to thrive—not just buildings and roads—seems to have gotten lost along the way. But the city does have a few public green patches besides the Sanayeh and the small open section of the Horsh al-Sanawbar. The Evangelical church downtown has a jasmine-filled vest-pocket park connecting it to the adjacent National Conservatory of Music. The development company Solidere, created by the late prime minister Rafik Hariri to rebuild parts of downtown, has added tiny gardens along the medians in the major roads that pour into the city center and is building a park on a stretch of landfill along the waterfront. The pest-management company Boecker has put in tiny flower beds in scattered spots around town, including some along the median at one end of Bliss, the street that forms the southern border of the AUB campus. But among the flowers, the company has also planted ugly, self-defeating signs nearly as big as the gardens themselves: BOECKER LOVES BEIRUT. Thanks, Boecker.

Since the reading last month for the Horsh al-Sanawbar book, I've been going to other evening events—lectures at AUB or nearby, given by academics, filmmakers, musicians, architects, or other speakers from Beirut or abroad—on nights when I've had no plans and haven't felt like staying home to read or watch a movie. One weeknight this month I attend a talk about graphic design by an American speaker in town from Brooklyn. I'm in-trigued by the sound of it—the topic is the link between design and social activism—but unfortunately the lecture turns out to be crashingly dull and vague. At the end, I decide to raise my hand and ask a question. The speaker has said over and over how much he believes in "designing in the public interest" but never bothered to explain what that means. I'm feeling a little shy about asking the question, but I push myself to do it, figuring there's a solid chance I'm not the only one wondering what he was talk-ing about. He seems glad to see a hand up; at least someone was listening.

As he answers, explaining how strong graphic design can play a role in influencing opinions and social activism, I realize that besides wanting to hear his reply, I'd also had an urge to signal with my question—in my American-accented English—*Hi, I'm American, too.* I've been feeling a shot of homesickness lately when I've overheard strangers in cafés saying they're from New York, or Americans chatting together on the sidewalk or within earshot of me, as I'd heard a few people in the row behind me doing at the lecture tonight. Part of me wants to say, *I'm one of you!*

At the same time, I've also been having the opposite impulse: the more I live here, the more I realize how much I enjoy speak-ing Arabic, finding my groove in it again, and learning all the new idioms and slang. Richard once said to me when I was trying to teach him a few Arabic phrases, "I love how emphatic Arabic sounds. So satisfying."

It's true, Arabic vowels are extra-enunciated, and at the same time there's a singsong lilt to the language, even more pronounced in certain regional accents. You can almost chew on the words.

The language is a mouth workout, perfectly designed for powerful opinions and towering romance and profound melancholy and noisy anger and explosive punch lines.

Since I got here, I've been badly wanting to sound like a native-speaking Lebanese again, not just like the typical emigrant who left during the war and never quite got her Arabic back 100 percent.

But it can be hard at times to practice Arabic in Beirut; the language issue is tortured here. Nearly everyone is bilingual or trilingual (almost always with French or English), but instead of treating their second and third languages as extra tools for navigating the world, many Beirutis treat English or French as their primary language even if they've never lived overseas. Walk into any swank restaurant or boutique or modern office in Beirut, and you're likely to be greeted in French or English first. Try to switch the conversation to Arabic, whether you're Lebanese or not, and you'll sense a resistance. That's less true in rural villages around Lebanon, or at working-class-run venues in the city like street food stands, or with taxi drivers—situations where Arabic is usually spoken first and often exclusively. But in many contexts all over Beirut, the French-or-English-first habit dominates.

"The Lebanese are trained from birth to leave Lebanon," my cousin Karim, the political scientist, says to me when I bring up the language issue with him. It's no wonder why: the employment situation in Lebanon is almost always bleak, not to mention the constant political instability. Companies around the world are now more equipped than local ones to hire educated graduates from Lebanon's best universities and pay them decent salaries. There are other reasons, too, for the country's outward gaze:

Lebanon's cosmopolitan legacy dates back to ancient Rome, when it was a crossroads for traders and travelers from Europe, Asia, and all over the globe. The country's recent past as a French colony is not so easily forgotten, either. Speaking multiple languages fluently, most commonly French and English, has a long history around here.

I can understand why the Lebanese want to practice and even show off our fluency in multiple languages, no doubt hard-earned while living or studying abroad for years during the war or going to an American- or French-run school in Lebanon. And I probably sound like a hypocrite when I get annoyed with the Lebanese for defaulting to French or English, since I'm still more comfortable in English myself. Sure, I do keep trying to override my English impulse and speak Arabic here, but I admit I'm proud of my English fluency and I sometimes get lazy with Arabic. Also, since I've had the chance to live in the United States for most of my life, I have zero moral high ground compared to fellow Lebanese who've spent most or all of their lives in Lebanon, and lived through the entire war here, and who want to prove that they can function in the bigger, more prosperous world.

Nonetheless, it's hard not to sense that many Lebanese are also running from Arabic, in a desperate bid to sound and feel Euro or American. The habit of avoiding Arabic in daily life feels to me like a sneaky, insidious sort of shame, an elevation of a borrowed identity over a Lebanese one. It's as if we're saying *Hey, the world doesn't like Arabs much, but listen, we're not Arabs!*

The other day I was reading a Lebanese news and culture website that was going on about how most Lebanese, allegedly something like 80 percent, are not Arabs but Phoenicians, descendants of a legendary, ingenious seafaring people who lived along this part of the Mediterranean coast from the fifteenth century B.C. and invented the alphabet. The Phoenicians are now considered by most historians to be just another name for the various Canaanite tribes who lived along this coast but were never unified as one tribe.

The Lebanese, however, especially the country's more historically West-leaning Christians, have always been enthusiastic about the Phoenician bit. Maybe a little too enthusiastic. Then again, that's no big surprise. There's a long history of Arab rejectionism in Lebanon. The country was carved out from the historic Bilad al Sham, or Greater Syria, region in part as a home for the Maronite Christians, who considered themselves distinct from the Arabs. After the defeat of the Ottoman Empire in World War I, the mutually beneficial relationship that the Maronites, living in the area then called Mount Lebanon, had been cultivating with France—the French protected the Maronites from persecution in exchange for a competitive foothold in the coveted eastern Mediterranean—resulted in a homeland for them and eventually in the nation of Lebanon.

In Wadad Cortas's memoir *A World I Loved*, she explains that for a number of years after World War I—from 1929 to 1943, when Lebanon was run as a French colony—most schools around Lebanon taught French and forbade Arabic, thanks to a calculated strategy by the French administration to instill a love of France and to erode any budding nationalist feelings in students. A tried and true colonial tactic, it worked beautifully in Lebanon. The effects have trickled down through the decades: French-speaking Lebanese parents continue the tradition by sending their kids to French-focused schools where Arabic is essentially a second language. And many of them speak mostly French at home, too.

These days there are also many American-run schools that teach primarily in English. Although those schools are aimed in part at the American kids of expat parents working in Lebanon, they're also filled with Lebanese kids who grow up speaking American-inflected English not just at school but at home, too.

Ironically it's my American friends in New York who most seem to love the sound of Arabic, and who keep asking me to speak it around them and teach it to them, and who listen in when I talk to my parents on the phone, even when it's in our typically Lebanese, half-Arabic-half-English mishmash.

"Hi, *keefik? Shoo akhbarik?*" Hi, how are you? What's new?

As proud as I am now that I'm getting comfortable again with my Arabic, I still have a long way to go before I can say I fully speak the language—my language. That's because Arabic isn't just caught in a schizophrenic battle with French and English in Lebanon; it's also splintered into so many regional dialects that people living in different Arab countries, even sometimes in different towns or neighborhoods in the same country, are often speaking what can sound like different languages. For instance, my Arabic is specifically the Lebanese dialect. Had my family stayed in Lebanon throughout my school years, or had I studied Arabic on my own in the States, I would have learned the formal version of the language, called classical or modern standard (*fus'ha* in Arabic), which is understood all over the Arab world, taught in schools, and used on TV news, in official speeches, and in literature. But now when I listen to or try to read formal Arabic, I strain to understand it fully, stumbling over words I'm not used to.

The other day I saw a funny article in a Beirut student-run newspaper called *Hibr,* which prints its stories in both English and Arabic. The piece was by a young Lebanese guy who was lamenting his generation's increasing escape from Arabic and lack of interest in learning the formal fus'ha. He decided to write his rant in Lebanese-dialect Arabic, which is weird to see in print. It's like writing for a Texan audience and using *y'all* instead of *you*. I understood every word of his piece, so rare for me when reading Arabic text, which is virtually always written in the more formal version. The student writer's point was that if the formal fus'ha is scaring off Lebanese youth, and they're not learning it so well in school, why not just embrace writing in *darej* (the local dialect) instead, since at least we'd be hanging on to some version of our language.

I can't see that happening anytime soon, but here's an encouraging sign: around Beirut lately I've seen a few posters that say SPEAK YOUR LANGUAGE! in big bold letters. And if that op-ed piece in *Hibr* is any indication, Arabic may be earning some coolness points with the new generation.

Another son of old family friends comes to Beirut for a visit one November weekend, with his wife and kids. They're living in Saudi Arabia right now because of his job with a multinational corporation, and one night that weekend they invite me out to a downtown lounge called MyBar with their Beirut friends. As I look for them in the bar, I walk past the stylishly dressed young men and women milling around the glossy, white-walled space—a glamorous but, to my taste, soulless vibe. What can I say? I like dark little pubs so much more, the divey bars cropping up around Hamra, and similar hangouts in Manhattan and Brooklyn. Our crowd that night is mostly Lebanese, a mix of Anglophone and Francophone types, and as we're standing around a high round table clinking our glasses of wine or whiskey-and-soda, a few in the group start asking me where I grew up, what I'm doing in Beirut these days. When I reply, in Arabic, that I've been living in the States but I've just moved back to Lebanon to see if it's still home, they automatically switch into English. I try to divert the conversation back into Arabic, but no takers. On this night, like so many others, it's a battle. I feel defeated. Do they just want to show off their English? Or have they decided I'm not Lebanese enough to speak Arabic with?

I'm in a similar situation a few days later. Over drinks with Mirna at a packed pub called Torino in the Gemmayzeh area, I notice she's wearing a cool strappy leather bracelet, and I compliment her on it. She tells me she bought it at a shop called Ants, a few blocks from my apartment. I stop by the store later in the week to scope out some early Christmas-shopping ideas. I walk in and find what's essentially a Berkeley head shop: incense burning, strummy sitar music on the sound system, and a wall hung with leather and bead bracelets and necklaces. A few hippie kids are sitting on Indian-print cushions on the floor and chatting in a mix of English and Arabic and French, and what sounds like Armenian, too. I ask a question in Arabic about the price of a bracelet I like, and one guy, curly black hair tumbling to his shoulders, answers me in English. Same when I ask another question, about whether a pendant hanging on the wall comes on a brown instead of a black leather rope. I can't tell if here at Ants, on this rainy afternoon, I'm in the same kind of language war I was fighting at that downtown bar the other night—or if this guy actually doesn't speak Arabic well enough to answer me, although he seems to understand it perfectly.

Returning exiles like me must be confusing—not just to ourselves but to everyone. What language to use with us? Many of us want to speak Arabic and get it back up to speed, but our accent hints that we haven't lived here in a long time. *How should I communicate with this person?* I imagine a Lebanese thinking. *Is she a real Lebanese, or is she one of those people who is just back for a little visit from the States and can barely speak Arabic anymore?*

I'm also starting to notice something funny about my English as the months go by in Beirut. Even though I can sound very American when I want to, I hear myself switching into a kind of Lebanese-accented English at times. In Lebanon, some English words get so Lebanese-ized that they become essentially Arabic. *Sorry,* for instance, becomes *suhrry,* the vowel clipped, the *r*'s rolled. Speaking certain common English words with a Lebanese accent is a halfway point between the two languages, a way of not siding too much with either one, and not sounding too Americanized. I hear myself doing it more and more. I wonder, though: the longer I stay in Beirut and work more Arabicized English words like *suhrry* and *okeh* (instead of *okay*) into my vocab, will I erode my hard-earned American accent? Yes, probably. If you fall into new pronunciation habits, over time they're bound to stick.

I'm wondering how much I should care about hanging on to my American English, even while I dust off my Lebanese Arabic—and whether I can re-earn my identity as a Lebanese local, linguistically at least, and still hang on to my Americanness. The languages are starting to battle it out in my head, or maybe they're learning to live together. More and more lately, as I walk down the street, I notice that I'm thinking certain thoughts in Arabic, like *What's happening to this building? Can I walk through this construction site, or do I have to go around the block?* I haven't had internal monologues in Arabic since I was a child. But other kinds of thoughts still come more naturally in English. *I need to get home asap and finish up that assignment*, for instance. Or *Richard, I wish you could be here right now to see this insane billboard*. When I talk to one of my American friends in my head, and talk to myself about certain subjects like work assignments, it's still always in English. But when I talk to the city, and have imaginary conversations with its streets and buildings and history, I'm surprised to find that I'm starting to address them in Arabic.

Another thing I'm noticing is that when I say my name out loud here—for instance, when I call ahead to book a taxi—I sound out my full first and last names even when the taxi dispatcher needs only my first name. In the States, it often takes forever to spell out my last name on the phone, and for transactions when I don't need it, I avoid it altogether. Here I feel a strange new kind of pleasure when I say my whole name, Salma 'Abdelnour, with its hard guttural *'A. Abdelnour* is a fairly common last name in Lebanon, and saying it out loud, Arabic sounds and all, makes me feel I belong here, that I'm owning my Lebaneseness, my Arabness. It's a relief after living in the States for so long, and after feeling, for as far back as I can remember, that my name is too foreign, too cumbersome.

Despite my American-versus-Arabic struggles, there's no doubt I've been looking forward to Thanksgiving, this quintessentially American holiday. Finally, the third week of November arrives, but first there's another big holiday: Lebanese Independence Day. On November 22, 1943, Lebanon officially won its freedom from France, and from that year on, Lebanon has celebrated its independence on that day.

Some obvious jokes to be made here, of course. This is a country that, while technically independent for nearly seven decades now, has hosted an ongoing series of invading forces, essentially a continuation of what the ancient Romans, Egyptians, Crusaders, and Ottomans started when they marched through this land over the past half-dozen millennia. We've had the American Marines in 1958 and again in 1982–84, and Israel in 1982 and again in 2006, not to mention Israel's occupation of southern Lebanon for twenty-two years until 2000. And there was also, of course, the Syrian occupation of 1990–2005, which ended after the Independence Intifada (aka the Cedar Revolution) in Beirut, triggered by the assassination of the vocally anti-Syria ex–prime minister Hariri in 2005. Although that year marked the official ouster of Syria from Lebanon, Syria still manages to keep its fingers in Lebanon's messy political cake mix.

Independence Day here isn't celebrated with quite the same gusto as, say, Fourth of July in the States or Bastille Day in France. Usually employees around Lebanon get the day off, the government throws a military parade downtown, and that's about it. As I was waking up today, I heard the sounds of the military parade in the distance—a series of gunshots, part of the traditional twenty-one-gun salute. But this time I was ready for the noises, wasn't startled by them as I was on that September night when I heard seemingly random fireworks and thought shells were raining on my neighborhood all over again.

I spend Independence Day morning making an apple cake from a recipe Zeina gave me. Earlier this week my mother's cousin Ramzi, always laughing and boyishly upbeat, had stopped by to drop off a big bag of red apples from the orchards near where he lives, in the town of Roumieh, a half hour from Beirut. I've been munching on them all week. But there are still about a dozen left, and in a phone chat with Zeina, she tells me about an apple cake she likes to make that uses up loads of apples. So I give it a try, stirring in brown sugar with vanilla, eggs, oil, flour, baking soda, more than a dozen sliced apples, and walnuts, and spicing it with cinnamon and allspice; the recipe is easy and quick. I try a bite as soon as I pull the puffy brown cake out of the countertop convection oven, wanting to taste it all gooey and hot before I let it cool. The apples have a nice chunkiness and sweet-tart taste, and the spices give the cake a subtle tingle.

Funny that on this morning, Lebanese Independence Day, I'm baking something that reminds me of American apple pie—although the apples themselves are Lebanese, and the allspice is a mostly Middle Eastern seasoning. And funny too that an hour later, when my mom's cousin (and Ramzi's brother) Sami and his wife, Najwa, call to invite me over again for lunch, we eat the breaded veal filet called *escalope* along with French fries, Western specialties popular in Lebanon. Fahimeh, their longtime Lebanese cook, makes both particularly well. One could almost say that escalope and French fries, called *batata miklieh* here, have honorary Lebanese citizenship by now. We've essentially adopted both and made them our own, especially fries, which come with almost every sandwich order and even sometimes show up as part of a meze.

I have no problem with giving escalope and fries honorary Lebanese status. I like almost any food when it tastes great. I may make part of my living as a food writer, but I'm not a food snob. I do wonder, though, about the local cuisine giving way to more cosmopolitan competitors. Here in Beirut, the hot new restaurants are almost always French, or Italian, or Japanese, or even American, with occasional exceptions. As much as the Lebanese profess to be proud of their cuisine, and to forever miss their mother's cooking, and as much as they teach their housekeepers to prepare the recipes they grew up with, when Beirutis go out to dinner or to impress, it's very often at a foreign restaurant.

Of course, it's easy for me to say all this when I've essentially just arrived back in Lebanon and haven't been eating Lebanese food at home nonstop my entire life. But I wonder if Lebanese people's feelings for the local cuisine, whether they crave it constantly or whether they'll take almost any other food as long as it's foreign, have to do with how much they personally love or resent life here, and how much they forgive or hate Lebanon for what it is or what it's become: whether pride in the country's ancient heritage, cultural complexity, and close-knit family life, for instance, trumps hatred of its depressing political scene, slumped economy, and seeming inability to get its act together. Do our eating choices, I wonder, represent an underlying passion for and vote of confidence in Lebanon—or an urge to escape at any chance possible?

Unlike escalope and French fries, my own national origins are Lebanese all the way through—but lately my paperwork is out of date. I need to renew my Lebanese identity card so I can travel all over the country without risking getting in trouble at checkpoints in certain restricted areas. Right now I have a temporary Lebanese ID paper called an *ikhraj qaid*, which I use as a supplement to my American passport to get past immigration at the airport (otherwise I'd need a visa to be in Lebanon longer than three months) and as a just-in-case document I carry around in the event I'm asked for ID at a checkpoint. But the ikhraj qaid just expired, and it's time to get it replaced, as well as apply for my real national identity card. For that I have to go up to Aley, a village in the Mount Lebanon range forty-five minutes southwest of Beirut, where my father's side of the family comes from and where all their descendants must, by law, continue to register births and deaths and marriages and divorces in person. Very old-school.

Josette drives me to Aley on a gray November morning and tells me to brace myself for a series of interminable waits in bureaucratic office after office. Once the forms are filled out in Aley, it can take months, even years, to receive the ID card. It took both my mother and my uncle Kamal, who were born and raised in Lebanon, several years to get their ID card renewals completed and sent to them. But incredibly, Uncle Kamal's American wife Diane, New York born and raised, whom he met and married while she was a year-abroad student in Beirut in the 1960s, recently received her renewed Lebanese national ID just two months after she applied for it in Aley. Classic. Fair-haired Westerners in Lebanon? Roll out the red carpet.

The whole identity card routine is almost comic in its hyper-bureaucracy—except that it's also a giant pain in the ass. Josette and I spend a half hour trying to find a parking spot along one of Aley's tight streets on this busy weekday morning, and finally we find one a ten-minute walk from the center of town. As we stroll toward the municipal building, I reminisce about childhood weekends in Aley visiting my grandparents during lulls in the shelling, when I'd play on the swings of their rooftop terrace and pick honeysuckle. My grandfather Jiddo Gibran always seemed so calm and Buddha-like, smiling as he'd hand Samir and me pieces of *kurbane*, a sweet briochelike bread traditionally eaten by Orthodox churchgoers on Sundays—and Teta Alyce was always more high-strung, worried, but loving as a grandmother and a wonderful cook.

Sadly there's no time today to lollygag along the Aley streets, now home to strings of terraced restaurants and shiny new hotels along with the dusty old shops and squat stone buildings over-looking the tree-lined mountains and valleys. Josette and I walk into the small, traffic-snarled center of town and climb up the stairs of the municipal headquarters and into the office of the lieu-tenant mayor of Aley. Dignified-looking in his gray suit and gray hair, he peeks out from behind a cluster of government workers milling around his desk, stacks of papers in hand, and greets us. He remembers Josette, who is always driving one family member or the other up here to do the ID renewals. He offers us cof-fee, and after the obligatory "how's the family doing?" chat, he sends us to another office so I can fill out some papers. One of his assistants accompanies us, a short, stressed-looking man who fast-walks through the corridors, his dress-shoe heels clicking along the tiled floors.

We follow as he zips through the hallways, outpacing the streams of men with briefcases who jostle past each other on their way into one of the many identical-looking doors. He opens the door to the room where we need to go, says a few words to the guy manning that office, and leaves. I wonder if he's just expedited the routine; maybe since our family's history in Aley dates back so many generations, he's asked the guy in charge to deal with our papers quickly and send us on our way. Josette and I grab seats on the faded blue sofa and stare at the Lebanese tourism posters on the wall. We then proceed to sit there for an hour and a half, watching various people walk in, ask a question, light a cigarette, leave, or sit down, and like us stare at the walls as the clock ticks on. After what seems an eternity, the mustachioed man in charge of that room turns his attention to us and hands me the forms I need. I fill out my name, address, family members' names, and so on. He waves us on our way.

From there we walk with our forms to yet another office, in an awkwardly laid-out strip mall around the block, with the oxymoronic name Royal General Services Mall. In a claustrophobic little room, we find a tiny, reed-thin man sitting with a stack of papers on his desk and a huge leatherbound book. A number of people are ahead of us in line, and we watch the man slowly handwrite people's names and information as they walk up to his desk to give him their filled-out forms. There's not a computer in sight; incredible. We sit in that office for another hour, until finally the man looks up, summons us over, and slowly handwrites my name into the giant book. Very slowly, the black ink swooping up and dropping back down with every letter: . . . n . . . o . . . u . . . r. Done!

Nope, one more stop: this time at an office where I have to get my fingerprints taken for the ID card. I stand in front of the fingerprinting machine, my palms facing down, fingers pressing hard onto the glass surface. One try, and we wait a few minutes as the guy in charge of that office squints at the prints as they come out of the machine. No go. Two tries, three tries, and finally he's satisfied that the fingerprints came through clearly. Okay, we're finished. The whole expedition, door to door (to door to door to door), took six hours. Nearly all day.

My reward for the Aley trip comes a few days later—but not the ID card, way too soon for that. It comes in the form of a fantastically soothing Thanksgiving feast. Turkey may not have earned honorary Lebanese citizenship quite the way escalope and fries have, but it might be on its way; I've been noticing lots of turkeys at supermarkets this past week, and I've found myself eyeing them with more anticipation than usual.

On Thanksgiving Thursday, I get dressed up in a caramel-brown dress and gold flats and walk through the Hamra streets, just a few blocks over to Bushra and Ziad's. It's twilight, and some of the boutiques, bookstores, and assorted other shops are closing for the night, their aluminum shutters rattling down, while others are staying open late, for the after-work shoppers who stream back home to the neighborhood as the sun sets. The restaurants and bars are already filling up, and the early-evening sidewalks are crawling with Thanksgiving-oblivious crowds.

I arrive to find a full living room, packed with a crowd that includes Ziad's sister and my parents' friend Umayma, who cooked that wonderful Ramadan iftar dinner back in September, here with her Palestinian-Jordanian husband, Nasser. I also spot my parents' old classmates George and Katia (my friend Zeina's parents); and a friend of Bushra's named Leila, who heads a department at AUB and who I'd heard mentioned might want to give me some editing work.

Bushra's melodic, Syrian-accented voice soon rings out, "*Yalla, tfaddalo.*" Come, help yourselves to the table. Dinner is served. On the buffet: an enormous golden-skinned turkey, resting on an antique silver platter; two pans of sweet potatoes topped with browned, melting marshmallows; rice with vermicelli noodles and pistachios, Bushra's spin on a stuffing; a saucer of traditional turkey gravy; and cranberry sauce in a blue bowl. I also spy something not normally present on a Thanksgiving spread: *harrak osb'oo*, a dish made with lentils, onions, tamarind, and cilantro, a Syrian classic and a Bushra specialty. There are also kibbeh meatballs, a lemony eggplant salad called *raheb*, and assorted savory mini-pies stuffed with wild greens or spiced beef or cheese.

I go easy on the turkey, choosing the thinnest, reddest piece I can find, and for old times' sake, I help myself to a big scoop of the candied sweet potatoes and a dollop of cranberry sauce. But what I'm really entranced with is the harrak osb'oo, a nuanced but earthy dish with pleasing sweet-and-sour notes. I need to get Bushra to teach me how to make this. I go back for seconds of it, and then thirds, and then force myself to put my fork down, though Bushra looks at my plate and says, *"Shoo? Maakalti shi!"* What's this! You didn't eat anything! You'll hear this from a Lebanese host even if you've just single-handedly consumed an entire turkey.

For dessert, Bushra serves *mhallaya,* a milky and slightly sour, cheese-based custard sprinkled with orange-blossom nectar and crushed pistachios, which is also Syrian originally and rarely seen in Lebanon. It's like the perfect marriage of a creamy rice pudding and a delicate panna cotta, with a subtle tang. Bushra also sets out two large pans of her signature apricot phyllo cake, similar to baklava in its layers of flaky dough hiding a sweet filling, but this chunky apricot version, made with fruit she bought the other day in Damascus—the famous Damascene apricots—is her own invention.

I get home at almost midnight, extremely stuffed but in a brighter mood than I've felt in days during this gray, increasingly chilly month. I've just spent one of the most joyous Thanksgivings in memory, in a cheerful group of old family friends reminiscing about Thanksgivings spent in years past with their grown-up kids in the States. The next night I get an e-mail from Richard about how he's been spending his holiday break in Boston so far: shopping for pants with his brother Jeff, a bassist in a band, and watching the Celtics, and eating oysters and chowder. He tells me the oysters made him remember a night when the two of us stopped in at the Oyster Bar in Grand Central during my October visit: "perfect happiness," he called it. I remember how that felt, sitting next to him at the old New York bar, picking out a couple dozen oysters from the East and West coasts, slurping them straight up or with just squirts of lemon, then walking through Bryant Park together in the late evening.

Memories of that night are rushing back as I read his e-mail. I'm thinking about how being with Richard, our time together, can feel like perfect happiness. I don't know what the rest of the year will bring for us, but right now this feeling is good; it's enough.

Before the week is out, I luck into two more Thanksgiving invites, both for the Sunday after the actual holiday: one from Zeina, and one from my Boston-expat friends Curtis and Diana. I say yes to both and get ready for a marathon day of nonstop eating.

Zeina gets nostalgic at times for the years she and Marwan spent living in New York, and today she's cooked up a beautiful, gorgeously browned turkey, which she serves, in a nice twist, with Lebanese sides—a dish of fresh okra braised in garlic and olive oil and called *bamieh bi zeit,* along with baba ghanoush, and mini savory pies topped with a wonderfully tart spread made with fermented yogurt, called *kishk.* Sitting around the table is a small, intimate group: her parents, George and Katia, Marwan, their four-year-old daughter, and the in-laws. We finish off with knafeh, the syrupy sweet-cheese dessert I love. A cup of Arabic coffee later, and a relaxed lounging session in the living room, and I'm off, whispering apologies for having to dash out so soon, but leaving the family in a mellow post-Thanksgiving trance.

At Curtis and Diana's a half hour later, I meet a few more friends of theirs, and we all sprawl out in the breezy dining room, the balcony windows open to the cool November air. I eat a bit less this time, limiting myself to one thin piece of a buttery, cheese-filled quiche and a bowl of richly sweet and spicy pumpkin soup—an autumn favorite here, thanks to the seasonal pumpkin bounty. I find myself chatting with James again, the only other person there who hasn't arrived with spouse and kids in tow. But today I'm not so worried about what meeting a cute single guy could mean for my romantic life.

I'm thinking about Richard's oyster note from yesterday. I'm crazy about that guy. I want another night like that, lots more of them.

DECEMBER

It's early December, and the streets around me in Ras Beirut are decorated with Christmas trees, along with leftover signs welcoming pilgrims from around the world for the Muslim Eid Al Adha holiday last month. Ashura, another Muslim holiday, is also happening in December. The entire month is riddled with events for both major religions in Lebanon, and so a slew of days off for businesses, government offices, and schools.

For me, this month is shaping up as a sequel to November's eating spree. My relatives and friends in Lebanon will be celebrating various holidays and ceremonies in December, in ways ranging from the faithful to the secular, all with one denominator common to most celebrations everywhere: food.

I've always looked forward to December, despite the last-minute gift-shopping stress and the wear and tear of a monthlong social and gastrointestinal marathon. Christmas for me still brings memories of gleefully unpacking the ceiling-high plastic tree from its enormous flat box in our Beirut apartment, setting up the manger scene with clay figurines of Jesus and Mary and Joseph and the Three Kings, and sprinkling the entire tableau with baby-powder "snow." Then, stuffed on our holiday dinner of lamb or ham roast and a big meze spread, off we'd go to the annual pageant at the Protestant church nearby, where we'd sing carols loudly, merrily, and in my case crashingly off-key. In those days, there was nothing like screaming along to loud organ music for an hour to take your mind off the war raging outside.

This year I'm not bothering with a Christmas tree since I'm in the apartment alone, but I do decide to plant some wheat seeds, a tradition in Lebanon to celebrate December 3, Saint Barbara Day—for the third-century saint revered by the Eastern Orthodox Church. When I was growing up here, we'd plant the seeds on a plate spread with wet cotton balls, and after two weeks or so, when the seeds had sprouted and grown to a few inches tall, my mother would repurpose the plants as grass for the nativity scene.

On this breezy, light-sweater December morning—the weather went up by a few degrees again yesterday, a warm front—I make coffee, sit on the balcony, and organize what my days will look like over the coming weeks: the work deadlines, gift shopping, and get-togethers. I'm especially looking forward to Christmas week, when my cousin Mona and her fiancé, Jia-Ching, arrive in Beirut from California to get married here. Then I'll be off to spend Christmas Day with my family in Houston.

I'm one of the few people among my friends in the States who doesn't find December hugely stressful and dispiriting. But in my own way, this year I'm channeling some of my American friends' angst. Even though the holidays, in all their rushing-around nuttiness, bring back happy memories, this year the religious and political realities—and obstacles—of life in the Middle East are weighing more heavily on my mind.

In America, practicing or ignoring religion is a mostly personal choice. In Lebanon and the Middle East generally, it's much more complicated. Intermarriage is still a big deal. It's becoming more common now but remains a hassle, and in traditional circles it's as taboo as ever. Some of my Christian relatives in Lebanon married Muslims but had to go outside the country to do it, since there are no legal interreligious marital procedures in Lebanon, although Lebanon does recognize mixed marriages if they take place outside the country.

My cousin Mona is the granddaughter of one of my mother's relatives, a Protestant who in the 1950s braved scandal and married an Iraqi Muslim. She had to face down plenty of disapproval at the time, but things haven't changed so dramatically since then. During her Ph.D. work at Berkeley, Mona met Jia-Ching, a handsome Taiwanese-American grad student, and they fell in love and got engaged. Her family adores him, but in order for the two to get married in Lebanon, where virtually all of Mona's relatives live, he's converting to Islam; there's no pressure from her family, but it's less of a headache all around. I've known other couples who have had to decide whether one of them will convert, or whether they'd have to just give up on the idea of marrying in Lebanon.

Whatever the hurdles, intermarriage is on the rise, and that bodes well. Lebanon needs all the mixing it can get in order to someday, with any luck, break up the religious-tribal mentality that continues to choke the country.

The ongoing lack of a civil marriage procedure is by no means the only religion-related inconvenience, shall we call it, of life here. The Lebanese government, ever since the country's independence in 1943, has been organized along sectarian lines, with political parties normally identified by whether they're Christian—usually Maronite, the most common Christian sect here and related to Catholicism—or Sunni, or Shiite, or sometimes a mutually beneficial alliance of two or more sects. As a result of a document called the National Pact established in 1943, the year of independence, the president is always a Maronite, the prime minister a Sunni, and the speaker of parliament a Shiite.

Whether Lebanon's sectarian system is, as some would argue, a delicate balancing act of competing claims to power, or a grossly unjust and outdated setup that perpetuates tribalism and favors certain sects over others even when they're no longer a majority, it's obvious that it's a giant mess. Maybe that's the only thing the Lebanese can agree about, in principle anyway. And many times in the recent past—from the first civil war of 1958, to the civil war of 1975–90, to a number of explosive instances since then—the sectarian system has brought Lebanon to the brink of total collapse. As a Sunni parliament-member friend of my father put it to us when my parents were visiting in October: "Sectarianism will be the end of Lebanon."

You can personally choose to live a nonreligious life here, and you can complain all you want about the injustice, absurdity, and dysfunction of the sectarian distribution of power. But year after year, sectarian-tribal realities continue to rule life in Lebanon, and the political system stays in place; call it inertia, corruption, or an age-old combination of the two. Lebanon may be, outwardly, a fairly unrepressed country, forever famous for its jet-set nightlife and risqué fashions. It may have the Arab world's least-persecuted gay scene (though it's still mostly underground), and a much-professed love of partying and sex and you name it, plus a political system that acts like a democracy thanks to its regular elections—however uninspiring or rigged—and absence of a dictator or theocratic regime. But it's still a long, long way from the separation of church and state, or mosque and state.

As if Lebanon didn't have enough of its own sectarian problems, it also tends to inherit some of the tensions and clashes of its neighbors, none of whom have set a particularly fine example of secular governance. That includes virtually all Arab countries as well as Israel, which, although it calls itself the only democracy in the Middle East, is primarily a democracy for those who happen to be Jewish—and significantly less so for the Palestinians, no matter how far back they trace their ancestry on the land. The strife down south in Israel between Jews and Arabs has had violent reverberations in Lebanon for decades, and so it, too, remains a roiling issue for the Lebanese, whatever their opinion of the situation.

As I get ready for a series of holidays, feasts, and social outings in December, I can't help thinking about what Lebanon's—and the Middle East's—religious divisions will mean for the country in the coming years, and what they may also mean for my relatives, my friends, and myself, not to mention for Richard and me. One December night, my mom's old friend Nadia invites me to go see a play by Ghassan Kanafani, a Palestinian playwright reportedly assassinated by the Mossad, the Israeli secret service, in 1972.

The play is about a Palestinian couple who returns to the Israeli city of Haifa in 1968, two decades after they fled in 1948 when Israel was created, and try to visit the house they once lived in. They'd left their baby behind in the house when they escaped back in 1948, in all the chaos and confusion surrounding the evacuation of the Arabs from Haifa by the Zionist military forces; when the wife went looking for her husband on that day of the evacuation, she wasn't allowed to come back to the house, so her baby stayed behind. When the couple decide to go back in 1968 to see what's become of their old house, they find a Jewish woman from Poland living in it, and they eventually realize that her twenty-year-old son, now a member of the Israeli army reserves, is the baby they'd left behind. The woman invites them in, tells them how she and other Poles were brought en masse in 1948 by the Jewish paramilitary organization Haganah and placed in houses all over Palestine, and how at the time she had noticed and felt uncomfortable about the lack of Arabs anywhere in sight. But she had nowhere else to go, and when she was given the abandoned house and found the baby in it, she moved in and adopted the child.

After the show there's a Q&A session. A young Lebanese guy in the audience raises his hand and says he thinks the play is groundbreaking in showing that many Jews who were brought to Israel as a result of the Holocaust weren't actively trying to displace Palestinians, but were themselves caught up in the horrors of the era, in Europe's extermination of the Jews in World War II, and were focusing on escaping persecution and death, not necessarily on colonizing the land. I hear booing from some people in the audience. I turn in his direction, to nod and signal to him that he's raising a point worth discussing, but I feel too intimidated by the crowd response to make an obvious gesture. Some members of the audience obviously took his comment as tacitly excusing the systematic erasure of Palestine, which didn't sound to me like what he intended to say.

Nadia and I walk over to her apartment after the play to catch up and discuss the show. Over tea, I confide to her something I've been anxious about at times: that Richard and I will have a relationship-ending fight someday over the Israel-Palestine issue, especially if Israel bombs Lebanon again, which it keeps threatening to do if Hezbollah makes another provocative move. Will his Jewish background and my Arab roots eventually clash? I tell her I'm worried that our opinions on the region, while overlapping in many ways, are not fully in line either. Maybe they'll present an obstacle in the future.

"Don't worry too much about that, Salma. You and I both worry too much," she says, giving me an affectionate smile and grabbing her silver-flecked hair into a ponytail. "Just think about your relationship on its own. Focus on all the things you love and value about it, and deal with any complicated situations if or when they come up. You'll find a way to manage them."

Nadia tells me to think of it this way: if Richard and I have a healthy relationship, politics doesn't have to be a central issue. It can often be compartmentalized as just a thing two people can differ on. We can disagree about some questions but still respect each other. She also promises me that we have her full support, and that mixed relationships are the only way Lebanon, not to mention the whole region, will eventually get over the sectarian bullshit.

I nod. I'm not quite as optimistic as she is, but I feel reas-

sured for now. I needed to hear this tonight. The sage tea we're drinking suddenly seems more fragrant, its forest scent filling the room.

I open the balcony door a few days later to a still almost balmy
mid-December morning, hovering in the low sixties. To do some
morning errands—the dry cleaner around the corner, a labneh
run at the grocery store downstairs—I've put on my jeans, a
bright blue top, and a pendant that says BEIRUT LIL-JAMI' (Beirut
for Everyone) in Arabic. I bought it at a jewelry store around the
corner and have been wearing it daily. As I adjust the pendant on
my neck, I stare at it for a second, realizing it might seem silly and
quaint to anyone who lived here throughout the fifteen-year civil
war and feels chronically burned out on idealism.

I don't blame anyone for resenting Lebanon for its eternal
dysfunction, and for never improving much politically or eco-
nomically, and for offering no real hope to those who've lived
through the war here and the constant explosive incidents since
then. I wouldn't be surprised if someone took a look at my pendant and scoffed, *Beirut for No One!* But I'm going to wear it
anyway and hope it doesn't seem too silly. Is it like the MEAN
PEOPLE SUCK bumper stickers I used to see around my college
campus in the 1990s? Here in Lebanon, though, a collective, post-
sectarian vision for the country is a far from obvious or widely
accepted idea.

Meanwhile, as the holiday season sneaks up, the political situation is looking hairy. Again. Rumors are heating up that if Hezbollah is implicated in the findings of the UN tribunal investigating
the Hariri assassination, the party is going to protest the results,
possibly by taking to the streets. I'm checking local news sites like
Naharnet.com every day now, several times a day. The constant

running headlines about Lebanon's impending political catastrophe are scary. Every reported incident of a scuffle on the outskirts of town, however tiny the headline or potentially nonpolitical the cause, is starting to make me a little nervous. For instance today: "Several men attacked each other by knives near Hadath and a woman was injured by gunshots during a wedding in Mraijeh."

I'm remembering how deceptively small incidents like these can, and have in the past, set off a much bigger conflict.

I ask my parents on the phone one morning about their opinion on the situation right now, which they're monitoring from Houston via online Lebanese news sites and Arabic-language newspapers, and I ask Umayma, who keeps close tabs on political news on the big-screen TV in her apartment. None of them believes there will be violence this time around. They all give me some version of "no one wants war again." But according to the local news, the political tensions are building up to a crescendo, and no one can predict where we're headed. I realize most media are in the business of sensationalizing any event, however small, but I can't help feeling slightly on edge.

One cool, overcast day, as I'm finishing some edits that are due to the university alumni magazine, I'm searching my files for a document I need, and I come across a pamphlet I'd brought with me from New York, titled "Emergency Preparedness Advice for You and Your Family." I'd received it in the mail years ago after 9/11, and while I was decluttering my Manhattan apartment last summer and getting ready to move to Beirut, I'd thrown it on a whim into the pile to pack in my suitcase. I find myself staring at it now. I'm supposed to be sitting at my laptop working right now, but what better distraction than an emergency-preparedness brochure from New York, circa a decade ago?

I flip through the pamphlet. There's a "Household Disaster Plan Checklist," divided in sections. "What to Have in Your Head: Decide where your family will reunite after a disaster." "What to Have in Your Hand: Copies of your important documents." "What to Have in Your Home: One gallon of drinking water per person per day."

As I page through it, my mind drifts back to the civil war days, when I used to take a strange comfort in helping my mother prepare a duffel bag of supplies in case we needed to escape to a basement shelter, a *malja'*. We did on many nights, when the shelling was too close by. I'm not sure whether I kept this New York emergency-prep brochure in my kitchen drawer in Manhattan as a practical guide to what I should have on hand, or just as a nostalgia trigger, albeit a dark one. I did contemplate packing an emergency kit in New York after 9/11 and again after the big East Coast blackout of 2003, although I never got much further than a few cans of beans that I threw away when their edges began to rust in my kitchen cabinet. Now, with that pamphlet here with me in Beirut, I'm wondering if I shouldn't take its advice and pull a few things together.

If the sinister drumbeat in the local news continues, I just might have a disaster-preparedness grocery trip in my near future. But for now I'll take comfort in my more seasoned and (somehow) optimistic elders, and—in true Lebanese fashion—in cocktail nights out with friends. One afternoon at midmonth, Mirna calls to invite me out for happy hour drinks at one of Beirut's old-school-hipster hangouts, Pacifico, on the east side. She's meeting some friends there, some of them former classmates and others colleagues from her urban-planning job. I walk into the crowded bar area and find the group, a coed bunch mostly in their mid-thirties. Mirna introduces me around, and as soon as we clink our glasses to toast the end of the workday, the conversation flows instantly. We talk about local bands we've been listening to lately (the Beirut retro-punk group Scrambled Eggs, the trip-hoppy Soap Kills) and eventually wind our way to the usual drink-session topics: work stress, family dramas, relationships. I notice how at ease I feel around this crowd, right from the start. Like me, they all spent their childhoods in Beirut and have at some point lived or studied or worked in the States or Europe.

It's rare that I feel so immediately comfortable in a group of total strangers, but this shared history does count for something, I'm realizing. I love making friends with people who have entirely different backgrounds from me, but even in immigrant-country America, I'm often the one person in a group who's slightly different, more "ethnic," and I still sometimes get self-conscious about that, oddly enough. Here, as a somewhat mixed-up, multinational Beiruti, I feel in my element in a particular way I haven't experienced for a very long time.

I stay for a few margaritas, Pacifico's specialty, and as always, I find the vibe of this place, sort of a Mexican cantina meets bistro, cheery and energizing. I've been here a few times during past summer trips. Once the beating heart of Beirut's Monot area—a small section of the Achrafieh district that was a nightlife center in the 1990s—Pacifico has hung on to its clientele, die-hard loyalists who still come here even long after Monot gave way to the Gemmayzeh area, and now slowly to the Hamra side streets near my apartment, as the place to find the hippest bar scene.

Mirna drives me home and drops me off in front of my building around ten P.M., and I decide to take a short walk to a street-food stand called Marrouche. I'm craving the chicken sandwich there, in my humble opinion one of the world's best: two crusty toasted sides of baguette slathered with toum, the garlic spread, and topped with shredded strips of grilled chicken and spicy pickles. Many times before, I've inhaled this sandwich so fast I've had to force myself to resist going for seconds.

Back at home, I water the wheat-seed plant I'm growing in my window before I climb into bed. My plant is looking healthy now. It's three inches tall, a miniature meadow of wheatgrass blades, sturdy and still growing. This kind of plant actually has a name, Adonis, after an ancient Greek tradition of planting wheat seeds to celebrate the festival of Adonis.

As I sprinkle water on my little Adonis, I realize that I know nothing about Saint Barbara, who inspired the December holiday in Lebanon for which this homegrown shrub is also a symbol. I wonder, is the California city of Santa Barbara named after the same saint? I do a little online research before bed and learn that the California city is indeed named after her, and that Saint Barbara is the patron saint of military engineers, artillerymen, and miners—in other words, according to a Wikipedia entry, "those who work with explosives."

Big surprise Saint Barbara has her own holiday in Lebanon. Growing this little wheat-seed plant is, it turns out, a symbolic two-for-one: the artillery god Saint Barbara and the debauchery god Adonis rolled into one. The quintessential Beirut shrub.

In the two weeks of December before Christmas, the social plans keep whirling. One Saturday night I go to my cousin Shireen's birthday party, which starts with a dinner of grilled steaks and Malbec wine at a dark, noisy Argentinean restaurant in Gemmayzeh, and ends with hours of dancing to a hip-hop deejay at a bar. Another night Karim and Hala invite me over for *kibbeh bi'sayniye,* a dish I love, a labor-intensive Lebanese classic. It's like a giant savory pie: the crust is made from ground lamb and bulgur shaped into a big circle, instead of the meatball shapes of the hors-d'oeuvre-style kibbeh, and stuffed with a layer of spiced ground beef, fried pine nuts, and strips of caramelized onion. Then it's baked until crunchy on top and served with mint-spiked yogurt to spoon over the slices, cut in triangles just like pie. The dinner gathering is small and relaxed, and the other guests there are Karim's friend Parag, an author who's in Beirut this week to give a talk at a conference; and Nicholas, a Beirut expat writer from New York who owns a bar in the Mar Mikhael neighborhood near Gemmayzeh. After dinner, we sit in the living room over more glasses of wine, and the subject turns to whether Lebanon is likely to have another war soon—Beirut's version of cocktail party small talk. The feeling is, probably not right now, but eventually yes.

The postdinner lounging session ends on a lighter note, as we talk about holiday plans, and I leave with a little more optimism that bombs will stay at bay for now. But as I walk outside, I notice the skies look ominous. After a long drought, it's raining like mad here tonight, and the wet weather is making the high-forties temperature feel colder. On my five-minute walk home from Karim and Hala's, I'm drenched waist to toe, my umbrella twisted and wrecked within seconds. But I'm glad to see this rain. Lebanon is parched and needs it. An epidemic of forest fires has ravaged parts of Lebanon and Israel over the past weeks. The thunder tonight is explosive and relentless, some of the loudest I've heard in my life.

When Mona and Jia-Ching land in Beirut later in the week to get ready for their wedding, their plane touches down in the middle of another deafening thunderstorm. I take them out to dinner the night after, for a quiet catch-up session. The last time I saw Mona was in California more than a year ago, and I've been missing her vivaciousness and sunny warmth. We go to an Armenian restaurant near Gemmazyeh and proceed to overorder like crazy—my weakness, always—feasting on small kibbehs stuffed with eggplant, and kebabs with a sour cherry sauce, and the tiny Armenian dumplings called *manti*, twisty-shaped, filled with minced beef, and topped with yogurt sauce. For dessert we sample delicate morsels of the restaurant's sweet-and-savory confections: candied eggplant, sugary walnuts, glazed chickpeas, and dollops of rose jam. Over dinner, we talk about plans for the coming week: a bachelorette party for Mona, a prewedding luncheon for relatives and family friends at a swank hotel, then a small vows ceremony for immediate family, followed by a huge party. Three days' worth of festivities, and lots to plan still. As we eat, Mona's cell phone lights up every few seconds.

Ilham, a cousin who lives in Boston, has also just arrived in Beirut. We grew up almost like sisters during the war; she and her brother, Kamal, lived directly upstairs, on the fifth floor of this building, with their mother, Nouhad, after their dad, my maternal uncle, died young of a heart attack. Ilham and I have continued our close friendship through the years with long-distance phone calls and e-mails. When we're both on the East Coast, we jump on the bus to visit each other a few times a year.

During her holiday break in Beirut this week, she's staying upstairs, in the fifth-floor apartment with Nouhad. Having Ilham in the building again is a joyous flashback, and when I stop by to welcome her back the morning after she arrives, I'm instantly comforted to see her face, her creamy complexion and honey-brown hair glowing as always. Ilham is an accomplished, well-spoken academic in her professional life, but when we're together, we quickly get silly, giggling and making funny faces at each other. We reminisce about the *Disney Disco* record we used to dance to in my bedroom—despite the pleas of our disco-hating older cousins—and about all the storage rooms and nooks we discovered in the building during our hide-and-seek games, before our families fled the war.

Today is a weekday, but Ilham and I are headed to brunch together at Umayma's: since it's the Muslim holiday of Ashura, it's a day off in Lebanon. Umayma has invited Nouhad—they're old friends from the neighborhood—along with Ilham, me, and a few other guests. The holiday honors the death of the Prophet Muhammad's grandson Ali and is mostly commemorated by Shiites, but Lebanese Sunnis often consider it either an optional fasting day or a time to get together with family and friends. Bushra and Ziad are there when we arrive, and also my great-uncle Cecil, who is visiting from London and has known Umayma for decades, since she's a childhood friend of my mom's. It's a typically laid-back and festive Ras Beirut reunion, old friends and family across generations and sects. Umayma and Nasser have put together a beautiful meze and set out a pot of *ful mudammas*—broad beans stewed in garlic, cilantro, and olive oil—which they serve with a tomatoey hot sauce on the side. We all relax and nurse cups of Arabic coffee for a couple of hours after lunch, lounging in the toasty living room, the temperature outside wintry and wet again, store awnings flapping in the wind.

The following Friday is Mona's bachelorette party, and I'm

one of the crew in charge of organizing the event. Mona insisted she didn't want a debauched night at a raucous Gemmayzeh club. She'd prefer something more original and ideally involving food. Since Mona loves to cook, I suggest doing a group cooking class followed by dinner at Tawlet, the Lebanese restaurant. I call to book the party, and with the help of a few of Mona's friends, we choose in advance a menu of dishes we want to make. A group of fifteen of us convene in front of the restaurant's open kitchen on the evening of the party, and a cooking instructor named Ahlam leads us into a fast-paced, hands-on class covering ten dishes, including *makanek*—spicy finger-size lamb sausages—and *sayyadiyeh*, fried fish resting on rice that's been cooked in a rich sauce of fish-head stock and meltingly sweet onions.

During the entire two-hour class, everyone is rushing around, trying to watch Ahlam and chat with each other at the same time, laughing, distracted, doing more socializing than cooking. Mona's friends have traveled from the States, Europe, and Dubai to be here, and they're dying to catch up. To cook, too, and to eat, but it's been months or years since some of them have seen one another. I'm excited to see Mona so happy, her bright blue eyes sparkling, and to feel so much energy in the room. I do manage to concentrate long enough to come away with a few techniques for making better baba ghanoush, and I also learn how to make *shish barak*, small doughy pockets stuffed with lamb and floating in warm garlic-and-mint-spiked yogurt.

Afterward we sit down to eat, and thankfully Ahlam has finished the dishes that we all only partly contributed to in our frenzied talking and socializing. The sayyadiyeh in particular is one of the best I've had, and though Ahlam has pulled together a gorgeous platter of it out of our not-terribly-helpful contributions, we destroy it in minutes, going back for multiple servings.

The Sunday night right before I leave for Christmas is the main event: Mona's wedding and the big party afterward. Earlier that day was the *katb al kitab*, the Muslim ceremony where a couple exchanges vows in front of their immediate family. Jia-Ching's parents flew in from Taiwan to be here for it. After the lavish prewedding luncheon I'd attended the day before for relatives and family friends, tonight I'm looking forward to the blowout party, planned mostly for the younger set, the cousins and friends of the couple. I spend the day doing my last bits of Christmas shopping and deciding what to wear to the party, a chic affair at the family home of Beirut chef Hussein Hadid, a nephew of the Iraqi-born architect Zaha Hadid, in the hilly Moussaitbeh neighborhood. I decide to do it up: I wear a sleeveless blue silk dress, gold heels, and a dark-gold layered necklace I found, long neglected, in my mother's closet in Houston on my last visit and "borrowed" with her blessing.

Ilham and I take a taxi together and still manage to get lost on the way, and at last we walk into the party to find Karim and Hala and a few other cousins mingling in the candlelit living room, decorated with antiques and contemporary art from all over Lebanon and the Middle East. In the back of the house, in the open kitchen and dining room, Hadid has spread out an eye-boggling feast of meats, including platters piled high with delicately arranged skewers of shish taouk and spiced-lamb *kafta*, along with bowls filled with all kinds of salads, artfully plated meze classics, and inventive crostinis, the best topped with goat-cheese labneh and sliced figs. For dessert there are shot glasses filled with various sweets, like the cinnamon-spiked rice custard called *mighli*, capped with a shower of walnuts, pine nuts, and shredded coconut. We all fill our plates at the buffet and our glasses with drinks, then eventually make our way to the living room to listen to the toasts. Mona's dad gives a touching, emotional speech thanking his daughter for following in her grandmother's footsteps and bringing yet another culture into our family: Taiwanese this time.

I go to bed late after the night of feasting, toasting, and dancing, and I fly to New York the next morning to spend a few days with Richard before heading to Houston for Christmas. I land at JFK in the early evening and take a taxi through the snowy Queens and Brooklyn streets. Back at his apartment, Richard is waiting for me and making us dinner. I find the door to his building open and let myself in without buzzing up, leave my bags in the lobby, and walk up the stairs to knock on his door. He lets out a "Whaaaat?!" when he sees me standing there, surprised because he'd been listening for the buzzer. He rushes up and hugs me. The *bucatini* are boiling, and he's finishing up the tomato sauce he's making, thickened with minced anchovy—one of my favorite pasta sauces. We pour red wine, hug some more, and kiss as the pasta pot nearly boils over.

Brooklyn feels cozy tonight in the snow. I always hear myself telling people I hate snow in the city; mostly I hate knowing we're still deep in winter. It rarely snows in Beirut, which is phenomenally great if I'm going to be there long-term; there's lots of snow up in the Lebanese mountains, but in the city it falls about once a decade. Tonight the white blanket outside is comforting somehow. Maybe it's just being back in New York, listening to the sounds of Flatbush Avenue, booming and relentless, the Brooklynese and the Dominican Spanish and the Haitian Creole and the Arabic on the sidewalk below as evening sinks down. New York is rolling over me in waves again, and being with Richard feels . . . right. My skin is tingling, a feeling I try to memorize in my cells, record forever, whenever it happens.

On Christmas Day in Houston, my parents, my brother, Samir, my sister-in-law Laila, and I go for dinner at my uncle Kamal and aunt Diane's house. My cousin Edward is in town from London with his wife, Mariah, and their kids. I'm the godmother to all three of them, and I rush up to interrupt them with kisses and hugs as soon as I spot them busily playing with their newly acquired Christmas loot with my cousin Rich and his wife Erin's two toddlers.

After Christmas dinner, when we're all sitting around the living room, Edward asks me where I'm staying in New York when I visit, since my Manhattan apartment is sublet. I think for a half-second then decide—here we go—and answer, straight up: "With my boyfriend."

A moment of silence. Edward gets an intrigued, twinkly look in his eyes. "Anything else you want to tell us?" Uncle Kamal looks over with a half-smile, a hint of paternal anxiety in his face, and asks: "So, this is serious?"

My aunt Diane jumps in. "The girl is happy. Leave her alone!"

Thank you, Auntie Diane. Thank you.

Uncle Kamal, an increasingly worried expression creeping over him, can't help himself: "I mean, have you two talked about a timetable or anything?"

I try to smile confidently, shake off this question somehow without any words, but an answer stumbles out: "Er, we're seeing

how it goes. Um, I guess we don't have a timetable or anything."
I pause awkwardly, then call out to my goddaughter, "Hey, Gigi,
bring that doll over and let's braid her hair!"

Later that night as I'm trying to fall asleep, my uncle's question, a predictable nudge from one of my lovingly nosy older
relatives, is running through my head. I start thinking, would it
be wise or dumb to bring up the big questions to Richard now:
*Do you think we have a future? Can you imagine us staying together?
Maybe even having kids eventually?*

But the truth is, I still don't know where I'll wind up after my
year in Beirut ends, or if Richard would even want to move there
if we stay together. And I still don't know if I want to have kids.
My feelings for Richard do make me consider things I didn't think
I wanted—plus I'm thirty-eight, so if I eventually want children,
there aren't exactly years and years left to ponder the question.
But we can't seem to even bring up the issue of where our relationship is headed, if anywhere, let alone talk about anything more
momentous. I'm afraid to scare him with big questions now, especially since I haven't figured things out for myself yet. Staying
close with Richard while I'm in Beirut has been feeling right to
me so far, but I still can't see the endgame from here. So what do I
accomplish, and what do I lose, by pressuring him to answer questions about our future and ambushing him with a clock that's supposedly ticking?

As of now, I'm feeling attached to my life in Beirut, and back
in the rhythm of the city, and it's hard now to think of leaving it
all behind, harder than I thought it would be in those rough early
weeks. Even so, there's no obvious answer to the home question
yet. Will I end up deciding Beirut is home and wanting to stay
there? Will I try to convince Richard to move there if I do? Or

will I by chance meet someone else in Lebanon? Tough to imagine right now, but who knows what will happen to our relationship as we try to navigate the coming months?

Still, despite a rocky start, I—and we—have made it through my nearly half-year in Lebanon. Will we survive the months ahead? Will Lebanon?

JANUARY

The international media can't get enough of Lebanon. Journalists covering the country, foreigners most of the time, usually write about it in one of two ways:

"Tanks are rolling through Beirut's streets! Again! Bloodshed and destruction everywhere! Stay tuned as we describe just what the F is wrong with Lebanon *this* time."

Let's call that Category A.

Or:

"Ah, this glittering seaside city, this jewel of the Mediterranean, this Paris of the Middle East. After decades of war and conflict, Beirut is back: thumping nightlife, beautiful women, stylish nightclubs overlooking bombed-out ruins. The Lebanese sure know how to party!"

We'll call that Category B.

If you guessed I might be responsible for some of those articles, you would be right. But just one or two. Small ones. Category B. The paltriness of my oeuvre wasn't from lack of trying. For years I pitched travel editors every story angle I could think of about Beirut: its dynamic food scene and nightlife, its insider hangouts, avant-garde style, and ancient heritage. And I pitched stories about Lebanese villages with fascinating histories and unusual foods or wines. But I was shot down at nearly every turn. Editors seemed happy to send me to Asia, Europe, Africa, and the Caribbean, to destinations dreamy or daring. But not to Lebanon. Those assignments, for some reason, mostly seemed to go to expats or travelers discovering the country for the first time.

So over the years I've resigned myself to reading article after article, in magazine after magazine, newspaper after newspaper, about Beirut as that delightfully paradoxical contrast of ruins and glossy modernity, feeling annoyed because it's such a goddamned predictable angle, and no one has anything newer or more insightful to say. But mostly feeling jealous because I can't get a Lebanon assignment to save my life.

I've been contenting myself with writing about my Beirut adventures on my blog—not quite the same thing, but at least I get to write exactly what I want, and how I want, and take up as much space as I want. I've also been idly wondering how many more times in the future of mankind journalists will find a way to recycle the "Beirut emerges from conflict to party again!" story.

In mid-January, I get my answer: at least one more time.

On January 12, soon after I return to Beirut from the States, the Lebanese government collapses. I realize a government collapse sounds like a crisis, a potentially terrifying emergency situation, but here in Lebanon it's just another eye-rolling day in the country's chronically dysfunctional political life. It's certainly not the first time the Lebanese government has collapsed, although to be fair I should point out that it's the first time in the entire past two calendar years. What's happened this time: Hezbollah has pulled all its parliament members from the government and cajoled some members of other parties into dropping out, too, in protest over Lebanese-government funding of the UN tribunal. Hezbollah is calling the tribunal corrupt and is still threatening to cause bigger trouble if some of its members are named in the Hariri killing. The "Lebanon Collapses!" news hits the headlines worldwide. E-mails and calls pour in from my concerned friends in the States and elsewhere: "Are you okay? What's happening there?!"

In truth, when I first hear the news, I do wonder for a moment whether this time the collapse is serious, and whether the appropriate response is "oh shit" or the usual yawn. I am, for the time being, leaning more to the "oh shit." I've been living in Lebanon for just a handful of months, and in the years since we moved away during the war, I'd been keeping up with the country's constant ups and downs mostly from a distance. I want to play the coolly jaded Lebanese local, but to be honest, I'm not quite there yet.

In the summer of 2005, when I was in Beirut on a brief vacation and stopped in to visit the Lebanese National Museum and see the ancient Roman ruins there, I'd heard a thunderous boom outside. I called my dad on his cell phone.

"Don't worry," he'd said, in typically Zen mode. "It's probably just a building being dynamited at a construction site."

After leaving the museum, I'd learned on the news that the big boom was a car bomb, a successful assassination attempt on a former Lebanese Communist Party leader and anti-Syria critic. For the rest of 2005, back in New York, I'd followed the news from Lebanon, and there was a string of similar assassinations of politicians and journalists.

One year after that assassination epidemic, I had watched the 2006 summer war between Hezbollah and Israel in nauseated silence in my New York apartment, strung out on anxiety and unable to sleep or concentrate on work. CNN was covering the war in the predictable way, meaning mostly from Israel's point of view, paying more attention to the tragic but smaller-in-number deaths of Israelis than to the hundreds of Lebanese civilians killed by Israel's stunningly disproportionate response to Hezbollah's reckless kidnapping or killing of five Israeli soldiers. I watched bombs fall on my city every day, all over again, that July and August, and could barely believe it was happening. But I'd been far away from the bombings and the wreckage and the death—safe in New York, or safer than in Lebanon at any rate.

Now here I am in Beirut, hearing "government collapse" news not from an ocean away. For this particular round of political chaos in Lebanon, I'm right here. And wondering, how afraid should I be?

A few calls to friends and family in Beirut confirm my other suspicion, the one that got trampled by my anxiety reflex: *Nah. Nothing to worry about. Not yet anyway. Come on, this is Lebanon. We're used to these breakdowns.*

"What? This? It's SSDD," says Zeina.

Leave it to a Lebanese to turn a jaded phrase—"same shit, different day"—into a handy acronym, ready to deploy at all the countless opportunities that spring up here.

But scary or not, this political crisis is definitely real in at least one way: it's another shiny new gift to an international media that can never resist a good "oh my god, Lebanon!" story. Here we have one once again. Catastrophe! Collapse! Lebanon in Danger!

So once we're finished with this latest news cycle, I wonder how long it will be until the inevitable "Beirut Is Back!" travel stories start streaming in.

Well, I hope I at least get to write one of them.

About a week later in January, once the international "Lebanon Collapses!" news cycle dies down—it lasted a good twenty-four hours before making way for news about the huge East Coast blizzard that same week—I get a call from an editor in the States asking if I'd like to do a big Middle East travel story. Sweet! At last! But . . . it's not about Lebanon. It'll be about Egypt. Can I get myself to Egypt as soon as possible and do a travel story for the next issue? Hmm. Yes. Yes, I can.

I go online and book a flight for the last week in January.

In the days before I leave for Cairo, the situation in Lebanon is tense, several orders of magnitude tenser than it felt when the government had its somewhat ho-hum meltdown two weeks ago. Things are taking a nastier turn. Hezbollah ratchets up its threats that it will raise hell if the UN tribunal goes forward with its predicted indictments, and a few scary, ominous street incidents break out in Beirut. One morning groups of men wearing all black are seen hovering on street corners all over the city. The men just stand there silently, and though nothing else happens that day, their presence causes panic, and schools send kids home for the day. Some businesses close, too. The incident is rumored to be Hezbollah's doing—as if to say, *Remember, we have our own militia, and we're fully capable of making things unpleasant around here.*

And we're not so ecstatic about the way things are going with the tribunal at the moment.

Meanwhile, Richard has bought his plane ticket to come visit me in Beirut in early February, so I'm particularly anxious about the developments in Lebanon, even more than usual. Will Lebanon become too dangerous to visit, yet again? Damn this place. Impossible to ever make long-term plans here. I talk to Zeina on the phone. She's depressed. Gone is the joking "SSDD" Zeina of a week ago. She tells me she hopes her daughter will leave Lebanon when it's time for college and never look back.

"There's no future here," she says to me in Arabic, her voice sounding far away this time, wilted.

She and her husband, along with most people in Lebanon, have to worry about crucial, high-stakes issues like whether to go on trying to raise kids or pursue a career here, whether to keep planning a future in this country. At the moment, my main concern is whether my boyfriend can vacation with me and prance around Lebanon for two weeks. That's a tiny bit less dire. Nonetheless this country has a way of squashing plans and dreams, big or small. And always when things are starting to look up again.

The night before I fly to Egypt, I hang out with my childhood friend Sawsan. She's living in California, doing a postdoctorate there, but is in Beirut this week visiting her parents. We go for drinks at the Hamra bar Ferdinand, and to an alleyway nearby that's crammed full of bars and usually a noisy, social crowd. But tonight all the hangouts we go to are barely half full. That's usually a bad sign around here. It takes a pretty nasty vibe to keep Beirutis out of restaurants, bars, and clubs. Everywhere we go, people are talking about *al wad'*, the situation.

At least Egypt will be a badly needed mental vacation, an

escape from this insane asylum, I figure. The trip will be hard work—fun, too, sure, but hard work no doubt. I have to make my way around Egypt and do all the reporting for this story in just five days, but at least I'll get my mind off Lebanon.

Off I fly to Cairo, on the sunny, mild morning of January 24, 2011.

I'd heard two days before my trip that antigovernment demonstrations were being planned in Cairo for that coming Tuesday, January 25. I rejiggered my itinerary so I'd leave Cairo for Alexandria on that Tuesday morning instead of spending the day in the capital, just in case there was any serious mayhem and violence stemming from the demonstrations. I'm slightly apprehensive but not too worried about the protests. I tell myself, with a sense of relief that I'll later be mortified to own up to, that Egypt has a tenacious dictatorship that will probably suppress any unrest before it spreads. Slim chance that the situation in Egypt could deteriorate so quickly—not like Lebanon always seems to. The Middle East–related anxieties I'm feeling that week are firmly fixated on Lebanon.

I land in Cairo around noon after the short flight, and in the afternoon I visit the Egyptian Museum, where I explore the mummy exhibits and peer into cases holding the fossilized remains of foods (beans, grains, prunes) that are, amazingly, still recognizable even though they date back millennia. I take an early drive that Tuesday morning to see the pyramids in nearby Giza before heading to Alexandria. Thanks to the nearly nonexistent crowds in Giza at the crack of dawn, the pyramids seem to rise up suddenly, almost unexpectedly, out of the dry and empty desert. After seeing so much film footage of them, I'm still startled by their almost cartoonishly large size and domineering presence. The view is unspoiled by crowds of tour buses, which I'm sure will start jamming the area within an hour. I'd wondered if the pyramids would be disappointing. But as I sit on a rock alone, staring up at the 450-foot-tall structures, built in the third millennium B.C., I start to think: *Whatever happens to Lebanon now, and whatever happens in Cairo during today's protests, will soon enough be buried in the dust, just like the pharaohs and all their worries and their belongings and the remnants of a once-dynamic civilization that's now stone and dirt.* I suspect I'm not the first person to have had these thoughts while staring up at the Giza pyramids. But the visit puts things in perspective like nothing else has done for me in weeks, and it turns out to be just the mind-bending experience I need after a rocky few weeks in Lebanon.

I head to Alexandria in the late morning, in time to escape the protests scheduled to kick off in downtown Cairo today. When I arrive and drop off my bags in my hotel room, I walk across the street to Alexandria's main waterfront boulevard overlooking the Mediterranean, and I stroll along for a few minutes, enjoying the soft breeze and staring out at ships in the sea. Suddenly I hear yells coming from behind me. I turn around and spot a small crowd forming about a quarter-mile away. I continue walking forward, looking over my shoulder every few seconds to see what's happening, and I notice the crowd keeps growing. Now it's tripled, quadrupled, and it's looking more like a riot, a mass of what appear to be mostly Egyptian men in their twenties and thirties streaming toward the waterfront in the direction where I'm walking. Moments later throngs of riot police, dressed in black, appear out of nowhere, running in from all sides and lining up in rows as they try to contain the thickening crowd.

I'm stunned at how the scene has just transformed, in minutes, from a calm, sunlit weekday-afternoon tableau—locals strolling, a smattering of tourists taking pictures of the curvy boulevard overlooking the sea—into a flash mob. As the crowd continues to grow and fill the area that stretches from the palm-encircled plaza near my hotel all the way across the boulevard to the shore, shouting protest slogans I can barely make out in all the ruckus, the riot police form a giant barrier around the crowd, and some cops are running amok in the middle, shoving people to the ground, holding batons and teargas canisters.

The protests haven't been confined to Cairo today, then. I later find out Alexandria is better known for its history of radical politics and activism than is Cairo, so no wonder the Egyptian uprising would kick off simultaneously in Alexandria. But right now there's no time for second-guessing my decision to come here. I need to disentangle myself from this thickening riot, pronto, or I'm going to be teargassed.

So far on this trip I've been speaking mostly Arabic, glad to be in an Arab country where people want to speak the native language with you—especially if they can tell that you speak it, too. No stubborn attempts to switch to English or French here in Egypt, not like in Beirut. My Arabic, even though I'm struggling a little with the Egyptian dialect, has already improved more in my two days here than it did in my first two months in Beirut. But on this particular afternoon in Alexandria, it comes in handy to be a foreigner, even an American one. It's not always the wisest move to loudly proclaim your Americanness in Arab countries that have a dicey foreign relations history with the United States, but at this particular moment in January 2011—partly because of the truce signed between Egypt's former president Anwar Sadat and Israel's ex-premier Menachem Begin at Camp David, Maryland, in 1978, and also because of the $2 billion in aid money the United States has been sending Egypt every year—the Egyptian regime and America are on decent terms. At the moment, the government is blaming mainly Egyptian civilians for the unrest, not foreigners just yet.

As I run to get out of the crowd, I come smack up against a riot cop who is blocking my way. He and his cohorts are holding their plastic shields end to end and creating an impenetrable barrier around the entire area. I opt for the I'm-an-American pose.

"Please, please, I'm a tourist," I beg the policeman in my best American accent, standing barely an inch from his plastic shield and the baton he's about to start swinging. I'm wondering if I have any chance of getting out of here before who-knows-what hell gets unleashed.

The policeman looks at me for a second. The riot cop standing next to him looks, too, says something to the other cop, and they both stand there, glowering at me. Then, ten seconds later—feels like an hour—they part their shields for a split second to let me pass.

I duck out of the mob and onto the other side of the police barrier, as the voices of the cops and the protesters merge into a louder and louder din. I'm relieved to be out of there, but wondering what may happen moments from now to the Alexandrians stuck inside the riot-police trap. They've potentially risked their lives to come out here and demonstrate against Hosni Mubarak and his cruel thirty-year dictatorship. For the first time since he took power, Egyptians may finally have the chance—now that a revolutionary movement has obviously built up enough momentum to get people into the streets today—to take back their country.

But clouds and clouds of teargas are about to engulf the crowd,

it turns out, and from a short distance away, I can see police officers beating protesters with batons. By this point I'm much farther
along on the boulevard, walking fast—not running, don't want
to attract suspicion, but walking as fast as I've ever walked in my
life—until I can't see or hear or sense the riots anymore.

But that evening I accidentally find out what getting teargassed
feels like. As I'm riding the Alexandria tram to a café, through
the streets of the atmospheric city—elegant townhouses darkened
by smog, and old coffee shops and bric-a-brac stores and pastry
shops, all crammed side by side along the sidewalks, the scent of
coffee in the air and the sea in the near distance—I hear someone
yell, "Close your eyes!" Suddenly I feel a painful burning in my
eyeballs and nostrils. Teargas is seeping in through the open windows; must be another raging mob of riot cops trying to break up
a crowd. All the passengers cover their faces and duck. In a minute or two, the gas dissipates, and my eyes and nose are still itch-
ing but no longer on fire. One woman is having trouble breathing
and scrambles out at the next stop. I continue along to the café.

What am I doing riding the tram to a coffee shop, in the middle of the historic Egyptian revolution of 2011? A fair question.
But in those first few days of the uprising, as hard as it is to imagine now, there was still mostly a business-as-usual feel, apart from
the scattered protests. I remember that feeling from the occasionally calm stretches of the civil war in Lebanon. When the mayhem
temporarily dies down, whether it's for a day or for a few hours,
you're not sure if something terrible is about to happen or if things
are settling back down, so you try to go about your life. You run
your errands and go to school or work if you can. In Lebanon during the war, you'd try to visit your friends and relatives, especially
if you've been cooped up for hours or days in a basement shelter

or at home. You take care of day-to-day business, more or less, as best you can manage and for as long as you can. In Alexandria, things seemed calm again that day, in between the protests, and so I tried to go on with my plans.

But Egypt isn't used to chaos on this level and hasn't seen it for decades, and the café where I've agreed to meet up with Raya, the guide I scheduled to take me around tomorrow, turns out to be nearly empty tonight. I spot Raya, a pretty brunette in her midthirties wearing glasses and a purple head scarf, sitting at a table alone. I ask her if our plan is really still on for tomorrow, and she assures me everything will be fine; the riots today were probably just a blip. But I notice there's an anxious expression on her face as she excuses herself to call home and check on her kids. When she comes back, she tells me about the history of one of the sites she's taking me to tomorrow: the Alexandria Library, the most prestigious of its time when it was built in the third century B.C.; Julius Caesar burned it down in the first century B.C., and it reopened in its current location just ten years ago.

Later that evening, as I'm just steps from my hotel, I hear more crowd noises and look back to see another throng forming down the street, holding up antiregime posters and chanting protest slogans. Cops are running in to break it up. This crowd is smaller than the riot I'd witnessed earlier, but it's scary—even if a little thrilling—to be so close to the action. I'm glad I'm safely back at the hotel.

The next morning the city feels quiet again, and according to the local news I hear in my hotel room, there are no reports of more demonstrations breaking out. I continue with my plans to see the Alexandria Library and National Museum that day. Raya picks me up in her car and shows me around the library's soaring, glassy new building and high-tech research facilities, and then takes me to the museum to see the collection of ancient jewelry and weapons from the days of Alexander the Great and Antony and Cleopatra. In the afternoon, I take a taxi back to Cairo. It feels like a normal Wednesday in Alexandria and along the highway.

In the early evening, as the cab pulls into Cairo, driving near the edge of Tahrir Square to take me to my hotel a couple of miles away, I start hearing loud crowd noises again. Suddenly streams of protesters come running out along the sidewalk past the now-stopped traffic, yelling "Gas, gas!" Clouds of teargas are blowing past our taxi, and masses of riot police are chasing after the demonstrators. My taxi driver just grunts and complains about the slow-moving traffic. I'm amazed he's only focusing on that, but he's an elderly driver (looks to be in his eighties) in an Arab country. He's probably seen some unrest in his day; maybe he was even driving a cab during the last Egyptian revolution, back in 1952.

I roll the taxi window shut on my side, and when the driver finally makes it to my hotel, I spend hours in my room that night flipping between the TV news stations: Al-Jazeera from Qatar, Al-Arabiya from Saudia Arabia, and CNN International. The protests have hit both Cairo and Alexandria again on this Wednesday evening, and the crowds have been growing, the cops getting more ruthless with batons and teargas. They haven't started shooting live bullets into the crowds yet; that will come later in the week. The cities are not yet swept up in giant masses of sit-ins. The Cairo protests in those first few days are happening mostly in the evenings and are still confined to certain parts of town, mostly around Tahrir Square.

Thursday morning: it's quiet again in Cairo. As I drink coffee in my room at the hotel where I'm staying, I read in the paper that the protesters are planning to resume the demonstrations tomorrow, Friday, after the noon mosque prayers. I'm relieved that I'll be heading out by then. As much as I wholeheartedly support the uprising, I don't want to be anywhere near the mayhem. I guess there's a reason I'm not a war reporter. Although the riots breaking out here are quite different from the war violence I grew up with in Lebanon, the atmosphere of chaos and danger makes me want to bolt, not pull out my notepad.

Speaking of Lebanon, the country has had some more hiccups in the past week, while I've been away. On the news in my Alexandria hotel room one night, I watched footage of an anti-Hezbollah demonstration in Beirut earlier that day—rioters protesting the group's antitribunal actions had burned tires on the streets. But the situation there seems to be calming back down.

My Egypt trip has been incredibly memorable—more than I could've imagined—and I'm desperate to come back here so I can explore the country better and hopefully do more travel reporting once the situation settles a bit. Even though I'm ready to return to Beirut now, I feel lucky to have been in Egypt at the start of a historic uprising. I got to watch as thousands, and eventually millions, of Egyptians risked their lives to try to transform their country—their home—into a place where they can live, thrive, have a future. I realize that it's one thing to leave the city where you're living and search for home somewhere else; it's an entirely more difficult, and arguably much more courageous, decision to stay put under tough conditions and go up against terrifying odds to transform your home for the better.

By the time I arrive in Beirut, a new prime minister is in place:

Najib Miqati, a Sunni multimillionaire from the north, who took office after the previous prime minister, the late Rafik Hariri's son Saad, was forced out by the government collapse earlier in the month. Miqati is trying to form a new cabinet by bringing together the opposing political parties, and there's some optimism that he'll get them to meet halfway, rebuild the government, and potentially agree to terms regarding the still-unreleased results of the tribunal.

I wonder, now that things may be settling down again, if it's time for the inevitable new round of Lebanon travel stories. True, there've been only a few weeks of instability this time, and no violence or war to recover from yet, but "Beirut Emerges from Conflict to Party Once More!" is an eminently recyclable story, and editors always need material. Journalists: Ready, set, go!

Meanwhile, it's looking like Richard can come visit in a week after all. Or, I wonder, should I play it extrasafe and talk him out of it? Selfishly, I don't want to, but I'm a little nervous.

As his arrival date inches closer, my anxieties seem more and more trivial compared to what's going on a few borders away. This is the first time in Beirut that I wish I had a working TV. In my hotel rooms in Egypt, I'd been glued to the set, watching the protesters march through the streets, cheering them on. But the only television I have regular access to here in Beirut is the one at T-Marbouta, the Hamra café where I work on my laptop sometimes, surrounded by a regular crowd of students and activist types. Lately that set has been tuned in all day to Al-Jazeera's coverage of the Egypt riots. I spend a few afternoons in a row at one of the café's corner tables, and I overhear people near me discussing the situation in Egypt, guessing at when Mubarak will finally step down. Every once in a while, as the footage shows a particularly egregious episode of police brutality, the buzz in the room grows, as everyone looks up from their laptops or conversations to boo and jeer at the screen. I can't remember a time in my life when televisions in Beirut were so fixated on minute-by-minute events in a troubled Arab country, and not Lebanon, for a change.

Day by day the tensions in Lebanon keep deflating—not the ones in my head, though. Although I'm less anxious about political unrest here for the immediate term, I've still been fretting: *What if Richard hates it in Beirut? What if it's awkward introducing him to my family and friends here? What if we can't make it through two straight weeks without driving each other crazy?* We've never spent this much time together.

Meanwhile the rest of the Middle East is in turmoil now, too. Populations all over the region have been inspired by Egypt's uprising and by Tunisia's, back in December, and are revolting against their repressive regimes: Bahrain, Syria, Jordan, Libya, Yemen. The potential for a major transformation is exhilarating. Nonetheless, the sense of uncertainty and danger, an unstable region teetering on the edge of something still unknown, is seeping in and rattling my dreams.

My own personal upheaval—my move from New York to Beirut—is so preposterously minuscule in importance compared to what's happening around the Middle East, it's embarrassing to even mention it in the same sentence, but I'm still feeling the effects of that shake-up. Will Richard's visit bring more tremors, another earthquake? Will we mesh here in Beirut the way we do on our more familiar turf, in New York, or will everything fall apart and end in a miserable breakup after his visit? Or worse, during?

FEBRUARY

I love February in Beirut. It's only a couple of days into the month—Richard arrives this week—and already the deep freeze I associate with February in New York is a distant memory. It's barely dropped lower than the fifties here so far, and as I watch locals pull their coats tighter and brace against the wind, I'm feeling like the hardy winter warrior; in New York I'm usually the cold-weather wimp. At least the sidewalks here don't get slippery with snow and ice, and the wind never gets so cold my face hurts.

It's not just the weather that's winning me over. Beirut life in general has been feeling easier, more natural with every passing week. Being away from Richard for long stretches of time hasn't gotten much easier, but now I'm finding more comfort in the life I'm building here. As I spend more time with childhood friends and cousins—deepening bonds we'd formed as kids—and as I hang out regularly with new friends and enjoy relaxed get-togethers with aunts and uncles, I'm realizing: Beirut is starting to feel more like home. Not just because I'm more used to it now, but because here I feel surrounded, literally on all sides—upstairs, downstairs, east, west—by people I care about and feel at ease with. Also, life in Hamra never gets dull, with all the little streets to explore and the cafés and bars to meet friends in. My old memories of the neighborhood keep mingling with my new discoveries. If I wimp out and leave Beirut now just so I can be near Richard and stop the long-distance angst, I'm probably going to feel a lot like I did when I was nine: *I'm not finished here. I'm being ripped away against my will.*

If Richard and I manage to stay together not just during his visit but as the weeks and months go by, it might not be so crazy to think he'd move here, too. Somehow we've been getting closer through our letters (well, electronic letters). We've been writing daily, and our e-mails have gotten more detailed, more like conversations, and more lyrical than phone chats. Our notes read like love letters but are also full of the flotsam of our days, the miscellaneous errands, the films and music and adventures and foods we've come across and want to experience together sometime, the things that are driving us nuts about certain people, the work annoyances, the social events and goings-on that are keeping us afloat, or glad to be alive, or sad to be apart.

"Dear S., New York was less brutally cold today. I fought the blues, and got out and about a little during my teaching day. I've been feeling inspired about my book again, which is good, but it also makes me impatient with work in a way that can get me down unless I get super-tough nuts. Tonight I watched the Celtics demolish the Cavs, and watched Obama talk to the country. Soon we'll be strolling on the Corniche together. Meantime I want you to have fun but be sure to be really safe. Not sure what that entails precisely, but if there's a question of staying out of a certain section of town that has delicious yogurt-drizzled dill cakes but is experiencing riots or something, please skip the dill cakes, OK? Miss you like crazy."

My recurring angst about his visit aside, I'm counting the days, practically the hours, until he gets here. It's odd, though, that we picked February for his visit. February is a loaded month. For one thing, there's Valentine's Day—admittedly the dumbest holiday ever, but here it also happens to be the anniversary of ex–prime minister Rafik Hariri's assassination in 2005. This month is also Richard's birthday, and I hope he'll be glad he skipped his annual party in New York to celebrate here instead. I so badly want him to feel comfortable in Lebanon. I can't help wondering if he will, though, and among my other concerns, I hope he won't feel in any way awkward about being Jewish here.

To my knowledge, there's no history of anti-Semitism in Lebanon, not the way there is in Europe and certain other parts of the world. In Lebanon, none of the sects, whether Christian, Muslim, Jewish, or you name it, has ever gotten along terribly well for long, but in various periods or places in Lebanese history, they've also gotten along beautifully; mistrust and sabotage alternating with friendly alliance among tribes is par for the course here. But Israel's penchant for invading, wrecking, and occupying this country is hard to overlook, sitting as we are just across Israel's northern border. And that history of invasions, massacres, and occupations, whatever its causes or attempted justifications, has bred resentment and suspicion of anyone with sympathies for the government down south.

I'm also worried that many of my relatives—for whom being just, humane, and intellectually honest includes defending the Palestinian narrative against willful erasure, and calling out Israeli land grabs and policies that brutalize Arabs—won't believe that I can be happy long-term with someone who is not only not Arab (most of my relatives can deal with that) and not Christian (the more liberal relatives I'm closest to won't care, even if others might) but a Jewish American with certain sympathies for Israel. Richard certainly doesn't have unconditional sympathy for Israel, far from it. He denounces the ways in which it has cruelly mistreated Palestinians and continues to. But he hasn't gone out into the streets to march for those causes, like certain of my Jewish friends in the States. I'd feel more comfortable bringing them to a cocktail party where political issues might come up. With Richard, I'm not as sure.

Nonetheless, I can't imagine basing my friendships and relationships purely on Middle Eastern political logic. Especially when there's no logic to this never-ending bloody mess, and when Lebanon, too, has a lot to answer for—not just the way it treats Palestinian refugees living here, but also its own history of intersectarian bigotry.

Politics aside, I've also been wondering if introducing Richard as my boyfriend to some of my old-school relatives will bring on a mortifying interrogation.

So . . . when are you two getting engaged, hmm?

Or, more terrifyingly:

Oh, you're visiting from New York! So you two are engaged? How lovely!

A couple of my cousins went through exactly that when they tried in recent years to bring a boyfriend or girlfriend on a trip to Lebanon. When I introduce Richard as "my boyfriend visiting from New York" to some of my more conservative family members, I envision *Annie Hall*—style subtitles running below the conversation:

Hi, meet my boyfriend. We're not engaged and have no immediate plans to be. But he's sleeping in my bed with me, in my parents' apartment, and they're five thousand miles away. Yes, I am a slut and a lost soul. But thanks for the coffee! We'll just show ourselves out now.

This may be the twenty-first century, but if you're Lebanese, even a cosmopolitan twenty-first-century Lebanese with an equally cosmopolitan twenty-first-century extended family, you'll know what I mean. This is treacherous territory. A full trifecta: my boyfriend is visiting even though we're not engaged; he's staying with me even though my parents aren't here to chaperone; oh, and also, he's Jewish (and therefore, in their minds, he's already taken sides on the Middle East).

Ever since I landed in Beirut last summer, I've been trying to figure out how people my age, the single ones, conduct a normal adult life in Lebanon. The tradition of living with your parents until you're married, even if you're in your thirties, is still alive and well here. Turns out the coping strategies come in many shapes.

A friend of a friend is a divorced thirty-year-old who is living back at home with her parents now and has a new boyfriend, but she can't bring him home. Well, for the occasional afternoon coffee with her parents in attendance, yes, but not for things that normal thirty-year-olds might do. Another acquaintance is thirty-eight, unmarried, and not in a hurry to marry, and she has a semiserious boyfriend she brings home and does whatever she wants with in her room; her parents don't notice, or pretend not to.

A good friend of one of my cousins is a lesbian in her thirties but has gay male friends she's close with, who live with their families in villages outside Beirut and who sometimes crash at her place in the city after a night out. Unbeknownst to her, she was being closely watched by her neighbors over the course of a few weeks recently, and when her parents came to visit from the States, a group of neighbors showed up at their door, rang the bell, and said, "Did you know your daughter has men stay overnight?" The parents laughed. They know their daughter is a lesbian. And they are fine with her lifestyle, with her girlfriend, and with letting her old friends crash at the apartment overnight.

So it depends on you and your family and on a whole web of circumstances. But living solo in an apartment, or living with a boyfriend or girlfriend, is still rare in Lebanon—getting less rare, especially in Beirut, but still all too rare.

No doubt about it: this is a deeply perplexed and perplexing place when it comes to sex. It's not just that Beirut in summer, with all its skimpy fashions both on and off the beach, is like the world's hottest runway show. Bars and nightclubs and parties are incredibly flirty scenes year-round, with couples often making out openly, even at gay bars, and going home together if there's no hovering, disapproving relative or neighbor on watch. (If there is, friends often organize group trips to the mountains, to ski in winter, or hit the beaches down south in summer—and for couples to have some private time and space.) But there's still virtually no sex ed in schools. And the Lebanese on the whole like to pretend, except among close friends and confidantes, that we're not having premarital sex, especially if we're women.

My mom's friend Nadia told me that in the 1970s, when one of her sisters decided to move into her own apartment in Beirut in her thirties without being married, she was doing something unheard of at the time. It was scandalous and led to much whispering and judging among neighbors and family friends, even though her parents approved of her decision. Slowly, very slowly, the idea of young women living alone in Lebanon has come to seem less outrageous, but it's still unfathomable to many.

Even my mother, while living in a Beirut apartment next door to her married brother's family in her twenties, after her parents died, got some needling questions from relatives concerned about her chastity: "Why not just move in with your brother?"

I'd like to think if I were alive then, I would've faced down the questions and lived alone if I needed or wanted to. Or would I have married, even if I wasn't madly in love or feeling ready to commit to a particular person for life, just to avoid being constantly judged and harassed? Or would I have just sucked it up and lived with my parents until I was ready to get married—even through my late thirties? Would I have done what I wanted and helped my parents turn a blind eye, found sneaky ways to avoid embarrassing them or bringing down the judgment of those who still insisted on tsk-tsking, even well into the twenty-first century?

I'm lucky to even have these choices, I remind myself. In another generation, or another country, or another family, I would probably have been married with kids a long time ago and would never even have considered the alternative. Or if I'd been determined or brave enough to postpone or dodge that path, I might have been banished.

So yes, I'm fortunate to even be hashing all this out right now. Fortunate but confused.

Before Richard arrives, I ask around for advice on how to explain his visit to people who might judge. Should I act like it's no big deal that he's here visiting me, staying with me, and horrors— no we're not engaged? Or should I just introduce him as an old platonic friend?

The opinions I get range from "Just do what comes naturally, no need to lie, and people will have to deal with it, and if they can't, then you don't need them anyway" to "You don't have to tell anyone; just say he's a friend; you know how the Lebanese like to talk and gossip and butt in," to the more paranoid "Cohabitation is actually illegal in Lebanon, so be careful" (although I haven't heard of any cases where the police went after a wayward couple). I want badly to go with option A, because that's the most natural and least absurd of the scenarios. But maybe I'll bend the truth just a little so as not to ruffle feathers.

It's an almost supernaturally blue-skied afternoon when Richard lands in Beirut. I go to the airport to meet him, and as he walks out the terminal door, an intense happiness washes over me, a warm tingly feeling. Yes, he's supposed to be here. With me. All I have to do now is make Beirut okay for him, maybe even incredible. Maybe we can live here together someday. But I'm getting ahead of myself.

We hug long and tight. I lead the way to the taxi stand.

"How did the trip go?"

"Pretty smoothly. I almost missed the connection at the Frankfurt airport because the flight out of JFK was delayed, but other than that, all good. Got my bags right away. The immigration line went really fast after we landed in Beirut. No one asked me, 'So, Meester Geelman, vat eez ze purpose of your visit to zees country?'"

"This isn't Nazi Germany."

"I know. Guess I was being paranoid for a second."

Richard's flight was the cheapest I've seen from New York to Beirut: just under eight hundred dollars round-trip. In New York over New Year's, when we found that airfare online and he bought his ticket, we'd high-fived each other. Bliss, excitement, a thrilling adventure on the way. And then five minutes later we'd gotten into a fight. I'd mentioned that maybe he should play down his Jewish identity when he's in Lebanon, because of the country's relationship with Israel and because people tend to assume that if you're American and Jewish, then you must be a Zionist.

In his family and in the Hebrew school he was sent to, Richard was raised to see the Holocaust as the defining event of this era, and he grew up learning about the history of persecution that Jews have faced in Europe and elsewhere at various points throughout history. Among my own relatives and the Lebanese in general, the Nakba—the expulsion of most of the Arabs from Palestine in 1948—has been one of the defining events of our times. It's had tragic repercussions in the decades since, on Lebanon as a whole and on the entire region, and it's also profoundly impacted some of our own relatives who married Palestinians and have half-Palestinian kids.

I understand how political views are shaped by, even if not necessarily always defined by, our families and the political and geographical contexts we all grew up in. Part of the problem, maybe the biggest part, of trying to resolve some of the region's seemingly eternal conflicts is that we're dealing with populations who grew up within different contexts, and who in most cases have trouble integrating the other narrative into their own.

When I'd suggested, just after Richard clicked "confirm" on his ticket purchase, that maybe he should be cautious about bringing up being Jewish when he's in Lebanon, at least until the people he meets get to know him better and feel unthreatened by potential political tension in the room, he'd gotten upset with me. My timing was admittedly awful—and I'd apologized for that, reassuring him that no Lebanese person, relative of mine or not, could ever pull us apart, or would even want to, if we want to be together. And anyway my family would be predisposed to love him, warm and funny and genuine as he is, not to mention that he's with me.

"Just please," I'd said, as we finally worked our way out of the angry cloud and decided to make the best of his trip, "lay off any 'rah rah Israel' when you're in Beirut?" I was joking. As if he'd ever say anything like that, or even remotely want to. But when it comes to the delightful relationship between Lebanon and Israel, you can never be too careful.

Ever since I got back from Egypt, I've been making a list of places I want to take Richard, and all the angles of this country I want to show him: Lebanon as beautiful site of ancient civilizations, and Beirut as crazy bad-ass city, gentle old Mediterranean port town, hipster-bar-scene central, and eternally mixed-up, schizophrenic, unstable, but ultimately lovable place.

On his first full day, I decide to take him on one of my now-patented long walks across the city to show him the sweep of it all, from Ras Beirut on the west side through downtown and on to Achrafieh on the east side. It's starting to rain as we set out on our walk, not ideal—but that's okay, I figure, it'll be more romantic, like in movie scenes where couples run through a darkening city, holding hands in the pouring rain.

Before we head across town, we pick up a man'ouche at the Hamra bakery around the corner from my apartment, and wind down to Bliss Street, then through the American University of Beirut. The campus descends downhill, along wooded paths and stone staircases leading through forested clusters and landscaped gardens planted with purple petunias, red hibiscus, and pink hydrangeas, all the way to the sea. Many of the campus buildings, graceful brick villa-style structures, were built in the late nineteenth and early twentieth centuries and are dedicated to the Protestant missionaries who founded the university—Dodge Hall, Nicely Hall, West Hall (named, coincidentally, after an ancestor of one of Richard's New York friends). A few more glassy modern buildings sit on the lower edge of campus closer to the waterfront. All over campus, peeks between buildings and through the branches of palm trees and pines bring cinematic views of the Mediterranean, and an underpass at the sea-level edge leads under the Corniche and to the university's own beach, a summer hangout for students and staff.

We walk through campus and exit out the lower end, crossing the street onto the Corniche. By this point it's raining hard, but we keep on walking and getting soaked, Richard gaping at my daredevil street-crossing technique, the only way to get anywhere as a pedestrian in Beirut. Cars won't stop on their own and rarely obey what few traffic lights there are, so, just as drivers do, you have to make a decision to cross and go with it, forge right through the traffic.

We continue toward downtown and head to the center and the Martyrs' Square statue of the Lebanese nationalist revolutionaries who were hanged by the Ottomans in 1919. Before the civil war, before I was born, the Martyrs' Square area was known as Place des Canons, or the Burj ("armory" in Arabic), and for anyone who has seen vintage postcards of downtown Beirut, that's the big palm-tree-lined square surrounded by lively pedestrian sidewalks and bus-ringed streets. A popular old guidebook called *Lebanon Today*, found on the bookshelves of many Beirut homes, including ours—it was published, poignantly, in 1974, a year before the war started, and predicts on page 187 that "Lebanon will always remain a haven of peace and stability"—described downtown Beirut this way: "The visitor would be well advised to mingle with the crowds in the Place des Canons itself . . . then the souks— narrow streets, frequently roofed—where you are carried along by the crowd . . . People often come here just to drink a lemonade or a fruit drink or taste the pastries or other dainties which they eat as they walk along."

But that prewar version of downtown Beirut hadn't been around very long by the time that guidebook was written. The statue of the revolutionaries had only just been erected in 1960, and the lawn and street arrangement that characterized the square and its surroundings before the civil war had been inspired by relatively recent French urban planning trends of the late nineteenth and early twentieth centuries. In a place like Lebanon, though, wrecked then rebuilt so many times over the millennia, starting way back before it was even a real country, the short-lived recent past becomes as sepia-toned as the ancient, hazier one. I feel wistful about Place des Canons even though I was never alive to see the way downtown looked back then. The Martyrs' Square reincarnation, with only that 1960 statue still present (albeit now bullet-ridden from the events of the 1970s and 1980s), has newer associations for the civil war generation like me. That part of downtown, a mostly flat and empty square ever since the war, is where the so-called Cedar Revolution happened in 2005, as masses of Lebanese gathered to protest Syria's postwar occupation of the country.

It's pouring even harder now, and Richard and I are both drenched top to bottom, as we head through the square and toward the ancient Roman baths and the parliament building. I'd wanted this walk to surprise and enchant him, give him a taste of the city's contrasts and complexity, but although he's being a good sport, we're both tired, soaked, and getting cranky.

On our walk, Richard has been transfixed by the noisy car-and-moped-crammed streets, the vendors selling fresh pomegranate juice and sesame bread from wheelbarrows, the chaotic mix of crumbling ruins and spanking-new buildings, and the sea that curves around, blue even on a rainy February day. But he's annoyed with the nonexistent sidewalks and the impossibility of walking here without pausing to defend your life from a speeding car or a perilous pothole every seven seconds. It's time for a break. He stops me at the next corner.

"Intense city, wow. Insane, and so cool, and exhausting. Drink?"

It's five o'clock, and we're walking now across Martyrs' Square toward Achrafieh, the mostly Christian neighborhood of old stone mansions and churches and posh boutiques on the east side of town. We try stopping at a couple of bars I like around here, first a place fittingly called Time Out, and then Pacifico, the bar I went to with Mirna and her friends weeks ago. No luck at either place; the doors are locked. This is when I learn that lots of Beirut bars, many of the ones in Achrafieh anyway, don't open until seven P.M. Not because of any puritanical law—just a widely shared feeling of *Why would you want to sit in a bar at five when it's not packed with people yet? What's the point of starting early? Pace yourself. It's a long night ahead.*

We take a service taxi back to Hamra, pick up a bottle of the Lebanese winery Ksara's Reserve du Couvent, an inexpensive, easy-drinking red that's ubiquitous in Beirut, and head back to the apartment. We spend the evening in, making dinner and watching a movie—*Pan's Labyrinth*, Guillermo del Toro's hallucinatory Spanish film, on a one-dollar pirate disk I'd picked up. It turns into a cozy night of pasta, wine, and a movie, just like any we'd have in New York. Simple, easy, pleasant. Incredibly pleasant.

The next morning, and every morning for the two straight weeks he's here, I wake up cheerful and rested—a personal record for me. Knowing we have days and days to spend together morning to night makes me feel a relaxed kind of joy that I somehow hadn't anticipated in all my anxiety about his trip. One day we wake up at six to take a bus ride, around two hours long, to the ancient Roman ruins at Baalbek, in the Beqaa Valley east of Beirut. We arrive to find we're the only ones at Baalbek on this rainy Tuesday morning in February, the first time I've seen the site so empty. But on past trips I've come here in July or August, when it's overrun with Lebanese visitors and with foreigners who've braved whatever political volatility happened to be in the air. We hold hands as we climb up the stone steps of the Temple of Bacchus, a grand, columned affair bigger than the Parthenon in Athens and built more than two thousand years ago.

"Whoa. Holy shit. I can't believe this place."

I stare out at Mount Sannine, covered in snow, in the distance beyond the valley and the pine trees. We walk over toward the Temple of Jupiter, the six giant stone columns that have made the cover of nearly every guidebook ever written about Lebanon.

"Want a commemorative Hezbollah T-shirt?" I ask jokingly, pointing past the temple to the row of vendors standing outside the entrance selling shirts with the militia's yellow and green logo: an outstretched arm rising up out of an Arabic-calligraphy scrawl of the word *Hezbollah*, and holding an AK-47. Baalbek is in a part of the Beqaa Valley controlled mainly by Hezbollah, not a fact that always makes it into the guidebooks. The roads in that part of the Beqaa are hung all over with posters of party militants and, Hezbollah being financed largely by Iran, of Iranian right-wing religious figures.

The sinister signage notwithstanding, I'm feeling proud of Lebanon as we walk around. These stone temples are so ancient, so shockingly well preserved through the millennia and the multiple invasions and wars. They radiate grandeur and timelessness. Few ancient ruins anywhere in the world rival Baalbek's, in my not-unbiased opinion—but Mark Twain agreed. After his visit to Lebanon in the nineteenth century, he wrote: "Such grandeur of design, and such grace of execution, as one sees in the temples of Baalbec, have not been equaled or even approached in any work of men's hands that has been built within twenty centuries past."

One night later that week we go out to a few Hamra bars with my cousin Shireen and some of her friends. Richard instantly gets along with the whole crew, but when he starts getting sullen later in the night—the music at the last bar we hit is too cheesy, he whispers to me, a sort of Euro club mix, and the beer he ordered is flat—we leave. I'm annoyed at the negativity and start to panic that things are taking a bad turn and he's already sick of Beirut; then I remember, we've had moments like this in New York. Cheesy club music makes me cringe but doesn't make me want to bolt out the door as quickly as it always does him. Plus, I decide to give him the ever-useful jet lag exemption.

On Richard's birthday, we're invited to dinner at Karim and Hala's. My cousin and his wife don't know it's his birthday, of course, but we decide to accept the invitation. I want Richard to get to know more of my cousins, since I consider them among my closest friends in Beirut and since it's less pressure, for now, than meeting a throng of older relatives. Besides Shireen, so far he's also met Josette, when she joined us for coffee one afternoon, and also my cousin Kamal and his wife, Nour, when they had us over for dinner earlier in the week. Those rendezvous all went beautifully, Richard appreciating everyone's fluent English and cracking jokes, lightening the mood—his specialty.

We walk into Karim and Hala's living room, and they greet us, Hala chic as always in slim beige pants and a cowl neck and stylishly cropped dark hair, and Karim the young professor in jeans and a sport jacket. Nearly every inch of their walls is hung with art and lined with bookshelves. We meet the small group of guests, most of them Middle East–focused academics like my cousin. The predinner conversation in the living room ranges from the latest news about the various Arab revolutions to some disastrous recent decisions by Israeli president Netanyahu, whom I know Richard can't stand either. But he decides, perhaps wisely for now, not to chime in.

At the dinner table, Shafiq, the guy sitting across from Richard, steers the conversation to whether the new Lebanese prime minister, Miqati, will ever be able to bring Hezbollah and the opposing March 14 Party together to form a cabinet. I can tell Richard is already annoyed with Shafiq: a thirty-something academic play-acting the wise old intellectual as he sighs and rolls his fingers around a string of worry beads. On top of that, Shafiq keeps diverting the conversation at the table into Arabic, when at least three people, the spouses of Karim and Hala's AUB friends, don't speak Arabic. I do get irritated when Lebanese insist on carrying on in French or English when everyone in the room speaks Arabic, but in mixed groups like this, with non-Arabic speakers, why not speak a language we all understand? Everyone is speaking English tonight except Worry-Bead Guy.

But Richard is less focused on the subtle linguistic swordplay than he is on the food. When we accepted the dinner invitation, I'd mentioned to Hala that he doesn't eat meat—but I'd also told her to please not do anything special. Richard can easily make a meal out of salad and bread and often likes to. Still, she'd gone out of her way, Lebanese-style, and put a lovely plate of roasted vegetables on the table alongside the roast beef, and served a sweet and spicy pumpkin soup, and several salads including a striking one made with red and yellow beets and goat cheese. Richard is clearly touched by the vegetarian-friendly feast and leans over to thank Hala as she sets out a dessert platter of *atayef*, small, blini-like pancakes I love filled with sugared walnuts. The chitchat around the table is animated, guests chiming in with witticisms about the eternal horror show of Middle East politics, in Lebanon and beyond. Eventually Shafiq decides to strike up a conversation with Richard, since they're sitting directly across from each other but haven't exchanged a word yet.

"Where are you visiting from?"

"New York."

"Do you have a connection to the Middle East?"

Hmm, I wonder, as I overhear them talk. *What does this*

question mean? Richard could easily pass for Jewish or Arab or lots of other ethnicities. Is Shafiq's question innocent, or is it a veiled interrogation?

"I went to Egypt once, about ten years ago," Richard answers, keeping things simple.

Pause.

"Also Israel."

Silence now between them. Neither Richard nor Shafiq hits that tennis ball again. Worry-Bead Guy pours himself another glass of wine and turns to the woman on his left to start up a new conversation. Richard looks at me, wondering if he played this right. I telegraph *yes* with my eyes. I mean, it's the truth after all. It could have sparked an interesting conversation, one that could've been conducted on mutually friendly and curious terms. But Shafiq didn't bite. Still, the dinner was fun and went smoothly all in all: no tussle at the table between the two of them, and no awkwardness that couldn't be drowned out with a few extra swigs of wine.

We decide that weekend to take an overnight trip out of the city and spend some time exploring a place neither of us knows. Reading up on local history, stumbling into intriguing sites, hidden side streets, strange bars, doing whatever comes up. We're good at this in New York. Let's do it in Lebanon. I ask around about cheap charming hotels outside the city, and based on an enthusiastic tip from Diana, we decide to go to Tyre and stay at a little inn called Al-Fanar. The inn is in Hayy al Masihiyye, the old Christian quarter, near the ancient port and the old souk. Tyre also has some of Lebanon's most famous ruins, and I haven't been here since I was a child.

We spend our first day walking around the old souk, eating

fresh fish on the harbor, where fishermen have slung their lines since the eighth century B.C. We drink frosty Almaza beers at a deserted but appealing little bar with ancient-looking arched stone ceilings. Our room at the inn, in a yellow two-story house, is perched right on the sea near the lighthouse and seems to jut directly over the water. As we crawl into bed that night, we look out the window. It's like we're actually in the middle of the Mediterranean. We sleep for ten hours straight.

We try to follow a map the next morning to the ancient Roman Hippodrome, one of the biggest chariot-racetrack remains in the world, but the rudimentary map we're holding leaves all the side streets out, and we get lost on the way. Two teenage boys, walking home from their college campus nearby, see us fumbling through the map, and one of them asks in Arabic if we need help. They end up walking with us for half an hour, to the perimeter of the Hippodrome, which turns out to be sealed off by a locked gate. All four of us start circling the huge area together, trying to find the entrance. I tell the two guys that we'll be fine, thanks so much for the directions. But they stay with us until one of them eventually spots an entrance, and they walk us over to it, then wave good-bye and dash off. Ah, the Lebanese. Rising to the occasion like champions, and going well beyond. So friendly and hospitable and helpful to strangers, more than I've seen anywhere else. Incredible that this same country specializes in bloodbaths, too.

The Hippodrome is deserted. We spot only an elderly man—must be a Greek Orthodox priest, with his long black robe, full graying beard, and huge silver cross on a chain—walking with a hunched-over old woman. In the distance we spot a young couple holding hands, teenagers probably looking for a place to make out. We nod hello at the woman guarding the front entrance, and she waves us in.

Inside the gate is an astounding sight: a huge oval-shaped lawn, where chariots raced in the days of the Roman Empire, is surrounded by a few stone bleachers, half-crumbled but still in decent shape considering they date back to between A.D. 200 and 600. A few meters away is the Necropolis, a burial site with marble and stone sarcophagi from the Roman and Byzantine eras. We walk through the enormous grassy field, then climb up to the top of a bleacher and zone out in the sun, looking out across the Hippodrome and the Necropolis, toward the edge of the city in the distance.

Later that day in the newer, more commercial part of town, we pass a few dozen store windows decorated with neon-pink stuffed teddy bears. Valentine's Day is in a couple of days. The Lebanese, at least the shop owners and restaurateurs, heartily embrace this holiday, and if Valentine's is not quite as inescapable here as in the States, the pink neon is still out in full force in Lebanon.

No idea what we're going to do for Valentine's Day—we haven't discussed it yet. For our second and last night in Tyre, we crawl into our bed in the middle of the sea and giggle like schoolkids at how unbelievable it is that we're here together, in ancient Tyre, a city that Alexander the Great tried to conquer more than two thousand years ago.

We're back in Beirut on February 11, the day Mubarak finally gives up in Egypt. Now the Shiites of Bahrain, who make up a majority of the country's population but have no representation in the dictatorial Sunni regime, are agitating for a revolution and getting brutally beaten and shot at. As with most Middle East news, it's rare when something good happens—say, Mubarak is gone! *Akhiran!* Finally!—without something nasty following on its heels: in this case, the violent suppression of the protesters in Bahrain, the Persian Gulf island nation off the coast of Saudi Arabia.

Meanwhile in Lebanon, there hasn't been much progress in forming a cabinet, but the political scene still feels relatively calm and uneventful now in mid-February. Still, Richard and I decide to lie low for at least the first half of the day on Valentine's Day, the Hariri assassination anniversary. I've heard rumors that protests might break out to commemorate his death and rail against the current government stalemate.

"Stay home. Don't go anywhere," Josette tells me on the phone.

"We won't. I promise."

In Lebanon, sometimes it's easier to just tell your anxious family what they want to hear. Then you just go about your business.

The protests, as it turns out, are a no-show, but a few high-profile parliament members from the March 14 Party announce they're going to give commemorative speeches that night. We concoct a last-minute Valentine's plan: after sleeping in late, we take a stroll from Hamra down to the Corniche, then over to Achrafieh, to wander around the winding streets and browse through bookstores, record shops, and whatever else we find. For dinner we go to Abdel Wahab, the restaurant where I'd taken the editor and TV writer from the States back in October, and I order a few of my favorite meatless dishes for us: eggplant fatteh, the sautéed dandelion greens called hindbeh, fattoush salad, and eggs fried in olive oil and sprinkled with sumac, a breakfast dish usually, but I love it at night, too. The food is mostly excellent, but the service tonight is a disaster, the waiters disorganized and apparently zonked out from the Valentine's rush.

But one waiter unwittingly earns his tip: he tries to speak Arabic to Richard, thinking him a local. In fact, a bunch of people around Beirut have attempted that, too, from the man who runs the grocery shop on the ground floor of my building, to Ali the concierge. Even in New York, no one can ever guess Richard's ethnicity: Indian, Iranian, Arab, Jewish, Native American, Spanish, Greek, Italian? He's heard it all.

I can tell he's flattered to be addressed in Arabic here, even if I haven't been particularly diligent in my attempts to teach him a few phrases so he can reply. I ask him over dinner if being mistaken for a local puts him at ease.

"It does actually," he says, as we spoon the eggplant fatteh onto our plates. "But everyone has been really friendly so far. I haven't sensed any anti-Semitism here. A big anti-Israel vibe, yes, but I get it. If I were Lebanese or Palestinian, I'd hate Israel, too. It's true, though, what they say about Lebanese hospitality, seriously."

After dinner we go see *The Fighter,* subtitled in French and Arabic. The crowd in the theater is rowdy, but tonight, amazingly, no one talks over the actors' voices or answers a cell phone during the movie, as often happens here. In fact, all the action-cheering noise from the audience makes the movie even more fun, as if we're watching it in a live theater. All through the balls-out brutal Hollywood boxing extravaganza, Richard pokes me with his elbow, smiles, grabs my hand. We survived Valentine's Day, our way: a deeply un-Valentine's movie, and a hearty, if spastic, last-minute dinner of some meatless greatest hits.

Before Richard got here, I'd been wondering if I'd be able to feed him well in Lebanon if we skipped the meat. Yes, Lebanon's cuisine is famously loaded with vegetables and legumes and many ways of getting your protein deliciously and without meat. It's tougher, in my mind, if you don't eat seafood either, but thankfully Richard loves fish. For lunch on his birthday, I'd taken him to Feluka, a restaurant on the Corniche with a sunny terrace overlooking the sea, and we'd ordered a platter of Sultan Ibrahim, a local fish similar to rouget. Deep fried and sprinkled with sea salt and lemon, it's hot, crispy, and tangy, especially fantastic with cold beer. That day Richard had declared Sultan Ibrahim his new favorite fish. One night at the apartment, I'd also taught him how to make *mujaddara*, a comfort food classic of lentils, rice, and fried onions. We'd boiled lentils, fried thinly sliced onions in a pan, and stirred them in with uncooked rice, seasoning the mix with cumin, allspice, salt, and pepper and simmering until the rice was cooked through. The mujaddara was a homerun, too.

"Let's make this in New York next time you visit," Richard had said as we ate the dish with warmed-up pita bread.

"I'll smuggle in some lentils from Beirut just for fun, although we'll find the same ones in Brooklyn, too."

On his second-to-last day, we head to the city of Byblos. It's gray and drizzling in the morning, but the sun is blazing by the time we arrive in the port town, forty-five minutes from Beirut. Richard is drawn to ancient crumbling ports, I'm finding, and happily this country comes through. No question, we specialize in ruins here in Lebanon—but many of them date back thousands of years. Byblos is considered one of the world's oldest continuously inhabited cities, spanning more than seven thousand years, and the remains here are from ancient Rome up through the Crusader era and beyond. The Lebanese call the city Jbeil, after its biblical name Gebal. It's like a theme park of ruins, a panorama of remains from Roman and Crusader stone castles and amphitheaters and

tombs, all perched steps away from the Mediterranean and excavated starting only in the early 1920s. In the distance, the Beirut
skyline wraps around the bay.

The waves are crashing hard here on the Byblos coast this
afternoon, and the sun is now shining fierce and strong. I imagine
a ship landing here in 3000 B.C., in the time of the Egyptian pharaohs, who would send boats to Byblos to collect timber from Lebanon's cedar trees for use in building their tombs. On my Egypt
trip in January, I'd seen an almost perfectly preserved ship in a
small museum near the Giza pyramids; the vessel was built around
2500 B.C., presumably to be buried with the afterlife treasures of
the pharaoh Cheops, and was made mostly with cedarwood from
Lebanon.

"Let's see if we can find Sultan Ibrahim again for lunch," Richard says after we walk through the Crusader castle and out into a
sunlit patch of grass overlooking the sea.

We do find it, at Bab el Mina, a restaurant on the harbor. Cold
bottles of beer, fresh seafood, the ancient port, the blue sea, and
both of us here on a gorgeous afternoon. Bliss.

On Richard's last morning, I take him to meet my great-aunt
Nida, who I adore for her wit and her stories, which I've dropped
by to listen to on a number of afternoons over tea. She's also the
one who'd said to my mom months ago, "Damn those men."

I'm nervous that she'll ask us if we're engaged. I give Richard
a heads-up.

"Don't worry. Let's go have tea with her. I like meeting your
family."

Nida greets us warmly, insists we eat the man'ouches she's set
out for us, and launches straight into one of her stories. She's the
best storyteller I've ever met and has a razor-sharp memory. She

speaks both Arabic and English in the same eloquent, punctuated tones, her hands growing animated, her eyes lighting up behind her glasses, her sharply elegant features forming into a smile or a generous laugh.

As we sip our tea, she tells us how she met her late husband, Freddie, in the 1940s. He was a friend of her brother's and was visiting Beirut from Cairo, where he had just started his career. He came by her family's house in Beirut to say hello and sat down for coffee with her and her parents and siblings. By the time he returned by ship to Cairo a week later, the two had already fallen in love. They started writing letters every day, and he told her he'd be back for her the next summer. Then one excruciatingly long year later, he wrote her at the beginning of summer to tell her that for work reasons, he wouldn't be able to come to Beirut that year. She was devastated, furious, and stopped replying to his letters. Then one day weeks later, she decided to write an angry response—the 1940s version of "Have a nice life"—but her mother intercepted the letter and edited it. "If God wills us to meet again, we will," her mom added at the end.

The following year, two summers after they first met, Freddie came back for Nida. She was icy to him the day he showed up at her family's doorstep, but he stayed for coffee with them, and slowly she started warming to him again, realizing her feelings for him hadn't died, and here he'd come all this way to see her. He proposed that summer, and they stayed married and in love until he passed away last September.

This is one of the best love stories I've ever heard. I wonder, though, how the story would have played out in the age of cell phones, texting, and instant messaging, when there are so many ways to communicate what's on your mind right this second—with no filter, no delay, and potentially disastrous consequences.

After their long-distance stint, Freddie and Nida lived in Cairo for a while but ended up moving back to Lebanon. Both had roots and family here, so the decision about where to make their home, if not a no-brainer, wasn't too tangled. In my case, it may not be so easy. Beirut was already starting to feel more like home to me before Richard arrived, and having him here for two weeks made it feel even cozier. My anxieties about his visit mostly vaporized as the days went by, and it felt easy and natural having him around.

As we kissed goodbye in front of the taxi that took him to the airport on his last day here, a voice in my head was saying, *Move here!*

But I didn't say it out loud. Another voice, much like Nida's mother's, took over, and I said something a little less hasty: "Safe travels!"

MARCH

It's coming up on spring this month and my birthday—and maybe even the birth of a new Middle East. It remains to be seen whether this season will bring changes beyond Egypt and Tunisia and overturn more regimes known, over the past century, mainly for cruelty and repression instead of for their ancient heritage or their artistic and intellectual contributions to civilization. But since Mubarak finally fell in mid-February, and before him Ben-Ali in Tunisia, the revolutionary wave has picked up momentum in nearly every country in the Arab world.

One afternoon in March, a few weeks after Mubarak's fall, I sit in at a talk at AUB by Rashid Khalidi, a historian and professor of modern Arab studies at Columbia

University. He's in town this week from New York to speak about the Arab revolutions—what everyone is calling the Arab Spring, even though it's still technically winter—and I'm curious to get some perspective about what's going on around the region from Khalidi, a Palestinian American and something of a celebrity academic both in the States and here.

What's different about these uprisings, Khalidi tells the crowd gathered in the university auditorium, is that for the first time in history, Arab populations are rising up not against a colonial occupation—which they've repeatedly done in the past—but against their own internal regimes, which have failed to deliver any kind of stability or economic growth or, perhaps most important of all, dignity.

Khalidi gets some cheers when he tells the packed room that for the first time in recent history, and maybe ever, Arabs are looking pretty good in the international media: "The way these revolutions are changing the American public image of the Arab world is astounding. It's a good thing, for the first time, to be an Arab in the United States."

Although he's a rousing speaker, he strikes some sober notes in his talk. He cautions against overoptimism, since it's not yet clear what will come next, if and when the other corrupt Arab regimes fall, and how the realities of postrevolutionary Egypt and Tunisia will play out.

And what about Lebanon? Khalidi doesn't say much. Even though the political stalemate here continues, nothing else is really happening at the moment. There's no dictatorship to overthrow; it's just the usual seesaw of inertia and instability. But the irony that Lebanon is now the quietest country in the Middle East escapes no one. How'd that happen?!

It's a relief that at the moment we're not on the verge, at least not the razor's-edge verge, of another civil war. Meanwhile, despite how inspiring it's been to watch the revolutions around the region, things are getting even more horrendous for the protesters in some countries, particularly in Libya, Bahrain, Yemen, and now Syria—each of the regimes crushing protests ever more violently and ruthlessly.

But the ground in the Arab world is indeed shifting in a way it never has before. Of all the years to move back to the Middle East, I've lucked into this one, if *luck* is the right word. Even if I've never been one of those journalists who run to a war scene for the adrenaline high—I'm more likely to just run—living in the Arab world as the entire region goes through dramatic changes is an undeniable rush.

During his talk, Khalidi quotes Wordsworth: "Bliss it was in that dawn to be alive, but to be young was very heaven." An optimistic flourish for these heady, dangerous times.

No one knows yet if a new Arab world really is about to spring to life. But something else, also miraculous, will be born this month: my brother Samir's first baby. She's actually due on my birthday, in late March, and with luck I'll be meeting her as a newborn when I visit Samir and his wife, Laila, in California in early April. Our parents are, needless to say, excited that one of their kids is finally procreating.

Before I head to the States to meet my niece, I have to write an essay about my Beirut experience for *ForbesLife* magazine and host my friend Claire from New York. She's been one of my best friends ever since we worked together at *The Village Voice* in the late 1990s, and she'll be here staying with me for a week and a half this month. Claire has been going through a breakup over the past few weeks, as well as apartment-moving hassles in New York, and she's eager for some Mediterranean-style eating, drinking, hanging out, and forgetting. She's a magazine journalist, too, writing mostly about art and pop culture, and hopes to find some inspiration during her visit. I'm hoping this trip will come through for her on all counts.

I've planned a full week of adventures for us, and I've also set aside a couple of days when Claire can be off to explore on her own while I work on my *ForbesLife* assignment. I'm looking forward to writing this piece, the first substantial article I've been assigned on Lebanon—and incredibly, it's neither about Beirut's wild nightlife nor about the catastrophic political scene, but just a meditation on what my life here is like now.

I've been excited to see Claire and get lots of catch-up time with her, but I've also been wondering if there's still any lingering tension between us from an argument we had when I was in New York around Christmas. It was nothing major—just confusion around a dinner plan we'd made for one of the handful of nights I was in town. We'd both been looking forward to spending time together but were crazed with tight schedules that week, and we'd ended up feeling rushed during our dinner. Hurt feelings and miscommunication ignited into a little fight, although we'd resolved it that night. But this will be the first time I'm seeing her since then.

My relationships with friends have been on my mind more than usual in these months in Beirut. As I've been cultivating some promising new friendships here and rekindling old ones, I've also been missing everyone I'm close to back in the States. But I've been noticing that with Lebanese friends, not just ones I've known since childhood but also people I've met more recently, I tend to have an easier time feeling confident and more like myself right away. My insecurities about seeming approachable, being trusted and valued, don't seem to kick in as powerfully here, and my fears of rejection somehow aren't as persistent or pronounced.

This can't have anything to do with the Lebanese being more easygoing or down-to-earth as a rule. There can be lots of artifice in social interactions in Lebanon, more so in some circles than others. Some friends of mine in Beirut complain about being fed up with superficial, status-obsessed Lebanese types, a common breed here. Years ago the wife of one of my cousins tried moving back to Lebanon from the States, before they got married, but didn't last long. She quickly got tired of the phoniness that's rampant in certain Beirut social scenes, and in the art world where she was working. Eventually, after they met and got married, they moved back here, and she gradually found ways to cope with the one-upmanship and snobbery when it came her way.

I think I've been lucky in the people I've met so far. Those whom I can't relate to I manage to weed out instantly. But between my new and old friends here, and my cousins, too, I feel surrounded by a wonderful bunch of unpretentious, creative, fun-to-be-around types—who remind me of my friends in New York—and oddly enough, I've felt comfortable and accepted right off the bat. No need to break each other in too much, no need to overcome my insecurities and look for reassurance in quite the same way as I've often needed to in the States. It occurs to me that the friends I've been clicking with here are versions of myself, pieces of who I might have been had my family never left Beirut. Spending time with them is, in a way, like reassembling a jigsaw puzzle, its pieces scattered everywhere—but, as I'm discovering, not scattered so far away.

Claire arrives in Beirut on a gorgeous, sunlit Saturday afternoon in early March. It feels like the first real day of spring, even though spring hasn't officially started according to the calendar. I walk down to the Corniche in the late morning and sit on a bench there for a while, staring out at the sea, at the snowy mountaintops in the distance, at fishermen and scattered groups of sunbathers in swimsuits on the seaweedy rocks below the Corniche, and at cyclists on the sidewalk. It's still ski season in the nearby mountain resort of Faraya and farther up in the Cedars, but down here along the Corniche, some brave Beirutis are already swimming. I guess it's true that in Lebanon you can ski in the morning and swim in the afternoon—one of the tourism ministry's favorite PR slogans and a longtime cliché in Lebanon. I'd always thought that claim was total BS, but on an early spring day like today, it appears to be no lie.

Claire buzzes up to my apartment at four o'clock in the afternoon, when I'm back home tidying up. She insisted on taking a cab by herself from the airport to my apartment, to get a better handle on the city; I've had that same urge in foreign cities. Because it's nearly impossible to give directions to visitors without resorting to famous landmarks (there are very few street name signs in Beirut), I told her to instruct the cab to go to the Mayflower, a boxy white-brick hotel near my apartment that became famous for housing the international press during the civil war, and the occasional celebrity writer like Graham Greene. It's not a particularly fancy hotel, but any taxi driver would know it, and from there it's a short walk to my place.

I run downstairs to meet her, and there she is in my lobby, smiling, her beautiful face and big hazel eyes lit up, curly light-brown hair catching the sunlight, not looking for a second like she just got through twenty hours in transit. Seeing her here brings me a jolt of comfort, as if my two cities, two worlds, two lives are coming together—sort of like they did when Richard was visiting, but in a more casual, matter-of-fact way this time, almost as if I've just run into her on the street, in Hamra by chance, instead of on Spring Street or Third Avenue in Manhattan.

She laughs as she tells me about the cabbie who ripped her off. There's an instantly relaxed vibe between us. I'm relieved that she seems glad to be here, and I sense her excitement for the trip. We put her stuff down in the apartment, she freshens up, then we head out for a sunset walk along the Corniche, the early-evening city lights along the boulevard's half-moon curve reflecting on the darkening blue-green sea. From the waterfront, we loop back up through the low Ras Beirut hills and into the Hamra area, and stop for drinks and a bite at a café-bar hangout near my apartment called DePrague. As we start in on a round of drinks and sink into a purple sofa in the dim, low-ceilinged room, it feels like we could be meeting up in the East Village or Brooklyn on any spring night this past decade, or back in the late 1990s when we were first becoming friends.

We can't stop talking, catching up on all the details we didn't get a chance to go into over e-mail or on the phone in these past weeks. We order some toasted halloum sandwiches because suddenly we're starving. The icy beers and crunchy baguettes slathered with the melted salty-white cheese are tasting good, and sitting with Claire feels soothing for me tonight, as it hopefully does for her. We linger for a while, then call it an early night after her long trip.

I take her for a walk around Ras Beirut the next day, after we take our time making coffee and eating labneh sandwiches, sprinkled with zaatar and olive oil, out on my balcony. Heading downhill from my neighborhood toward the waterfront, we walk past the abandoned Holiday Inn, a twenty-six-story modernist tower built in the 1970s; right around the hotel's grand opening, the war broke out. The hotel ended up getting used instead as a base for various militias, and all of its floors were bombed out or repurposed as platforms for shelling enemy militias and keeping a watch on goings-on for miles around. The building is now a hollow shell but still standing, a shattered, bullet-ridden museum piece of the war. Claire pulls out her camera to take a picture of the hotel, which has probably been photographed by every visitor to Beirut ever since the war. Immediately two cops materialize from behind the front gate and speak to us in English.

"What are you doing?"

"Oh, I'm sorry. I just took a picture. Is that okay?"

"No. I need to see your photos."

The policemen grab her camera and look through her pictures. They must have looked through every single one, including shots of her with friends in Brooklyn taken weeks ago, and of her cat Oliver. Finally they decide we're okay. Claire is panicked. I'm startled, too—I'd never expected to be stopped for doing something just about everyone who has walked past the Holiday Inn has done, many times. Then I realize the officers are probably just bored, flirting with us, nothing better to do on this sleepy Sunday afternoon.

A little later, as we reach downtown, Claire tries to shoot the view from near the Grand Serail, the parliament building, from a spot that turns out to be too close to one of ex–prime minister Hariri's mansions for the security guards' taste. We're stopped again. Same routine. Two guards emerge from a doorway and ask to see her camera. Again, they look through all the photos. Oliver the cat is becoming an international star. I've only been stopped once before, on a summer visit one year while trying to take a picture of my mother's Ahliah school nearby, also apparently too close to the ex–prime minister's house. But today armed guards seem to be coming at us from all directions—a big help in my efforts to make my friend feel welcome here.

Other than that, walking around the city with Claire feels mellow and pleasant. We talk sometimes, stay comfortably quiet other times. We stop in at the Virgin shop downtown to look for Arabic music; surprisingly for an international chain store, it has an extensive selection of obscure local bands and musicians. Funny, too, that all the Virgins in the United States have closed, but the Beirut branch lives on. Claire looks through some Fairuz disks, and we ask one of the guys who work there if there are any great new albums from Lebanese or Palestinian bands. At the bar the other night, we'd heard one we liked, and we asked the bartender about it and learned it's the Palestinian hip-hop band Dam. They don't have it at Virgin, but she ends up buying a few disks the guy at the store recommends, one by the local group Fareeq al-Atrash (their name a play on a famous singer from the 1930s, Farid al-Atrash), and another by Rayess Bek, a Lebanese rapper.

As we walk out of the store, cross Martyrs' Square, and keep strolling eastward, to the winding, tree-lined streets of Achrafieh, Claire asks me what's happening on the Lebanese political scene these days.

"Oof, you really want to know?"

"I've been trying to read up, but it gets confusing. Things

sound a little dicey again lately. Could there be another war soon?"

"There could, though probably not right away—the government is stalemated at the moment. But you never know here. Tensions have been brewing off and on. If war eventually breaks out, it would be along different lines than the civil war was: it would likely be more of a Sunni-Shiite divide this time than a Christian-Muslim divide."

We stop at a bakery to pick up man'ouches, and because Claire wants to know more, especially since the revolts elsewhere in the Arab world have been in the news daily, I give her my two-bit summary as we stroll along. I explain that mass popular revolts are unlikely to happen in Lebanon at this point since we do have elections and a quasi-democracy, and most groups do have some kind of voice in government—even though the system is a mess.

From the quiet Achrafieh side street where we're wandering around, headed nowhere in particular, we can see the downtown mosques and some nearby church spires. I explain that of Lebanon's two main political groups right now, the March 14 Party is mostly identified with the Sunni sect and the rival March 8 Party with the Shiite community and Hezbollah, although both parties have some members of other sects, including Christians, mixed in. I mention that the president still always has to be a Christian, and that there hasn't been a census taken in Lebanon since 1932—the Christians have been blocking one—but it's clear they're no longer the majority. She's curious about the population breakdown, and I say that based on some rough estimates I've seen, Shiites are now around a third, Sunnis a quarter, Christians somewhere in between those two fractions, and the remaining numbers divided among minorities like the Druze.

"It's unbelievable that the president still always has to be a Christian," I say as we round a corner and start walking along a downhill street. "But most of the real power now is actually with the prime minister, who is always Sunni. The entire system is ridiculous, and personally I'd just love to be able to elect whoever is going to fix up this place—at least fix the electricity and water and roads, and speed up the Internet so it's not running like in a fourth-world backwater."

"Last night I tried sending an e-mail, and it took half an hour to send."

"Just wait till the power goes out while we're in an elevator," I warn her. "People visiting Lebanon usually freak out the first time that happens to them. Then you just get used to it—you count to a hundred and it comes back."

During Claire's visit, we don't spend every single day together, and luckily for her, I don't subject her to my political soapbox on a daily basis. On some days I suggest a few plans she can do solo, my way of giving her space and letting her explore on her own, especially so she can take her time at art galleries she might want to write about. I could also use a little more time to work on the Beirut essay that's due the day after she leaves.

One afternoon when Claire goes to see Baalbek, I spend the day working on my article at T-Marbouta, the activist-hangout coffee shop. I can pass hours there at my laptop, drinking strong coffee, snacking on the café's surprisingly good fattoush salad, and enjoying the laid-back but scholarly vibe. At a nearby table, I overhear a group of guys organizing a meeting of a political activist committee to discuss how they might help the protesters in Bahrain, who are still being violently attacked by the country's regime and military. One guy says to his friends, in Arabic: "It's going to be impossible now to stop this wave in the region. Every regime that tries to stop it is going to fail eventually, like Mubarak, even if it takes way too long for it to fail."

Then the group starts talking about a conference at AUB this week that's trying to draw attention to the parallels between the political situation in Israel—where Arabs don't have the same voting or citizenship rights as the Jewish population—and South African–style apartheid. Part of the aim is to support the Boycott, Divestment, Sanctions (BDS) movement, modeled after the divestment efforts that helped bring down the apartheid system in South Africa. I overhear one of the guys mention that this same week in March, ninety-five cities around the world are hosting events to call attention to BDS as a form of nonviolent protest of the inequalities and the ever-expanding settlements. I read later that the list of musicians who have supported BDS and canceled performances in Israel over the past few years has been growing and includes Elvis Costello, Carlos Santana, the Pixies, and Gorillaz. (But a few months later, in July 2011, the Netanyahu administration would outlaw all cultural and economic boycotts in Israel.)

I don't end up making it to the AUB conference, but the conversation I listen in on as I'm writing my article at the café makes me wonder whether an event like this—which seems a way to bring attention to historical patterns, open a dialogue, and advocate for change through nonviolent means—would get any traction in the United States, where criticism of Israel is more muted. I haven't been politically active for most of my life, but living in an environment where certain grim realities are inescapable— tensions and miseries around the Middle East have a way of spilling across borders—is making me feel engaged in new ways. I start wondering how I can be more involved in calls to reform Lebanese politics, for starters, instead of just complaining about the situation. I decide to keep a lookout for activist events or rallies happening around Beirut, in case the Arab Spring inspires any kind of movement here in Lebanon.

Just as in New York, or in any city or country that's famous for certain tourist attractions, locals often don't visit the sites until they have guests to show around. Incredibly, I've never been to see the legendary Cedars of Lebanon, which are mentioned again and again in the Bible. I decide to use Claire's visit as an excuse to finally go to the north and see them. This is my first March in Lebanon since I was nine, and I hear the trees up in the mountains are still snowcapped—supposedly the best way to see them. So I figure *yalla*, let's go.

We take a bus up the northern coastal highway, veering into the mountains and winding up the twisting roads toward the Cedars, about two hours from Beirut. On our way there, the driver monologues to himself in Arabic about the lame driving skills of everyone around him, alternately making cracks about the too-slow or too-swervy cars on the road, and getting riled up and impatient. The trip is harrowing—he plays chicken with every oncoming car on the narrow mountain roads, to see who gets to stay in their own lane and who has to duck out of the way, and he seems to just barely dodge every vehicle that comes along. He manages to pull this all off with confidence and shocking skill, but my heart is thumping through my sweater. We arrive, finally, to find the Cedars all covered in snow, just like in the tourism posters. The red-roofed houses in the nearby village of Bsharri are capped in white, the rocky cliffsides plunging down into the forested Kadisha valley.

We get out of the car to walk around the forest, our boots and jeans quickly sinking into the knee-high snow. It's dead quiet up here. The ski season is winding down, and some resorts are starting to close for the spring and summer. I realize I love off-season tourism in Lebanon: an empty Baalbek with Richard in February, a serene Cedars forest with Claire in mid-March.

The snow-covered Cedars look so much more majestic in real life than in the pictures, their thick trunks rooted firmly into the hillside, their Christmas tree branches feathering out to the horizon, the needle-shaped green leaves covered in frosty white. After we each walk off on our own to stare out at the forest, then come back to take pictures of each other and smile silently at the magic of being here, we finally get our fill of the trees. We head over to see some monasteries in the nearby Kadisha valley, which housed Maronite Christian patriarchs in the Middle Ages. In the fourteenth century, during the Mamluk era, named for the Muslim empire that was based in Egypt and annexed parts of Lebanon, the Maronites and the Muslim rulers at one point had a friendly alliance in the Kadisha valley, as Christians and Muslims also did in other areas in Lebanon at various periods.

After walking through the cold, tunneled corridor of one of the monasteries, stopping to peer at an early printing press used here centuries ago, we walk onto the terrace and look out at the towering mountains and at the remains of a tiny hermitage built into the rocks above, where monks would hide out for months or years at a time.

One other thing I've been curious to see up here is the region's enormous, tennis-ball-size version of the kibbeh meatball, made mainly in the town of Ehden. Before we take a bus back to Beirut, we stop to try some at a small family-run restaurant. It's my first time eating the legendary Ehden kibbeh balls, and I immediately fall for them. The huge spheres are made of a mixture of lamb and bulgur, grilled to a crisp, and stuffed with a filling of toasted buttery pine nuts, bits of juicy ground lamb, and fried onions. The giant size makes perfect sense to me—more to love. Even without the Cedars, I would have been happy to take a trip north just to dive into a plate of Ehden kibbehs, topped with generous ladles of fresh, snowy yogurt.

I'd been toying with the idea of throwing a cocktail party while Claire is here, to introduce her to a bunch of my Beirut friends at once and also to return some invitations. But I have another motive, too. Sana, a daughter of old family friends who lives in Dubai, is in Beirut this week—she'd e-mailed a few weeks ago to ask for help brainstorming names for a new store she's adding to her jewelry business. We don't get to see each other much but have kept in touch over the years, and a while back she'd sent me a couple of pieces as gifts—a leather pearl-and-metal-studded bracelet that wraps around and around, and that I wear almost daily, and a striking dark gold ring with a stone the color of cocoa. Since she's in town on business and I'd love to see her, I decide to host a casual focus group for her in the form of a small party, inviting some friends and cousins over to hang out and try to help her come up with the perfect name.

Claire and I spend the day of the party running around my neighborhood to buy mini-man'ouches, fatayer, and bottles of wine. I mix a drink of sparkling water with basil, grapefruit juice, and honey, while Claire arranges the pastries on platters and sets out glassware. I program a playlist (Soap Kills, Coltrane, The Roots) and set out scratch paper and pens in the living room.

Sana arrives first, looking hip in her gamine-short hair and army-green pants, and after I introduce her to Claire, she tells us about her recent adventures poking around Europe and North Africa to find talented young jewelry designers. As we chat, and Claire and I double-check that the living room looks presentable, Sana shows us some pieces of jewelry she discovered—sparkly brooches that evoke the 1920s and 1940s, stackable cocktail rings with unusual stones, ropy leather bracelets, eye-catching stuff. Outside it's pouring buckets, and I'm guessing some people will flake out because of the weather, but within half an hour everyone is here, dripping wet but in high spirits.

I greet my cousin Shireen and my friends Mirna and Diana and show them to the drinks table. Also here tonight are Hala, and Zeina's friend Maria (Zeina couldn't make it today), a smart and warmly friendly Ph.D. student in history who splits her time between Massachusetts and Beirut. Another guest is a distant cousin named Sumaya, a sharp-witted editor and mother of two who moved back to Beirut from Bahrain recently.

Sana is soft-spoken and intellectual but has a smart business sense, too, and tonight she's prepared what she wants to say and how she'd like to introduce her new jewelry shop to the group. I help quiet everyone down so we can get started. She starts off by explaining that she's looking for a name that will sound edgy but approachable, and potentially unisex in case she introduces a men's line—a name that says the line is stylish but original, personal, and wearable. Also, the name needs to be short.

That's a lot of ideas to communicate in just a word or two, but judging from the enthusiasm in the room, the guests feel up to the challenge. There's a lull for a while, a lot of sipping of wine and munching of man'ouches and quiet jotting down of ideas on scratch paper. Five minutes later names are flying around the room: Take, Sweet, Yours, Daydream, Shuffle. Lots of one-word ideas, a jumble of verbs, nouns, adjectives, images.

Then someone calls out, "How about Loot?"

Sana pauses for a second.

"I like Loot. I really like that."

"Loot!" "Loot?" "Looooot!" Everyone is saying the name at the same time, rolling it around.

"Does everyone like Loot?"

"Yes!" shout seven people.

"But wait," a voice pipes up. "Doesn't *lootie* mean 'gay man' in Lebanon?"

In this still sadly homophobic culture, that brand name may not work so well after all. Two hours and dozens more ideas and joking-around breaks later, we have some strong contenders but haven't quite nailed the perfect name. Still, I'm feeling good about all this. I look around the room and think, *I'm lucky to know these women, to have them in my life.*

Most of us here tonight have at least two if not more national or ethnic identities. Some of us are at a major crossroads in a relationship or career or other significant life issue. But we're all trying to make a life that feels grounded and authentic, no matter where or how we're living. Being with these people, admiring their warmth and humor and strength, makes me realize once again that I wasn't completely crazy to return to Beirut. Without consciously knowing it, the chance to experience this exact feeling is a big part of what drew me back, that elusive sense of being so comfortably in my element, woven into the fabric of a group whose lives and personalities resonate so strongly with me.

Who knows where half of us will be next year? But this feels like home for me, right in this moment. Here in this room, none of us is 100 percent Lebanese, whatever that means, or 100 percent from any one place. We all have complicated lives and are trying to merge all the divergent strands. But here in this room, I'm feeling 100 percent normal. Okay, 87 percent—let's not push it. But wow, that's a strange new feeling.

On a Saturday night a couple of days before Claire flies back to New York, I take her to a show at the Music Hall downtown. On weekends the cabaret-style theater hosts an eclectic series of bands who each get fifteen minutes to play, and the shows tend to last late into the night. Reservations are a must, but I don't end up calling until the last minute, and it turns out there are no seats left in the theater—but one stool is still available in the bar area. The reservationist tells me we're welcome to reserve and share it. Sounds like a tight squeeze, but we book the one stool and arrive at ten thirty, just as the show is starting. A host shows us to the bar and points at two side-by-side stools, and Claire and I high-five each other that we've lucked into two whole seats instead of having to split one. We settle in and order drinks, and a hilariously terrible Pink Floyd cover band comes on for its short set, playing an overwrought version of "Comfortably Numb." Next up is an African American female singer impersonating Prince and doing a spitting-image version of "Kiss." Our tickets come with a half-dozen free drinks each, and we decide to take full advantage, especially since we're sitting right at the bar and don't have to wait for table service. We order another round.

A young Lebanese couple soon appears right in front of us, and the host apologizes and tells us they, too, had booked only one stool. It's time to give up one of our seats. Damn. But by that point, a classical Arabic band is on stage, and the crowd is up and dancing to old Lebanese songs everyone recognizes. Several more Arabic bands follow, playing their quarter-hour sets, and Claire and I are both dancing, drinks in hand. We donate our lone bar stool to the couple, too, so the poor chivalrous guy next to us can sit down and not have to keep leaning on his date's seat back all night. We end up staying until the show winds down around four, six drinks into the night, and as we walk out of the theater, we realize we're pretty drunk. We stop by an all-night café on Bliss Street to eat halloum sandwiches, and both wake up completely hungover around noon the next day.

We're not fit for any ambitious plans as we pound down cup after cup of coffee in the kitchen, and eat up all the bread and cheese in the fridge and the leftover pastries from the focus group party, in an attempt to recover from our Music Hall binge. But in the afternoon, we manage to venture out to visit my mom's cousin Afaf Zurayk. Since she's an artist who has worked in both Beirut and the States, and Claire had expressed an interest in chatting with her, I wanted to make sure the two of them could meet. Afaf's Hamra apartment is soaked in sunlight when we walk in. She makes us a pot of mint tea, and we all sit around for an hour, discussing the art scenes in Beirut, D.C., New York, and cities around the world; I mostly listen. Afaf has been working as an artist most of her life and has interesting comments about the evolution of art in the

Middle East, and the conversation seems to snap Claire instantly out of the stupor we both feel from last night. It's as if the two have known each other for months. I mostly content myself with gazing, bleary-eyed, at Afaf's hauntingly beautiful abstract paintings on the walls, and wishing Claire lived here, too.

Claire is eager to go to the northern city of Tripoli the next day, her last full day in Lebanon before she leaves on a late-night flight. She'd read about an unfinished pavilion there built by the famous Brazilian architect Oscar Niemeyer that had been abandoned in 1975 when the civil war broke out. She sometimes writes about architecture, and Niemeyer is one of her design icons, known for his fluid, often space-age-looking buildings, and also for having created Brasilia, the capital of Brazil.

The day we're planning to go also happens to be March 14, the anniversary of the Cedar Revolution in 2005 and the namesake of the March 14 political party. I'm wondering if mayhem might break out while we're in Tripoli. For one thing, it's where Lebanon's controversial new prime minister, Najib Miqati, comes from, and sometimes politicians' home bases ignite during tense times; for another thing, in the past few years Tripoli has had a number of shelling incidents. A great idea to go up there on the anniversary of the March 14 revolution? I'm not so sure.

I take a small poll. Umayma says, "Go. Tripoli is worth seeing, and it would be a good adventure to take Claire on while she's here. I seriously doubt there's anything to worry about tomorrow."

Minutes later Josette calls just to say hi, check in, see if I need anything; her twice-weekly call, so sweet and thoughtful, and so reassuring for her since, like much of our family including myself, she's a chronic worrier. I mention our Tripoli idea.

"No, absolutely not. Don't go. Not on March fourteenth. I don't think it's safe. Well, ask your dad anyway if you really want to go."

Well, I'm not twelve—and anyway Umayma said it's okay. So I figure: *Let's just go.*

Claire doesn't seem anxious at all, and I'd feel slightly ashamed chickening out, especially since I'm the supposedly jaded local in our twosome. Claire tells me I shouldn't feel I have to come along, if I need to get some work done or have any hesitation about the trip. I think of sending her off on her own, so she can have a solo adventure and so I can finish up my Beirut article. But the truth is I want to see Tripoli, too. Many Beirutis, especially Christians, tend to be snotty about Tripoli, considered a much more Arab, much more majority-Muslim city than Beirut. It's the second biggest city in Lebanon, but it's too far north for Beirut-centric locals who have no specific business or family up there. So far I've been guilty of that laziness, too. And I even have an ancestor from there, my paternal great-grandfather Jiryus, who lived in Tripoli until he moved to Beirut in 1905 to teach at AUB.

Also, if Claire goes to Tripoli and gets lost or doesn't make it back to Beirut before dark, I'm going to have to dash up there, worried sick, to find her. We're both adults and well traveled, but I'm the local. So I decide, *khalas,* that's it. We're both going.

We take a public bus the next morning from Charles Helou station in Achrafieh for the hour-and-a-half ride. It's a smooth, mostly scenic ride up along the coastal road, past Nahr al-Kalb, a river by the highway where successive conquerors of this land over the centuries have left commemorative plaques celebrating their invasions, from the Babylonian king Nebuchadnezzar to Ramses

II, the Roman emperor Caracalla, Napoleon III, and the French Mandate era's General Henri Gouraud. We pass by the sixteenth-century Mousayliha castle, on the side of the road, mostly in ruins but an attraction for tourists who drive by and get out of the car to climb it. When we arrive in Tripoli, the bus drops us off within walking distance of the old souk, but we quickly realize it's not obvious how to get to the souk from where we're standing. I ask for directions in Arabic, and Claire asks if we can stop somewhere and use the restroom first.

We walk into what looks like a spacious old café and turns out to be a roomful of men sitting at tables playing backgammon and smoking argilehs. Not a woman in sight. Every one of the men stops and stares at us as we walk in. The man behind the counter rushes up to ask us in Arabic what we're looking for, and I wonder for a second if I should say "Nothing!" so we can dash out immediately. But I tell him we're looking for a restroom, and he says, "Just a minute." He disappears behind a wall, then comes back to say, "You're welcome to use this one." Claire looks at me. I shrug. "Go in and see. I'll wait right here." Five seconds later she's back. She silently mouths "no," and we leave. Turns out there was just a urinal hole built into the floor, and it smelled vile. The guy working there had graciously offered it to us even though it's obviously meant for the male clientele, but maybe he should've just sent us on our way.

"What was that place?" Claire asks.

"Just one of the typical all-male hangouts of the Arab world. You don't find this kind of thing in Beirut anymore much, but it's still alive and well all over the region."

"I feel weird that we walked in on them like that."

"I'm glad we jolted them a little. I guess I should respect their privacy, but it's about time they got used to seeing a woman in the doorway."

On the way to the souk, we pass by a famous pastry shop called Abdel Rahman Hallab and stop in for Arabic coffee and some morning dessert: *osmalliyeh,* a tangle of vermicelli noodles fried until they're crunchy, and topped with a creamy, soft white cheese and a drizzle of the sugar syrup called ater.

We find a busy weekday hustle-bustle at the souk, when we arrive on foot a few minutes later. We wind through the mazelike alleyways, past vendors selling fresh fish splayed out on ice beds, butcher stands with whole sheep hanging from hooks, rotisseries with rows of roasting chickens, and women shopping for vegetables with their kids in tow, haggling over prices. In one corner of the souk is one of Tripoli's old *hammams,* public baths. We open the door to peek in the entrance, and a man dispensing towels up front asks in Arabic if we need help. I tell him we'd like to visit an old hammam. He says this one is for men only. "Is there one nearby for women?" I ask.

"No, but you're welcome to come in if you just want a tour. Hold on."

He disappears inside and comes back a few minutes later.

"Ok, it's ready. Come this way."

We follow him into the main hammam area, room after room of tiled baths and saunas. A few men wearing towels step out of the way and nod as we walk by. I guess he told them to cover up; there's company coming. We emerge into a salon area, a square-shaped room lined with rug-covered banquettes for lounging. He offers us tea. We politely decline, and I ask if I can buy a few bars of soap from the stacks on shelves against the wall. It turns out they aren't for sale, only for use in the baths. But he gives me a price if I want to buy some, fifty cents each, and I take two—at least some contribution, albeit a feeble one, for his time and hospitality.

One end of the souk leads through a series of twisting alleyways into the city's old soap factory, Khan el Saboun, now mostly a string of shops selling soap and surrounding a big tiled bath, which looks as if it hasn't been used in a century. We buy some soap made from olive oil and keep walking through the alleys and past more meat and fish and produce vendors. At a bakery on the edge of the souk, we pick up a snack of the sesame bread called *kaak* filled with melted Picon cheese—the blandly creamy processed cheese I grew up with and used to make fun of with my school friends. Somehow the cheese has also become a ubiquitous filling for kaak, but when served warm and slathered on the inside of the ring-shaped loaf, it becomes hypnotically good, its slight saltiness melding with the tastes of sesame and toasted bread.

It's nearing lunchtime, so we hop a service taxi to the port area to walk along the waterfront and make our way to a seafood spot. So far we've encountered only Arabic speakers in Tripoli.

"I know I said you didn't need to come if you didn't feel like it," Claire tells me in the cab, "but I don't think I could've ever found my way around if it was just me."

"You would've figured it out," I reply. "But it may have taken a few hours longer. I have the worst sense of direction, but at least I can help with the Arabic!"

I'm glad I decided to join Claire on this trip. I'm loving the adventure of exploring a new city and feeling like a tourist in my own country again. We stop for lunch at a restaurant I'd heard about called Silver Shore near the harbor—today it's filled with a business-lunch crowd of mostly men in suits—and we order a platter of fresh fried Sultan Ibrahim fish piled high. We voraciously attack the plate and smile at each other, happy and full.

A digestive walk along the waterfront after lunch, and a half hour sunning our faces on the rocks along the beach, and we're ready to investigate the Oscar Niemeyer pavilion, also known as the Tripoli International Fair. We take a service taxi there and arrive to find what looks like an enormous landscaped park surrounded by a gate. There's hardly anyone inside. Reminds me of the day Richard and I ambled around with those college kids looking for the Hippodrome in Tyre and found the area deserted.

The guard at the gate asks us where we're from—the compulsive Lebanese question—and I say, "Beirut and New York." He waves us in. Ahead are a half dozen futuristic-looking concrete structures of various shapes and sizes, seemingly abandoned and part rusted. There's a huge St. Louis–like arch, and a hollow dome, and two other structures that look like life-size spaceships. We climb up one of the concrete spaceships on a rickety rusted metal stairway and look down onto the city. Only a couple of other people are in the park today. We spot a skateboarder on one of the Niemeyer-built ramps—all the curvy surfaces in this park must be heaven for daredevil skaters—and a group of three blond tourist-looking types walking around. There's a woman in a tracksuit taking what appears to be a brisk cardio walk. Other than that, silence—just these wild, surreal-looking buildings.

We walk around, take pictures of each other, then venture into the dome and find an echo chamber inside, and a shallow pool of black-looking water surrounded by a small empty amphitheater. I'm having *Blair Witch Project* flashbacks. I hurry back out. The peaceful green park is a restful break from the noise of the souk, and we're too entranced to leave the pavilion right away, so we stroll around for a while and eventually head back to the gate. I ask the guard in front if anyone ever uses this pavilion, and he says yes, they have a book fair coming up next month, and they use the grounds sometimes for car shows and other exhibits. But the main building, an exhibition hall space that reminds me of the Javits Center in Manhattan, seems to have been deserted for years; we see only shattered glass inside when we peek in.

I ask my parents about the pavilion on the phone a few days later. They've never been to see it, either. Dad says he hasn't heard anything about it in years but remembers construction work on it started when he was in engineering school at AUB in the 1960s, and a few of his friends had worked on the project until it was abandoned at the start of the civil war.

Claire and I take a bus back to Beirut that evening, and before we get on, I double-check with the driver that this is an express ride to the city. "Of course," he answers. But before we pull out of Tripoli, we stop at a coffee shop, and the driver calls out to the passengers—the bus is packed with about three dozen people—to ask if anyone wants coffee. We stay parked outside the café for half an hour while the driver picks up coffee, cup by cup, and hands it to everyone on the bus who put in an order. I'm marveling at this absurd mutation of Lebanese hospitality, but finally we're off. Not so fast, though: we make about twenty ad hoc stops on the way to Beirut, dropping people off by the side of the road, picking up passengers on the sidewalk. It takes nearly three hours before we're back in Beirut. Express indeed.

I'd been wondering if Claire would be sick of me by now, her tenth day in Beirut, but the vibe between us is still feeling comfortable and easy. Back in the city, we get together for a drink with our former *Village Voice* colleague Kaelen, whom I had run in to at the restaurant Tawlet in the fall. We meet up at Ferdinand bar in Hamra and reminisce about our *Voice* days and compare impressions of Beirut. Kaelen has been happy living here over the past decade and writing about the art scene—she seems to have taken to Beirut from the start. Slim and stylish, her dark hair in a chic layered cut, she could pass for a native Beiruti at first glance. How strange for the three of us to be reuniting here, but somehow it seems natural—as if, once again, this Hamra street were a side street in the East Village, the three of us popping into a bar near the office after work.

On our way home so Claire can pack and catch her late-night flight, we stop briefly at a café to smoke argilehs. She'd been wanting to try one, and I like smoking a water pipe, but I don't do it much these days since apparently the pipes are worse than cigarettes, and I technically quit smoking years ago. The apple-mint tobacco tastes light and sweet, and the air feels like early spring as we sit on the café's outdoor terrace and watch people walk by on their way to nearby bars and restaurants. A couple of pretty young Asian women pass by, wearing the shapeless pink-pajama uniforms that employers here make their domestic workers wear. Back at home we listen to the Rayess Bek hip-hop CD that Claire had bought at Virgin while she packs, and we reminisce about favorite moments from her trip. We squeezed in a lot in her week and a half here, and it all flew by so fast. I hug her goodbye before I go to sleep; in a couple of hours, in the middle of the night, a taxi I've called for her will be picking her up to take her to the airport.

The next day, to distract myself and fight the postvisit loneliness, I drag myself to T-Marbouta café to work on my magazine essay. I spend the entire day there finishing up the piece and snacking on the spicy Armenian sausages called *soujouk* and on fattoush salad, and drinking glass after glass of frozen mint lemonade. In the afternoon, I click send on my story. *Akhiran*. At last. Done.

The next week I'm off to the States to do my taxes, visit Richard for a few days, and head to California to meet my soon-to-be-born niece. I arrive in New York in late March, on the night before my birthday. I've barely told anyone I'll be in town, since my trip will be short and I usually don't like making a big deal about my birthday—but I'm hoping for a mellow dinner with Richard that night, at home or out.

Walking into his apartment as he runs up to hug me is heart-thumping, electric. The time away this year, tough as it's been for us so far, seems to be confirming that what we have is worth hanging on to, even if the questions—will things really work between us long-term?—are still crackling in my mind. He tells me he's planned where we'll have my birthday dinner tomorrow, and winks deviously. I wake up the next morning jet-lagged but looking forward to the day.

When he gets off work, we meet up for drinks at a bar called Brooklyn Social and end up having several rounds of Dark & Stormys. Richard tells me he's planned a sushi dinner for us—am I game? Yes. I'm desperate for great sushi, which I can't seem to find in Beirut. Three drinks in at the bar, I realize I haven't eaten since my early lunch—nine hours ago.

On the walk to the sushi restaurant, I'm a little woozy from the three strong rum cocktails on an empty stomach. But we're both in an upbeat mood, gossiping about the bickering couple sitting next to us at the bar. As we stroll, Richard jokingly says maybe we should stay away from any political topics tonight; over dinner or drinks, we've tended at times to latch on to some Middle East–related subject or other, and then not let it go for hours. The debate can be fun and thought-provoking sometimes, less so other times, but when it happens, it always takes over the night.

"Okay," I say, and smile. "I won't mention the Israeli Apartheid Week conference at AUB last month."

"What was that?"

I start to explain, but wait—politics. I didn't actually mean to get into it tonight. I was only half-jokingly bringing up the Middle East right at this moment. Better stop now. But it's too late.

Over and over again in the past, we've agreed to disagree about whether any state should be defined by its ethnic or religious identity. But the mention of the apartheid conference, which I hadn't even attended, opens up a subject—whether Israel should be considered an apartheid state—that neither of us really feels like arguing about at the moment. I'm stupidly thinking I can just blithely bring up the topic and then quickly drop it and continue with our jolly sushi plan.

He takes a deep breath. I can tell he's not in the mood for this subject right now. But I hazily forge ahead with it. "The problem is that Israel refuses to see itself as a state that belongs to all of its people. Defining itself as a specifically Jewish state means non-Jewish Arabs, no matter if they were already living in Israel long before it became a state in 1948, don't get the same rights."

Richard is shaking his head: "There are ways to fix that problem without giving up the idea of Israel as a homeland for Jews, in a time when they don't necessarily have anywhere else in the world where they're guaranteed not to be persecuted. The

Holocaust is a pretty recent memory. Wasn't Lebanon established initially as a homeland for a Christian minority that felt itself to be in danger?"

"Yes, but take a look at Lebanon. It's not exactly an example of social justice or religious harmony."

On our way to the Japanese restaurant, we both make half-hearted stabs at changing the subject, but mostly we keep trying to win points in the debate—which neither of us can seem to stop.

While we walk, I ask Richard to explain the difference between South African apartheid and the reality in Israel, and as I press him on the issue, I hear the cadence of his voice rise. He's feeling attacked. I'm feeling frustrated that we're both now in combative mode, each backed into different corners.

We're taking faster strides on the sidewalk now, our argument heating up, getting louder by the second. We're each still trying to make headway in the debate, but I wonder if, instead, we're just sinking into the quicksand that drowns so many Middle East arguments. The so-called debates I see on the Middle East among TV pundits, or in op-ed sections of newspapers, usually get nowhere for the obvious reasons: opposing sides refuse to see past their own familiar positions and to try to reconcile them with the complex realities and struggles of another side. They talk past one another, each in their own bubble.

I've always admired Richard's sense of empathy, his instinctive generosity of spirit, and his sharp rhetorical skills—even in the middle of our nastiest arguments. He and I both like to see ourselves as rational debaters who value humanity and ethical integrity over doomed tribal thinking. But in a part of the world where so many populations feel victimized and are trying to find their safe corners—and where "Arab" and "Jew" are loaded identities—will it always be so maddeningly hopeless to get past the insular thinking, the paranoia?

When he cringed at the word *apartheid* tonight, I thought of how Middle East issues are usually framed in the United States, and how certain questions are silenced before they even have a chance. I need to be able to talk about sensitive subjects with Richard, and vice versa, but I wonder if we're coming up against the usual boundaries now. Can't we discuss tangled Middle East issues like these together—fearlessly, and also empathetically?—or will one of us always feel misunderstood or attacked? For us these debates aren't just intellectual swordplay; we have personal ties to the region, and the emotions run deep.

He and I often do break through the walls when we talk about these subjects, but right now we're just slamming into them. I'm sad, flustered, wondering if we're destined for a life of doomed fights about the Middle East.

I hear myself muttering, "We should just break up now."

Is it the cocktails talking? I'm too upset and confused to think straight.

Richard's Beirut visit last month had been a success, and none of the anxieties I'd had about it beforehand—will identity issues get in the way? will we have a big meltdown?—had come true.

I guess the train wreck was bound to happen sooner or later.

Richard glares at me and storms off.

APRIL

A few days ago all these thoughts were skipping through my head: the baby, a clandestine New York visit, northern California in spring. A break from Beirut. The hard-earned end of winter, and a celebration not just of my birthday but of the general okayness, the bliss even, of life when happy events unfold one after the other and you're feeling tuned in, grateful, ready to enjoy them.

Now my birthday's been ruined, and my relationship is on life support. I'm heading to California in a couple of days, and I'm going to be a mess meeting my niece for the first time. She'll be only a few days old, but surely it won't escape her notice that her auntie is a wreck. It's not so easy to hide emotional chaos even from babies, I'd imagine.

After all the hard work trying to make this relationship last from across the planet and for so many months, it's amazing how easily things fell apart. In barely a few minutes. Roadkill from a badly timed spat about—what?—politics, damn it!

The next day I text Richard while he's at work.

"Bummer the night ended the way it did. Drunk debating—not good."

"Yeah. Let's talk."

When he gets home from work, I smile, mumble "Hi," but he shakes his head. My "We should just break up" comment from last night is hanging in the air. Last night after our sidewalk fight, we'd both ended up back at his place; all my luggage was there, and it was too late to try crashing anywhere else. We'd gone to bed without a word. Tonight we're standing in his living room, silent again, staring out the window onto the brick-red town-houses across the street.

"I want to talk," I say.

Richard shrugs. "There's nothing to talk about anymore."

I walk away, pace around the apartment, and head into the kitchen. I open a bottle of wine, pour out two glasses, and set them down on the coffee table in the living room. We both keep standing there, neither of us sitting down, or touching the wine, or saying anything.

True, I'd been wondering ever since we started dating if politics would wreck this relationship eventually. But even when we've had huge arguments, we've managed to recover from them, our mutual affection and respect winning out. Then, last night, I'd hurled that break-up comment. As angry as I was, that was an unfortunate and sudden outburst. It was hurtful to him, as I'd intended it to be right at that moment.

Apparently he hadn't just forgotten about it during his busy workday. Now he's looking distant and worn-out as we stand there in his living room, still quiet, not knowing what to say or do. If he's decided we should in fact break up, I'll have to change my return ticket and leave New York early, or stay with a friend for my last few days here. I don't want to. But I wonder if we've pushed things too far this time.

Eventually I venture this:

"Listen, we're not always going to agree. Not about politics, and not about a lot of things. The way we argue about certain issues drives me nuts sometimes, but we've always found our way back. I feel about you the way I want to feel about someone. It's going to get politically dicey between us sometimes, but I'm pretty sure we can handle it."

He doesn't answer. For half an hour, neither of us says anything. I leave the kitchen and go to his room, shut the door, and lie down on the bed.

An eternity goes by. An hour, maybe two.

Then a rap on the door.

"So, want to watch the end of the Celtics game?" It's his voice. I can hear it behind the door.

Yeah. I do.

The morning after, he gives me a hug and a kiss before he heads to work. We both crashed hard as soon as the game ended. Although I hardly ever watch sports, this was a badly needed distraction, and I guess we'd spent our frustration and anger and were determined to move on without rehashing the whole nasty night. The game showed up just in time. Good thing, too—not only because an hour of raucous cheering helped melt the frost and get us back on track but also because I have to do my taxes today, and I need every positive vibe I can scrounge up.

Before I leave for California that Sunday—my taxes all done and mailed off, stress level ratcheted back down—Richard and I decide to have a Saturday adventure. We take the train to the huge Chinatown in Flushing, Queens. The plan is to gorge ourselves on Szechuan food and explore a neighborhood we both want to get to know better. It's a tank-top day, with a warm breeze, spring hitting early. We arrive in Flushing at midday and join the sidewalk fray along Main Street and Roosevelt Avenue—masses of the old and young, Chinese mostly but other ethnicities mixed in, too, street vendors lined up in front of buildings, pedestrian and car and stroller and wheelbarrow traffic fighting for space. Smells of roast duck, hot soy tea, and spices are everywhere. We peer at the tiny map on my cell phone screen and make our way to a Szechuan restaurant I've been wanting to visit called Spicy and Tasty. The small square dining room is lit up in fluorescent bulbs, not the most atmospheric, but based on the dishes I'm spying on the tables around us, I can't wait to start eating.

When I go to restaurants with Richard, I usually skip the meat right along with him—even though he always says "Don't!" But I like to order so we can share everything and maximize the dishes we can sample, unless there's a meat dish I can't resist. Today we easily find enough nonmeat dishes to fill our table and order enough for five (in true Lebanese style): cold noodles with red chili sauce, sesame yam balls with red bean paste, squid with peanuts and hot peppers, shrimp and pickled turnip in spicy sauce. Bright bold flavors, spiciness, crunch, heaven.

Stuffed after our gluttony, we head for the 7 train out of Flushing, and on the way we wander into a Chinese bookstore. We end up in the language section, reading to each other from an educational handbook that attempts to teach American conversational phrases.

" 'The pork chop was tender and large, yet tasteless.' "

" 'I don't like my wedlock.' "

" 'Many people crave politics.' "

That was our last day together for a while. Plans for the next few months are up in the air. I'll be in Lebanon. He likely won't be able to take enough days off from work to visit me in Beirut again this spring or summer. So it's back to the long-distance life. It hurts to leave, stings badly every single time. We've been building up that muscle, the two of us, but it's still tough, no doubt about it.

And I'm off to California.

When I first see my baby niece Marlena's face, in Laila's lap, in their home on a lush green Oakland street, all I can think of is a phrase from one of the English handbooks in Flushing: *"You are the cat's pajamas."*

It's such a joy to look into Marlena's pink marshmallow face, her enormous dark eyes and soft brown hair, one minute an exact duplicate of Samir, and then instantly like a mini-Laila. I hold her and stare at her while she sleeps, and I have this strange feeling that I'm holding part of myself. Marlena is not even my own daughter, but the feeling that comes over me when I hold her catches me off guard.

Over the next three days, I get lots of time to hold her and stare into her small blush-cheeked face, while Samir is at work and Laila takes occasional breaks to shower and return phone calls and do things you can't always do as a brand-new mom when you're responsible for the survival of a tiny living thing. I can't get enough of rocking Marlena in my arms, singing her lullabies (terribly out of tune, I'm sure she can tell), and jangling the colorful mobiles I dangle above her chocolate-brown eyes and raspberry mouth. I realize how much I already love being an aunt. She's snagged my heart completely, this miniature thing.

My time in California flies by too fast, and soon I'm back in Beirut. My acquaintance Joumana, the one I'd met at the book event in October and who lives in Dubai, is in Beirut helping organize an event called TEDxRamallah. It's a spinoff of the annual TED conference in California, which brings together speakers to give brief talks on various "ideas worth spreading." I'd promised her over e-mail that I'd be there. The Middle East edition that Joumana is helping put together will invite a variety of speakers from around the Arab world to give short talks about innovative entrepreneurial, cultural, and activist ideas coming out of the region. It will take place live in the Occupied Territories, with a simulcast at a Beirut theater.

This is the first time a spinoff TED conference is happening in the Arab world, and another of its goals, besides creating a forum for progressive ideas from around the region, is to bring in speakers from the Palestinian refugee camps. The hope is to spread the message that despite the bleak conditions of the camps, plenty of ambitious, creative thinkers and entrepreneurs are living there and undertaking projects the rest of the world rarely gets to hear about.

The Beirut simulcast kicks off on an April morning in a bare-bones auditorium called the Sunflower Theater on the city's southeast side. It's early on a Saturday—the event is scheduled for eight thirty, but as always in Beirut, nothing starts on time. I wander in at ten to find I've missed only the first few minutes, and I sit down to hear an American woman named Gisel Kordestani, Google's director of new business development for Latin America and Asia-Pacific, give a charismatic talk about the possibilities of Internet activism. She's followed soon afterward by Fadi Ghandour, the founder and CEO of the Jordan-based shipping company Aramex, who pioneered a program called Ruwwad for Development that teaches entrepreneurialism to disadvantaged Arab youth.

Over the next couple of hours, I also hear Palestinian writer Raja Shehadeh, author of a lyrical book called *Palestinian Walks*—well reviewed in *The New Yorker* and *The Economist*—talk about the rural landscapes he grew up with in Palestine in the early twentieth century, and Lebanese Brazilian director Julia Bacha discuss her recent documentary *Budrus,* about Palestinian villagers' nonviolent efforts to resist the takeover of their land. Alice Walker, the Pulitzer Prize–winning poet, speaks after the lunch break and tells funny stories about her hard time getting past the Israeli checkpoints to make it to the event. An activist named Amal Shahabi, who lives in a Palestinian refugee camp in Sidon, tells of the challenges she faced in opening a center for the elderly and creating educational and social resources for her disabled son and others like him in the camp. Suad Amiry, an architect and a Palestinian-Israeli peace negotiator, closes out the day on a lighter note when she reads excerpts from her hilarious and moving memoir *Sharon and My Mother-in-Law: Ramallah Diaries,* about the years she spent juggling the stress of life in the Occupied Territories under Ariel Sharon with the challenges of living with her ninety-two-year-old mother-in-law.

On this day in April, there's been a sudden heat wave—it's eighty-five degrees and brutally humid, for spring anyway, much too soon to start in on a long sweltering season. After the event, I look for a taxi outside, and as I walk past condo tower after strip mall after condo tower in this monotonous neighborhood on the east side, I think about the idea of home for refugees—that at some point life in the camps, especially for the second generation, becomes itself a home, if just potentially, ideally, a way station to a more permanent and life-affirming kind of home. But I can see how waiting endlessly until a seemingly hopeless situation improves, until a temporary home is replaced by another refuge, can feel like a waste of a life or at least of years. And here today, as I sat and watched the speakers, some of them from the camps, I saw people who are engaging in their life as it stands now and making a home, even if—with any luck—a temporary one, in conditions the rest of the world might pity or even scorn.

The TEDx event makes me realize I have no real sense of what the Palestinian refugee camps in Beirut are like, or what the families who live there go through. Out of negligence, mixed in with shyness about intruding nosily or cluelessly into other people's lives, I haven't yet made an effort to visit. I ask Diana if she would mind taking me along with her sometime. She's working on some documentaries in the Shatila camp, and she offers to take me one day this spring and introduce me to some of the families she knows who live there.

Shatila is near the northern edge of Dahieh, Beirut's enormous mostly Shiite neighborhood, which I've also been wanting to get a feel for. Dahieh contains about a third of the total Beirut population, but as with so many parts of Beirut and of Lebanon in general, if you don't live or work or have family and friends there, you probably rarely if ever go. I'm curious to walk around Dahieh and have also heard there's great discount shopping there. One overcast and blessedly cool day in April, Shireen and I jump in a service taxi and go. Earlier that day I'd mentioned casually over the phone to an aunt that I was on my way to explore and do some shopping in Dahieh. "Be careful!" she pleaded, and I flinched at her overreaction. Beirutis who've never been there predictably look upon the area with fear since much of it is poor and run-down, and there's Hezbollah signage everywhere; the party built up a strong following there by providing infrastructure like schools, hospitals, and utilities to poor, disenfranchised Shiites who faced discrimination and neglect by the government. But my aunt's advice is not completely unfounded: if you're not a local there and you're acting like a dumb tourist, you might stand out.

Because Beirut is still Balkanized in many ways, its neighborhoods mostly inhabited by one sect or the other, certain insular-minded locals can get paranoid and wary of outsiders wandering aimlessly around their neighborhood. If you're a Muslim and especially if you happen to be wearing a head scarf, you'll likely be made to feel uncomfortable in certain conservative Christian neighborhoods in the city and will often be prevented from buying or even renting property there. If you're Christian, or even if you're Muslim but not Shiite, you may feel uncomfortable in parts of Dahieh. But Shireen and I figured that if we dressed modestly—jeans and a long-sleeve top—we'd be fine. The service taxi drops us off in the middle of Dahieh, in front of a minimall selling everything from furniture to cosmetics to toys, but we decide to walk around outside instead of going in.

The streets here are wider than in Hamra, less tightly jammed, but the buildings, some of them shabby-looking especially after multiple wars, their balconies surrounded by faded curtains meant to keep out the sun, remind me of some run-down parts of my own neighborhood. There's a smattering of pedestrians on the sidewalks, and street vendors push wheelbarrows piled with vegetables or the sesame bread kaak. I notice a few other local women shopping along the street and not wearing head scarves. After a failed attempt to find a restaurant called Buns and Guns we'd heard about that opened here a few years ago—a kitschy fast-food spot with militia-themed decor and menus shaped like missiles—we learn it closed recently. We spend the afternoon taking a leisurely stroll along the sidewalks, stopping at housewares shops and produce stands and buying good-quality discount-priced kitchen items—a mortar and pestle for Shireen, stacking bowls for myself. We stop in at a fancy pastry shop to buy some atayef, the small pancakes I love, stuffed with crushed walnuts and the clotted-cream-style filling called ashta, for half the price of what they'd run at a similar store in Achrafieh or even Hamra.

In New York, I'm always dreaming up plans to see parts of the city I don't know yet, and after more than a decade there, I still haven't spent enough time getting to know the Bronx, or Staten Island, or Queens. But sometimes the right mood, the right weather, or the right companion translates into instant motivation for adventure or a new angle on the city. Same in Beirut: my frames of reference have always been Ras Beirut and Achrafieh mostly, but as with any neighborhood in any city, staying there gets both stifling and myopic. I try to force myself to get out of my comfort zone, whether just to stroll or to go to a party or a cultural event, to get a lens on the rest of the city. Post–civil war, Beirut is wide open again, at least in theory. The militia-patrolled Green Line dividing east and west Beirut is gone, and the *you stay on your side and I stay on mine* mindset has loosened, even if it still lives on for some. There's no reason not to see the full stretch and scope of the city, even if it's uncomfortable sometimes in unfamiliar neighborhoods, even if the locals pick up on the *I'm not from here* signs flashing on your face.

I remind myself: *Be respectful, modest, and friendly, stimulate the economy a little, and don't be an ass.* The usual rules. It's hard for me to feel at home in a city if I can't poke around in the corners and take it all in, maybe not all at once but as a goal—and if I can't do my minuscule part to keep it from ghettoizing itself.

Suddenly it's near the end of April, and—flashback to pre-Thanksgiving—I'm wondering if I'll land an Easter invitation. I may not consider myself religious, but Easter is a huge deal in Lebanon; it's called Eid al-Kebir here, the big holiday. Jesus's purported rising from the dead on that day involves much more celebration and dressed-up churchgoing and ceremony in Lebanon than it does among Christians in the States. Every candy store, pastry shop, and supermarket in Lebanon's Christian or mixed areas is festooned with Easter chocolates and decorations for weeks ahead of time, and plans for big family gatherings are made early and slaved over.

Just when I'm resigning myself to spending the holiday alone, I get two tempting lunch invitations, one from my mom's cousin Nadim and his Armenian wife, Asdghik, a terrific cook, and one from my great-uncle Cecil. He'll be visiting from London for Easter, spending the holiday at his country house in the southern town of Marjeyoun with his daughter Zelfa, who'd come to Beirut with him and her family back in September. Since I don't get to see them much, I accept the invite.

I've been curious to see the Marjeyoun house. Cecil has invited my parents and me to go in summers past, ever since the Israeli

occupation of the south ended in May 2000 and going to Marjeyoun became less of an ordeal. But the timing never worked out for
me during any of my rushed minivacations to Lebanon.

For the trip there on Easter Sunday, I've hitched a ride with
Kamal and Nour; they're also invited down for the holiday. The
drive takes us through Sidon, an ancient port town with a busy
souk and modern buildings rising up in the shadow of Crusader
castle ruins, and then farther south, into a gradually more mountainous and green, more sparsely populated, stunningly beautiful
part of Lebanon. The towns thin out, dotted here and there along
hillsides, the winding road curving around and through mountain
passes, with herds of goats bleating as we drive by, valleys planted
with wheat in the near distance, snow capped Mount Hermon way
out beyond, and crumbling Beaufort Castle, a strategic site for the
Crusaders in the twelfth century, perched on a mountaintop a few
kilometers away. Trucks pass us in the opposite direction, swerving by on the hairpin cliffside roads. Every time, somehow, both
cars make it in one piece, barely skirting past each other and man-
aging, amazingly, not to tumble off.

When we reach the outskirts of Marjeyoun, we're stopped at
a military checkpoint. Because this volatile part of Lebanon is so
close to the Israeli border and is heavily patrolled by the Lebanese
army and UNIFIL, the United Nations Interim Force in Lebanon,
visitors must have Lebanese identity cards or other documents
granting entry. NO FOREIGNERS, says a sign above the checkpoint.
Luckily I'm spared a huge headache since my Lebanese ID card,
the one I applied for back in November, finally came through two
weeks ago.

We pull into Cecil's street, and he greets us at the front gate.
As we park the car and get out, I'm struck by the loveliness and

charm of the old one-story stone house, on a tree-lined lane just off Marjeyoun's small central souk. Cecil restored the house decades ago, after it was neglected for years when his parents died. A garden that leads up from the front gate to the door and wraps around the side of the house is alive with flowering rose and jasmine and geranium bushes, planted in between tall pine trees. It's heaven here, so serene, and the scent of flowers everywhere instantly calms any nerves rattled by the harrowing roads.

We all gather on the terrace out back, sitting on antique white wrought-iron chairs, drinking freshly squeezed blood-orange juice and catching up before lunch. Cecil, dapper in his tweed jacket, dark purple tie, and wispy white hair, leans over and says that like me, he too had at one point long ago decided to look for home in Lebanon. He had grown up in England, his parents having emigrated there in the late nineteenth century, but after he finished graduate school at Oxford, he decided to restore his parents' old house here and rebuild his family's roots in Marjeyoun.

His mother's family used to farm the land in Ibl, a town nearby, also part of the greater Marjeyoun area; its name means "valley of springs." Cecil tells me the region has a rare and long-standing mixed-sect population of Sunnis, Shiites, Druze, and Christians, mostly Orthodox. Cecil's grandfather, a Protestant, had converted from Greek Orthodox during the nineteenth century, when American missionaries were spreading through Lebanon.

Zelfa calls us to lunch, a feast of roast lamb with roasted caramelized squash, onions, and beets; *foul bi zeit*, freshly shucked broad beans stewed in olive oil and garlic, which Cecil made; various eggplant dishes including baba ghanoush and the lemony salad called raheb; rice studded with pistachios and golden raisins; and thick, tart yogurt made from local goats. For dessert, there's traditional Easter *maamoul*, powdered-sugar-dusted cookies stuffed with crushed pistachios or dates.

I guess I've gone on a few too many times today about how smitten I am with this house. "It's your house, too," Cecil insists, "since it belonged to your great-grandfather"—and he and Zelfa suggest I stay the night and join them the next day for an Easter Monday lunch at their neighbors' house. Before I've fully thought it over and said yes, Zelfa has already made up my bed, a four-poster queen size in the guest room, which has its own balcony shaded by mulberry trees. I sleep nine hours straight that night and wake up to birdsong. Beirut feels like a continent away.

Cecil's house is rustic, its high whitewashed walls mostly empty but hung with a few paintings by Iraqi artists from the 1950s, an interest his late wife, Furugh, had in that period. With an antique crystal chandelier and all the artisan-sewn striped-silk cushions strewn about, the effect is of subtle style, a sharp eye lurking behind an overall sparseness. Next door at their neighbors' house the following day is a different scene altogether: ornate Persian rugs, lots of embroidered textiles and sofas and cushions, the shelves brimming with pottery and antiques, a display of wealth. The house is packed with at least forty people today, and as I enter with Cecil and Zelfa, we're led into the side room, a traditional chamber in Arab houses called a *liwan*, furnished with a U-shaped banquette. A dozen men are sitting and chatting and fingering their worry beads, including the local Orthodox priest in his full black robe and chains hung with big silver crosses. We shake each man's hand, one by one, saying *"al massih qam,"* Christ has risen, the Easter greeting, and Cecil stays in the liwan as Zelfa and I walk out to meet other guests.

Within ten seconds, we're surrounded. Everyone wants to ask

Zelfa about Skandar, her eighteen-year-old son who has starred in all three *Narnia* movies, the most recent released just months ago.

"My kids have watched *The Lion, the Witch and the Wardrobe* at least a dozen times. My daughter has the biggest crush on your son. Is Skandar here this weekend?" one woman asks Zelfa in Arabic.

"No, he's spending Easter in England this year."

"When is he coming to Marjeyoun?"

"He was just down here on a visit with university friends a few weeks ago, but they've left."

"Dommage!" Too bad!

With promises of signed photos made all around, and perhaps even some face time with Skandar on his next Marjeyoun trip, Zelfa grabs my wrist, and we head toward the Easter table. The priest emerges from the liwan, gathers the guests around, and says an Easter blessing, then *"Sahtain,"* or *"bon appétit."*

For this, my second holiday feast, the table is spread with a whole roasted lamb, and an enormous stack of the stuffed grape leaves called *warak bi inab,* and of stuffed lamb intestines known as *fawaregh,* piled high into a huge cake. There are also multiple platters of *freekeh,* roasted green wheat topped with cinnamon-scented chicken; rice-and-meat-stuffed zucchini called *koussa mehshi,* ladled with goat yogurt; and bowls of tabbouleh and fattoush salad. It's an incredible spread, and well worth having stayed in town overnight.

In the early evening, I hitch a ride with some of Zelfa and Cecil's neighbors back to Beirut. We stop along the way to buy fruits and vegetables from a vendor by the side of the road, and I pick up a bunch of the small sweet bananas grown in the orchards outside Sidon, and a bag of the loquats, called *askadinia,* that are in season now and taste like juicy orange candy. A perfect top-off to one of the best Easters I've had, and not just one this year but two. Just as at Thanksgiving, I'd been convinced I'd spend the holiday alone but then lucked into invites to multiple celebrations—and I feel as grateful as ever for my people's love of food, feasts, and any occasion to live it up.

Back in Beirut, I'm feeling, not for the first time, bloated and overfed. I could probably live off the double Easter feast for weeks, like a camel. But before the month is out, I read about an obscure local holiday in a book called *The Rural Taste of Lebanon*, and I can't resist investigating. Apparently on the last Wednesday of April every year, some Beirutis celebrate the day the Prophet Job healed himself by jumping into the sea, and they do so by picnicking on the beach, swimming, flying kites, and sharing a dessert called *moufattaka*, a sweet, sticky rice and turmeric cake that's labor intensive to make, befitting Job.

The celebration apparently tends to happen mostly in the vicinity of Ras Beirut, among the Greek Orthodox and Sunni communities there—and most visibly in a beach section called Ramlet el Bayda. It strikes me as oddly specific that the holiday involves one particular Christian and one Muslim sect, and one corner of the city.

My mother grew up around Orthodox and Sunnis in Ras Beirut; maybe she'll know something. I call her and find she's heard of *urb'it Ayoub* (the Wednesday of Job), but she's never heard of any such picnic celebration, or of eating moufattaka in honor of Job. She asks Umayma, who has heard that people sometimes picnic and fly kites on that day. But no one else I ask has heard of this holiday.

I must get to the bottom of it. On the *urb'it Ayoub* day, I go to a pastry shop called Makari, which I'd heard is known for its moufattaka. I walk in to find that indeed, the shop is selling platters of moufattaka for the special day, and plates of it are sitting on every surface in sight. No other pastries are available today at the shop. So far so good. But when I buy a small moufattaka and head to Ramlet el Bayda, I find only a few scattered people on the beach. No kites. No moufattaka anywhere, as far as I can tell. There are a few groups of sunbathers scattered on towels on the sand, some smoking argilehs or playing cards, but no noticeable picnics in sight.

I've brought a labneh sandwich I made at home, along with the moufattaka. I sit down on the sand and begin to unwrap my sandwich. In a minute, I sense someone hovering over me. I look up and find a young guy in a white polo shirt and a visor standing a few inches away and peering down at me.

"Biki shi?" he asks. Is anything wrong?

"La." No. "Okay if I sit here?" I ask, half-sarcastically, annoyed at the intrusion.

"Sure. Just wanted to make sure you're okay."

I'm irritated with his question because it feels so tiresomely Lebanese, Arab, this assumption that if a woman is eating by herself, then something must be wrong. Even in Beirut, where so many women are fiercely independent and can dress as they please, drive, succeed in business, and generally act the part of the freethinking twenty-first-century woman, sexist attitudes and traditions stubbornly intrude.

I later learn that Ramlet el Bayda is a paradox: an upscale residential area with expensive condos and a clean sandy beach that, apparently, was known in the recent past as a prostitution

zone. I wonder, then, if the guy in the visor was some kind of security guard. Was he wanting to arrest me, or wondering if I'm
a lost soul in need of help? I was wearing jeans, a long-sleeved
T-shirt, and sneakers—hardly effective hooker gear. Was he
there to guard the beach for the mysterious holiday? Doubt-
ful, since there was barely anyone at the beach. Was he possibly
flirting? He didn't have that vibe at all; he just seemed puzzled
and slightly disapproving. A few minutes after he walked away,
I noticed him sitting on a bench a short distance behind me,
gazing in my general direction, looking vaguely official despite
any recognizable uniform.

Another paranoid question popped to mind: Did he suspect
me of being some kind of spy? I was sitting on the beach alone,
and there had been military ships at sea that day, just off the coast,
but that's not terribly unusual. Still, in Beirut these days, Who's a
Spy? is a popular little parlor game. Suspicions easily swirl around
foreigners who speak multiple languages, or anyone whose job
requires frequent visits to political hot spots around the country
or region. The speculation can be nothing more than amused
curiosity, or just a side effect of the jadedness that comes from
living in a place like Lebanon. A relative of mine was once joking to me, or half-joking, that a new American neighbor of hers,
who'd arrived in Beirut days before the 2006 summer war and introduced himself as a refrigeration systems engineer, must have
been up to something shady. I've heard rumors that two homeless
men who always sprawled on the sidewalk outside the AUB campus gate were Mossad spies. And that various street vendors and
workaday locals roaming the streets of a particular neighborhood
day after day could be undercover agents for the government—
mukhabarat, secret police—or foreign intelligence moles or who

knows what. One of my aunts once told a dinner guest he had "espionitis," the disease of assuming everyone in Beirut is a spy.

The night before the Job holiday, I'd watched on DVD the film *Beirut Open City*, about a filmmaker suspected of espionage when he tries to make a movie about a shooting incident in Beirut. The movie's atmosphere of a security-goon-infested, tense, post-civil-war Beirut was still with me as I sat on the Ramlet el Bayda beach, even more so after Visor Guy appeared. In this paranoid city, everyone might be up to something, or nothing, or might think you're up to something—even if you're a woman alone, wearing sneakers, jeans, and a long-sleeved shirt, and eating a labneh sandwich on the beach on a sunny April day.

The intrusion by Visor Guy reminded me—an unwelcome but I suppose necessary reminder—that this country is still fucked up, in insidious ways that go beyond the obvious infrastructure and political problems. And expectations of what is and isn't done can be hypocritical and embarrassingly archaic, sometimes when you least expect it. Maybe wandering the nearly empty sands of Ramlet el Bayda alone in a still-traumatized and suspicious city is not quite the same as my solo New York adventures, like taking the ferry to Staten Island to check out the Tibetan museum there, or walking from SoHo to Hell's Kitchen to eat Portuguese cheese bread. But at least my Job Day adventure—even if it didn't shed much light on the strange holiday—convinced me of one thing: if I'm ever going to make Beirut my city again, I'll have to take the weird stares, the nosy questions, the "what's a woman doing eating lunch alone" glares, and just press on.

MAY

After that Ramlet el Bayda day, and nine months in this crowded and intrusive city, I'm feeling claustrophobic. It's not an unusual emotion here. Most Beirutis I know get cabin fever on a regular basis. Lately I'm counting myself among them—the locals I mean, not the mere visitors. Ironically perhaps, the more I feel at home in Beirut lately, the more I realize I need a break.

I'm getting the urge to run and hide from everyone, just shack up alone somewhere for a few weeks and read, work quietly, stroll, meditate, recharge. I also figure I might as well escape the city for a while because—well, because I can. The freelance world may not be the highest paid or most secure, but it has one fantastic fringe benefit: I can, in theory, work from anywhere.

I have some writing and editing assignments to finish over the coming weeks, and besides that I just want to spend time outdoors and feel the rhythms of Lebanese life outside the high-octane insanity of Beirut. Some time along the mellow northern coast might be nice, and maybe a couple of weeks trying out the quiet village life down south. I sketch out a plan that will get me out of the city for most of the blue-skied month of May.

First, my northward destination: Amsheet, a town an hour up the coast from Beirut. I'd read about a campsite and adjacent little hotel built in Amsheet in the late 1960s, a hippie-backpacker pit stop dating back to the optimistic prewar days. I book myself a cheap room there for the first half of May—before the summer high season kicks in—and pack up the army-green camping backpack I brought with me from New York. I explain to everyone I know that I'll have intermittent phone and e-mail access this month, then lock up my apartment and hit the road solo.

The coastal highway from Beirut north to Amsheet runs along a stretch of stunning rocky cliffs plunging down to the bright blue sea. But before that, the road runs past clusters of drab white concrete buildings on the northern edge of Beirut. Anyone paying close attention will notice on some of those walls a series of trompe l'oeil landscape murals, a gentler, more bucolic version of the city's ubiquitous graffiti. One building has a wall painted with a scene of birds flying in front of a window, its curtains parted to look out onto the soft blue sky. An urban prisoner's escape fantasy?

My taxi driver to Amsheet immediately strikes up a conversation—the usual routine here. Every interaction in Beirut, even a trip to the grocery store for a roll of toilet paper, can feel like a *ziara*, a social visit. In just about any cab ride in Lebanon, especially a long one, the personal asides will soon start tumbling out, unsolicited. With any luck, the driver will have a salty wit to keep the captive chitchat from turning bleak or too awkwardly personal. After the usual "what's your name? where are you from?" questions, my driver opens by telling me he never would've guessed he'd end up driving a taxi. Explains that he doesn't even own his cab. He used to be an accountant with four successful branch offices around the city, but he went broke during the war. I've heard similar stories from taxi drivers in Beirut before. Maybe they're all true.

The driver seems to be in a sour mood today. Like other cabbies I've ridden with, he's stressed out lately by the rising cost of gas, not yet reflected in the standard taxi-ride rates, and he curses the economy. Then he screams out the window at a pedestrian who is just trying to do his best to cross a gridlocked intersection. I excuse myself to put in my earphones and listen to music instead. The sun is beating through my window. We're edging out of the city now, and in my head I'm already miles away.

As we approach Amsheet, the rocky coastline curves around the crystal-blue sea, the water visible from high up on the road, like driving up the Pacific Coast Highway from San Francisco. My taxi pulls into the campsite, tucked into a hilly green enclave of conifers and bursting pink bougainvillea bushes, and adjacent to the driveway is the small inn where I've booked a room. The forested grounds are scattered with tents and wooden huts, and I see a few camping vans and groups of what appear to be twentysomethings sitting around in swimsuits drinking beers. After I exit the cab, my backpack slung over my shoulder, I check in at the cluttered reception office, then walk along stone steps winding through flower bushes and grassy patches down to the sea. From the rocky beach, a ladder attached to a wide flat stone leads directly into the waves. It's a windy day and the water is whipping high, but a few blond, European-looking campers are swimming in the waves, shrieking and giggling at how cold the water is. I climb back up the steps and walk along a pathway to the inn to find my room. I open the door to a bare-bones but clean, comfortable space with a queen-size bed, a kitchenette with just a fridge and sink, a turquoise-tiled bathroom, a sitting area, and a terrace outside overlooking the cliffs and sea. Perfect. This is all I need.

I settle in, then walk out to the terrace with my laptop to stare out at the sea and start in on my day's work. I'm drinking tea I've brewed in the water pot I brought with me, and my bare feet feel good on the cool stones. My cell phone is switched off, and I'm already feeling relaxed. I could do this for weeks on end.

Each morning in Amsheet, I walk up a hill behind the inn and set myself up with my laptop on one of the carved-rock benches a short distance from the main campsite. I love this quiet, with just the sounds of the sea below. One afternoon the sun fades in and out every minute or two, blazing hot when it comes out, cool and windy when it vanishes. A strange weather pattern, this, like a new season kicking in every few minutes. I take off my long-sleeved shirt, when the sun first comes out bright and strong, and sit for a few minutes in my purple tank top and white cotton work-out pants, which roll up easily to become shorts. I soon realize I could easily put the long-sleeved shirt back on and take it off every few minutes, roll and unroll my pants; the temperatures are changing so dramatically, each time the sun and clouds shift position. The sea looks rough today, the bright blue water rolling and punching against the cliffs.

I spend much of my time in Amsheet just like this: propping myself on a bench for hours every day, staring at the Mediterranean, the cliffs, and my computer screen. I'm writing up an interview with a New York chef for the travel magazine *Afar*, and editing a batch of articles for the Lebanese American University campus magazine. I'm in that narrowly focused, intensely productive zone, a work mode I crave and find hard to reach in Beirut, where every few seconds the jackhammers crank up next door or a street vendor screams out his goods for sale. The inn is in a sleepy part of town, but a few cafés down the road make competent versions of classic Lebanese dishes, so I keep the fridge stocked with baba ghanoush, fattoush, and mujaddara, and sometimes I order in a hot dinner delivered to my room: lentil soup, skewers of spiced lamb kafta, fried cauliflower with tartar sauce.

On my fifth day, I take a break from work and decide to do some exploring. First I take a half-hour walk along the two-lane road that leads north from Amsheet to a bakery I'd heard about, called Furn al Sabaya. It's down a twisty path that leads away from the road, and is marked only by a small sign in Arabic. The place is run by four sisters who bake using organic flours and who, among their specialties, have perfected an unusual dessert and also invented meatless versions of Middle Eastern meat pies. The bakery has a few shaded seats on a patio and some gingham-covered tables inside, and I sit chatting with one of the bakers as she steers me to what I should try. I find I'm not wild about the meatless *lahmbajin* flatbread, the ground meat replaced here with bits of crunchy wheat, but what I do instantly love is the *muwarraka* pastry that the bakery is known for, made with layers of phyllo dough wrapped around a filling of crushed walnuts and sugar, then rolled, shaped into a long cylinder, and twisted around and around like a coiled snake. I munch on the crisp, salty-sweet muwarraka as I walk back out to the road and follow it to the main Amsheet town intersection.

My path forks from there along an uphill road that leads into the hills of Amsheet, dotted with spectacular old houses overlooking the sea way down below, through purple jacaranda trees and pink hibiscus bushes. This time my walk takes more than an hour, and when I reach the top, I wind around through quiet residential streets and stop to look at houses built in the nineteenth century by the rich silk merchants who once lived here. The houses are made of yellow or white stone and have classic Lebanese features: balconies with wrought-iron railings in a variety of colors and designs—mint green, or lavender, or turquoise, with straight or swirled bars—and those arch-topped windows capped with fan-shaped glass that I hope never disappear from houses in this country. The views down across the valley and toward the sea are breathtaking.

A thought blows through my mind: *I love Lebanon. I really love it here.*

What does it mean, to love a country? Especially a place like Lebanon, which doesn't always make it so easy. Is loving your country the same as nationalism? My feelings for Lebanon—admittedly stronger on some days than others—seem more visceral than ideological. My love of Lebanon is not love for the idea of Lebanon, or in any case not the way the country was envisioned in the early twentieth century as a protected Christian homeland, or the way it's currently run. In any case, I've always had trouble with the idea of nationalism, anywhere. I understand that nations can't function without the loyalty of their citizens, but nationalism seems to me a lot like organized religion. Do I have to believe this is a great country, just because I was told to as a child, or because I was raised here?

But despite its past or present political baggage, Lebanon is an enormously diverse and complex place, a country with phenomenal—if mostly abused so far—potential as a meeting place for a great variety of cultures and ideas and ways of life. It also covers an undeniably beautiful patch of land. And the truth is, I do love this patch of land, even more now than ever before. I might love other countries, too, and believe in some of their political ideologies more than I believe in Lebanon's dysfunctional system at the moment. But I love what Lebanon could be, if it could ever clean up its political mess. If it could ever start putting its incredible diversity, talent, and beauty to better use.

And I do love this coastline, and these hills and valleys and mountains and trees and flowers, and this sea. Always this sea.

I return to Beirut on a mid-May weekend so I can show up at a political demonstration I've been hearing about, scheduled for that Sunday. I almost never go to demonstrations in New York, a reflex left over from my Berkeley days, when my friends were always en route to one protest or another and the contrarian part of me got bored with the everyone's-an-activist culture. I'm not exactly proud of this. But here, the more I complain about the endlessly murky, corrupt political system, the more I feel I should walk the walk a little more. Adding one more body to a thin crowd of Lebanese optimists feels, even if it's hopeless, still somehow vital.

On Sunday morning, I walk down to the Corniche to join the rally, calling for a secular political system in Lebanon. It's organized by a group called Laïque Pride (*laïque* means "secular"), responsible for organizing the first big demonstration for the cause last spring. This time last year Lebanon's secularist movement—it also goes by the terms *antisectarian* or *anticonfessional*—was a mostly low-profile idea. This year it's picking up momentum, partly because the revolutions around the Arab world have inspired more vigorous stock taking in Lebanon, along the lines of: *We may not have a dictatorship here, but it's time to get rid of the religion-based division of power.*

Another secularist organization called Isqat al Nizam (Down with the System) has recently been setting up a daily stand in front of the Ministry of the Interior headquarters. The group also held a few well-attended rallies of several thousand people while I was visiting California this spring. The time seems ripe—maybe, finally—for the secularism movement to get some traction.

The Laïque Pride rally today is a march, starting from a central spot along the Corniche near the huge McDonald's and the Hard Rock Café, heading to downtown and the parliament building. It's a strong turnout on this Sunday afternoon, at least several thousand people, it looks like—teens up through the elderly, and families with their kids, and women in the hijab and others in skimpy tank tops, and stray passersby joining up midway, a whole eclectic mass. Banners with secularist messages are everywhere, hand-written or produced on fancy print-shop computers. The Laïque Pride organizers, a small group of men and women who look to be in their late twenties and early thirties, are sitting on the back of a pickup truck at the front of the crowd, holding megaphones and chanting: *"Shoo deenak? Ma khassak!"* What's your religion? None of your business! The whole troupe of us marches, following the truck and chanting, for the hour it takes to walk slowly through the streets that run from the starting point on the waterfront and into the center of downtown.

The confidence and momentum of the crowd keeps gathering strength along the way, with alternating hollers of *"Shoo deenak? Makhassak"* and *"Al sha'ab urid, isqat al nizam,"* "The people want the fall of the system," a chant inspired by the protests in Cairo's Tahrir Square. We also call out a plea to parliament members to vote yes on draft legislation to update the personal status law. That change would allow mixed-sect couples like Mona and Jia-Ching to wed in Lebanon in a civil marriage, instead of having to convert or marry outside the country, and could open the way for more secular-minded legislation.

Even though the Lebanese government still seems a long way from turning secular, the concept itself isn't new in Lebanon. It sprang to life and died a quick death over and over again before and during the civil war; the treaty drawn up to end the war, 1989's Taif Accord, specified a phase in which Lebanon would do away with the sectarian quotas in government and move toward a nonsectarian system. But this obviously hasn't happened yet, and beyond the renewed calls from activists and the occasional politician, it seems nowhere near happening.

Ending the religion-based system that is strangling the Lebanese government won't be nearly as linear as the process, however long and arduous, that led to Mubarak's fall in Egypt. As usual in Lebanon, when it comes to making changes, there are no credible strategies yet, a scant few inspiring political candidates to back, and no immediate hope of making real and sustained progress. Getting rid of the sectarian system is, for the time being, still a somewhat utopian goal. No politician is backing it in any vocal or significant way. Sectarianism is too deeply ingrained, the habit of thinking in terms of one's own tribe—Maronite, Sunni, Shiite, Druze, Orthodox, Protestant, or whatnot; Christian or

Muslim—is simply second nature to too many Lebanese. Electing politicians who profess loyalty to various sects is still widely seen as the only way to avoid persecution and advocate for day-to-day basic needs (electricity, water, and so on) in the various religious enclaves. Not to mention that most political and religious figure-heads of every sect in Lebanon gain too much from the status quo; marriage procedures, for instance, currently require red tape that's simply too lucrative for the priests and imams and religious powers-that-be to surrender without stubborn resistance.

Some of those skeptical about getting rid of Lebanon's religion-based setup argue that a secular one-person-one-vote system that does away with the prearranged distribution of power among religious groups would be doomed. That it would, for instance, allow a radical Islamist government to take over, if Shiites are now the most populous group, as most estimates guess, and if the conservative or Hezbollah-supporting voices among them end up winning. Or else a right-wing Sunni regime could take over, if conservative Sunni politicians were to win. Or else a Muslim-baiting Christian administration could end up running the government—although Christians are by virtually all estimates no longer a majority, so a secular Lebanon would mean the long-overdue end of a locked-in Christian presidency.

It's a tangled issue on all fronts, with no easy way forward. But even if I have my doubts that getting rid of sectarianism is a realistic goal anytime soon, showing up at the Laïque Pride rally, and marching and chanting with the crowd, felt like an adrenaline kick.

But, funny thing about Sunday's Laïque Pride rally: even though it drew a big crowd—around ten thousand, according to an estimate in the French-language Beirut daily *L'Orient—Le*

Jour—and even though it blocked the streets in a busy part of the city and drew tons of attention from passersby and drivers trying to get through, there was virtually no other coverage of the march apart from that article in the paper. Why? Because the Laïque Pride rally happened to take place on May 15, the anniversary of the establishment of Israel as a state in 1948—commemorated across the Arab world as Nakba Day, the "day of catastrophe," when millions of Palestinians were dispossessed of their land.

Thousands of Palestinians and other sympathetic protesters from around the Arab world marched from Lebanon and Syria to the Israeli border on Sunday, and although the Nakba protests were nonviolent and the demonstrators unarmed, some of them tried to breach the border. Israeli soldiers shot at them and killed fourteen protesters and injured more than one hundred. It was major news internationally. The antisectarian march in Beirut? Barely a blip on the radar of the local media.

Shortly after the Laïque Pride and Nakba Day rallies, I'm scrolling through QifaNabki.com, a blog run by a Lebanese graduate student at Harvard. The writer says he "couldn't help but notice the sad juxtaposition of the two marches scheduled for last Sunday," and adds: "A friend of mine regularly chides me for imagining that any of Lebanon's problems will ever be solved before the Arab-Israeli conflict is settled. On days like yesterday, I think he's probably right."

That following Monday I was planning to leave Beirut again and start the second half of my rural exile; I'd decided to go back to Marjeyoun, my great-uncle Cecil's town down south. He and Zelfa are back in London now and the house is empty, but they'd left me a set of keys in case I ever wanted to return. Since the town is right near the Israeli border, I decide to postpone my trip by a few days, to see if the Nakba Day events will ignite any further violence down south.

Meanwhile I sign on to take a road trip with my cousin Josette and aunt Marcelle up to Akkar, a region in the far north of Lebanon, considered an eternity away by most Beirutis. If you're Lebanese and not from Akkar, you've probably never been there, even though it's just two and a half hours by car from Beirut. This week a group called the Association for Protecting Natural Sites and Old Buildings has organized a rare free tour to take anyone interested up to Akkar to visit Tell Arqa, a hill thought to have been inhabited by a series of ancient civilizations and currently the site of a major archaeological dig, and to see the spectacular forests and waterfalls farther north.

When I arrive that morning to meet Josette and my aunt at the departure site, in front of a church in Achrafieh, I find three vans waiting to take the signed-up guests. From what I can tell, the crowd gathered in front of the vans is virtually all Lebanese. I overhear only one foreigner, a French graduate student studying at AUB.

The roads winding up from Beirut to the far north are dicey in parts, and the drive is tiring and sometimes treacherous, so even though the trip isn't so long, it makes sense that car-weary Lebanese who have never been to Akkar would jump at the chance to take a rare, not to mention free, sightseeing bus tour up there. The organization hosting the tour normally sets aside just one van for its various trips around the country, but apparently more people than expected were interested in seeing Tell Arqa and the Akkar landscape. When we arrive at Tell Arqa, the vans let us out, and we climb up a steep hill covered in pink thistles and red poppies.

An archaeologist from the Sorbonne, the university sponsoring the dig, is waiting for us at the top.

He explains that the dig is attempting to uncover houses and artifacts dating back thousands of years, to the ancient Romans and beyond. Right now only some stone structures are visible in the dug-out sections of the hill, possibly used at one time as baths or rooms. Even though ruins of ancient civilizations are scattered up and down the eastern Mediterranean—and construction sites in Beirut still often turn up stone formations from centuries or millennia ago—Tell Arqa seems to hold extensive and still-unexcavated remnants of past civilizations. It feels like a rare privilege to be here as the dig is under way. Depending on what they find here, I wonder if one day in the near future, Tell Arqa will become as important a stop in Lebanon as Baalbek or Byblos.

A little later, as the vans take us from Tell Arqa up into the curvy cliffside roads north of the site, an enchanting green vista slowly comes into view: steep forested mountainsides, plunging valleys, craggy white-rock cliffs, tall crashing waterfalls. So this is Akkar. At times, I've heard it described as mostly a string of poor villages and monotonous stretches of forest or farmland. In fact it's a gorgeously varied landscape, and seems to spread for endless miles up into the sky and the horizon. Scattered houses and farms dot the landscape here and there. But mostly it feels empty up here, like a film set for a mysterious green planet far away.

"*Shoo hal dini?*" What is this world? asks an elderly man sitting behind me in the van, talking to himself. For such a tiny country, it's incredible how much its own people, including myself, don't really know it.

When we arrive in Beino, a town farther north into the Akkar region, we get out again, this time to walk around a forest preserve created by a billionaire and former parliament member named Issam Fares. The spread covers hundreds of acres of trees and green hillsides, home to populations of birds and deer and a variety of flora and fauna. The forest vistas and nature paths through the preserve are breathtaking, especially against today's clear blue sky. Guests have to make an appointment in advance to tour the park, and it seems a shame that such a dreamlike landscape isn't left wide open to the public, to wander into and discover. Later I find that almost no one I mention this forest preserve to has even heard of it.

Outside the park, Josette and I stroll around together for a while to look at the humble but classic, graceful Lebanese-style houses on the residential side streets. We eventually rejoin the group and pile back into the van for the ride back to Beirut. The mountain air smells fresh through the open windows, and I gaze outside nearly all the way home. This trip felt like a journey to another country, and I didn't have to cross any borders to get so far away—even if it was only a couple of hours up the road.

In Beirut that night, I check local news sites and learn that the area around the southern border is calm again. I'm looking forward to being in Marjeyoun again. In the same week, I'll have gone from way up north in Akkar, down to one of the southernmost points in Lebanon.

Two days later I'm on my way, and the driver I've hired for the ride pulls into the quiet center of town, with its cluster of little shops and small family-owned restaurants, just minutes from Cecil's house. From town, a few one-lane streets lead up a hill to a smattering of cottages and farms, and the driver drops me off on the leafy street in front of the house. I open the black metal gate to Cecil's garden. Just as I did on Easter weekend, I wind my way through, gazing at all the flowers as I pass by—the pink and white rosebushes are in full bloom now, and the geraniums are thriving all over the garden. Cecil employs a gardener who works on the property all year, and it shows in this blooming little oasis. I unlock the wooden door and walk into the living room. It's a thrill being here alone. I throw open the terrace doors, put my bags down in the guest room, next to the four-poster bed, and make myself a cup of tea.

Here, too, as in Amsheet, I spend hours each day outside, working on my laptop or taking walks. I eat very well but a little more ascetically than in Beirut, which feels good for a change. There's a bakery down the street that makes excellent man'ouches, which I pick up for breakfast or lunch on some days, and I stock up on local sheep cheese, tart yogurt, tomatoes, and cucumbers from a nearby farm, sold at a tiny grocery nearby. For dinner I make simple soups—tomato, lentil—or pastas, or sometimes one of my favorite solo dinners: sardines on toast, with a little mayo and hot sauce. In the afternoons, I snack on sticky-sweet mulberries and on *janarek*, tart green plums that have a short season in spring. And as I sit on the terrace, I drink pots and pots of tea, put my feet up on the balcony rail, stare out at the mountains in the distance, the green valleys and farms, and the stepped garden that descends in row after row of pine trees, lemon trees, rosebushes, and jasmine branches.

One day, at Cecil's urging, I go visit his friend Hussam, who runs the local grain mill down the hill from the house. Hussam comes from a Shiite family that first put down roots in Marjeyoun around 1900, and he and Cecil have been friends for decades. Cecil encouraged me to visit Hussam and his mill because, as he put it to me over Easter, my generation has lost touch with where food comes from. He's right, of course; that also happens to be the mantra driving every food trend in the States over the past decade (backyard chicken raising, rooftop gardening, farm co-ops). Hussam's mill grinds the wheat grown on farms nearby, along with sumac seeds, zaatar, and other spices. In the shop in back he also has burlap sacks of herbs and grains sold by weight, and all manner of the fruit, vegetable, and dairy preserves the Lebanese call *mouneh*, including jars of olives, jams, and local goat cheese rolled into balls and soaked in olive oil.

I introduce myself to Hussam, who looks to be in his late fifties. He smiles, his tanned face wrinkling around the eyes, a warm expression as soon as I mention Cecil. The electricity has just gone out, he tells me, so the grain-grinding machines are down, but I should come back another time to see how they work. I buy a bag of dried marjoram, or *mardakoush*, as it's called in Arabic, to make the smoky-sweet herbal tea my late grandmother Alyce used to make for me in her house in Aley when I had a stomachache; and I pick up some zaatar and freekeh, the roasted green wheat, so richly nutty-tasting when cooked in butter and chicken stock and topped with pieces of spiced roast chicken.

When I thank Hussam and start to leave, promising to come back another time, he insists I stay for a cup of coffee out back with his family. I try to decline, saying I need to get back to the house. As usual in Lebanon, "No thanks, I really can't just now" is an unacceptable answer to an offer of food, coffee, or hospitality. I end up sitting on the veranda out back, overlooking the plots where Hussam's family grows strawberries, lettuce greens, lemon trees, and askadinias. The mountains rise up in the near distance behind the farm and span the horizon from east to west. Hussam's wife is wearing a pink apron and a head scarf and sitting on a chair with a neighbor, trimming parsley for tabbouleh. I shyly introduce myself and apologize for the intrusion, and Hussam's wife puts her hand on my shoulder, smiles, says, *"Ahla w sahla,"* You're welcome here, and goes into the house to brew a pot of Arabic coffee, despite my protests.

Hussam tells me that in the century since his family and ancestors have been on this land, a mix of Lebanon's *taifis* (sects) have always lived here together in peace. "I'm Shiite, and we've always been friends with the Christian families, and there are Druze here, too, and we all live together," he tells me. "Where else do you see this in Lebanon?"

It's a shame that this kind of coexistence among sects only happens in rare places around Lebanon—Marjeyoun, and my Ras Beirut neighborhood in the city, and a handful of other spots—where the various groups happened to establish footholds next to each other decades or centuries ago. Otherwise, intermixing is still slow going, when it happens at all. Towns and neighborhoods all over Lebanon have become set in their ways, wary of outsiders trying to buy land or establish any kind of beachhead.

Back at the house, I don't feel like sitting still in a chair and opening up the laptop just now. If I'm going to hold a metal object in my hand this minute, it's going to be an instrument that feels a little more tied to life here, not so much to my Beirut or New York realities, to the breakneck high-tech work pace. I decide to water the geraniums, the only task Cecil and Zelfa have agreed to assign me, probably more for my own pleasure than for the geraniums'. I wonder if the gardener has just watered them himself, but I can't tell. I find a tin pail hanging on a wire trellis, and I fill it up in the stone fountain in the front garden. Then I walk from the front of the house past the flower beds on the side, the jasmine bushes sending out their perfumey scent, and on to the back of the house, to the stepped terraces, and I rock the pail back and forth, throwing splashes of warm fountain water on all the geranium beds I can find.

Someday I hope I can bring friends here to Marjeyoun. If they're not Lebanese, they'll need special permission to visit, unless the country finally lifts the ban on foreigners in this area. I want them to smell the flowers and the pine trees, sit on the white iron chairs and the blue cushions on the terrace with me, drinking marjoram tea, gazing out on the mountain in the distance. It still has snow in streaks running down from its very tip, but for how much longer? Will the snow last into midsummer? I want Richard here with me, too, and I don't want to call this Lebanon and that Israel, and me here an Arab, and him there a Jew. Just both here, both there, or wherever, the important thing being the smell of the trees, the sound of those tittering insects—are they crickets?— and the bird I'm hearing now with its loud *wa-wa-wa* call. The important thing being the sounds and the smells and the air and life—and whoever loves it here, on this land, can live on it, work it, be here, and that's all. But we're not there yet and maybe never will be, the region, the world, human civilization. Not nearly there yet. But I'm here now, in this garden in this town, and I want these minutes and hours to linger like this, suspended in time, to always be here, at least as a memory, even when I'm not here.

I stop in front of an exploding white rosebush to smell the flowers, and I hold myself there, not walking now but just standing, leaning near the branches, the white rosy perfume taking me instantly back to the parks of London, when my parents would bring Samir and me there for a few weeks at a time to escape Beirut and the war. We'd rent a flat in London each time, but once we stayed with my great-uncle Albert and his wife, Odile, in Oxford, and helped pick the crabapples from their trees out back, and slathered black currant jam on buttered toast every morning. That thick smell of roses—was it the garden in Oxford? Or the London rosebushes? Holland Park, Regents Park? Playing in the lawns, running through the gardens, the war so far away.

Walking out the gate and along the winding street that runs up the hill, I stroll by the houses next door to Cecil's, some lived in now and some falling apart for years, their arched windows smashed, the stone partly eaten away, or bombed, or just decayed somehow. Along that street, the smell of jasmine follows me from a neighbor's garden, the bushes pushing over onto the street, the way they do here in this country, the jasmine delicate but fighting for its space in the air, never to be ignored or forgotten.

I walk back to the house and notice there are more geranium plants I'd missed the first time, and I spot another watering pail, the real kind with the spray nozzle. I go over to the fountain, fill it up with the buggy warm water, and sprinkle the rest of the plants. It's an arm workout, carrying around a pail full of water, and walking up and down the stone garden steps makes me feel stronger. I'm hauling the water and stopping again to smell the white roses, and in my head I'm humming the old song about country roads. Can I make a home in the country, in a place like this? I think maybe yes, for the first time. A dream to have long quiet stretches like this, walking and sitting and working in a garden, and blocking out the rest of the world.

Just feeling the space and air. Just these breezes, these pine tree smells, this earth, and learning how to care for a garden like this, and how to just sit and just be.

JUNE

Summer is sliding in, slow and easy. I come back to Beirut to find a cool breeze still blowing, the heat not yet crushing down into every corner, every wrinkle. So rare, this languid start. By now it should be sweltering, burning, godforsaken. The big fat SUVs driven by the summer tourists and luxury-label shoppers from the Persian Gulf region, gigantic vehicles that would usually be jamming the Beirut streets by now, are only trickling in. Not yet a traffic-stopping battalion.

Maybe this won't be a crowded summer, the Arab Spring having quashed urges to travel much in these parts, or to get so close to Syria. Or maybe Lebanon's own brewing problems will keep visitors away: in recent days, some rallies in northern Lebanon showing solidarity with antiregime protesters in Syria, and others expressing support for Syrian president Bashar al-Assad, have turned violent. Also now, in early June, anxiety is still humming over what will happen when the UN Special Tribunal releases its conclusions on the Hariri assassination; when one set of results does finally get released weeks later, nothing much happens—for now—except some speeches by the accused Hezbollah party denouncing the credibility of the findings.

But other ominous events have been happening lately, side effects from the Syrian strife or local harbingers of tension and trouble. The other day in Sidon, less than an hour south of Beirut, a bomb went off at the headquarters of the UN Interim Force in Lebanon. I was in a service taxi on my way to dinner at Kamal and Nour's house in Achrafieh when the news broke.

"Oof, ballashna," said my taxi driver. We've started, meaning "Here we go again with war."

"Oh no!" said a middle-aged woman passenger sitting in the backseat next to me.

The driver turned up the volume to hear what happened. The news report said the motive behind the bombing was a mystery. Six Italian officers posted in Sidon had been injured in the explosion, but no reported deaths so far.

"Oh," said the woman next to me, idly turning a page in her fashion magazine.

The driver switched to another station, Arabic music.

Is that boring, six injuries and no deaths? Not quite the drama we'd expected? I've noticed that Lebanese, myself included, often talk about political tensions in an animated tone, full of anticipation. I flash back to that comment Josette made to me once, about war being like salt and pepper here. This country has been through so many bloodbaths, and is so often on the verge of another, that I wonder if too much serenity for too long can seem disorienting or dull or even ominous in its own strange way.

Maybe brewing conflict, scary though it is, also sometimes plays an oddly comforting role here. I wonder if it can put the stagnation of a life in perspective, give a palpable reason for depression, unemployment, a failing marriage, a life stunted or in disarray: there's a war on, after all. In peacetime, as dysfunctional and stagnant and infuriating as life can be in Lebanon, the excuses aren't as obvious.

That could be why fireworks go off every day somewhere in Beirut—whenever a child's birthday or family celebration or store grand-opening seems to call for thunderous booms, the adrenaline bump of an explosion, a familiar soundscape of urgency, fight-or-flight, repurposed for ceremony and heart-thumping thrills. But fireworks still make my nerves jump every time; that sound of shelling is uncannily exact.

Despite the mostly mellow start to this summer, the no-sweat weather and traffic so far, Beirut is closing in on me again. I've been spoiled by the country air, the solitude, haven't missed the interrogating stares on every street corner. The minute I walk back into my beloved Beirut apartment, a place I've missed as I would an old friend, I'm ready to bolt out for the countryside again. But I want to let Beirut wash back over me. I want to enjoy being here this summer, really milk my time here, because this is the season when Beirut truly comes alive—or tries to, in the summers when there's no war, no invasion.

Also because I'm thinking about leaving Lebanon soon. Not yet, not this month. But before the summer is out, I might be back in New York. I've been struggling with the question of whether

I can stay in Beirut long-term ever since I got here last August, and much more so lately, as my one-year anniversary approaches. The truth is, I can't quite decide if I want to stay or go. Beirut drives me nuts, yes, but it's gotten under my skin this year again, and now I know it's not going anywhere, whatever becomes of this crazy country. I'm feeling at home here again, finally, and I know I could live here. I could stay on. I'm surprised to feel this way. A year ago I wouldn't have guessed this is how things would turn out.

Also, I don't know if I can bear to leave this apartment. The living room balcony looking out over Ras Beirut, the sea in the near distance, the traffic noises from Hamra Street, the smell of man'ouches from the bakery around the corner, the orange sunlight filtering through my bedroom curtains—these spaces and sensations are like extensions of my body. I've never felt this about a room or a house or an apartment anywhere else I've lived, in Texas or California or New York or any other city or state or country.

And: I love Beirut. I love it desperately. I know that now, and I know it in a deeper way, with more qualifiers but also much more certainty than I did before.

In spite of all the reasons to stay, all the emotions and attachments and arguments that keep cycling through my head as the weeks go by, I'm torn in other ways. For one thing, I'd rather not live on another continent from the person I'm involved with. Beirut will be here forever (well, who knows), but having a relationship that feels this natural, and durable through a slew of challenges, happens too rarely and can't be willed to happen any old time. It's happening now, and I'm hoping it will keep on growing if it's meant to. It's either an inconvenient obstacle to staying in Lebanon forever—or a confirmation that I miss my New York life just as much as I feel reconnected here in Lebanon. I'm feeling tugged in both directions, some days stronger toward Beirut and other days more toward New York. I need both cities in my life somehow, need to find a way to bring together the places and people that give my life meaning, wrap my life around them as best I can.

Here is one stab toward a resolution: right now it's easier for me to live in New York than for Richard to move to Beirut, although I suppose we could continue the long-distance relationship for a while longer. I've known plenty of people who've had it geographically worse than we do.

I still have some thinking to do, and I haven't figured out exactly when I'll return to New York if I do. But as much as Beirut feels jarring to me now, immediately after my blissful Amsheet and Marjeyoun escapes, I want to get my fill of it.

Shireen and I go out one night to see the African American jazz singer China Moses perform her renditions of Dinah Washington songs at the Music Hall. Midway through a soulful cover of "Is You Is or Is You Ain't My Baby," Shireen whispers to me that we should make a list of places to explore this summer, plan a few memorable Lebanon adventures together. Because after agonizing over the decision of whether to stay or go, she's decided to move back to the States in a couple of months.

I flash back to what a few people said to me when I landed in Lebanon last summer: *"Beirut is a transitional city. People you meet are always about to leave."*

But don't many of us also return? Shireen and I both did. We came back—to find Beirut again and our place in it. We're both surprised by how attached to it we're feeling now, more than ever, and how ambivalent we are about moving away. In Shireen's case, she's dating a guy who has just moved back to the States after a few years working overseas, and there are more job opportunities for her there. There's also more space in America, as everyone I know who has lived there notes: physical space, personal space.

My month in the countryside has made me even more aware of the near-lack of public space in Beirut. But here I am nearly a year into my stay, and I've still never been to the Horsh al Sanawbar, the pine forest on the southeast edge of the city, so I tell Shireen we should put it on our Summer Adventures list. As I'd learned at that reading I went to last fall for the launch of the book about the Horsh, most of the park is closed to the public, but we're curious to see whatever parts we can. We take a service taxi there one morning and get dropped off in front of the fence that encircles the park and separates it from the busy avenue running along one side. We walk along the fence, up and down the avenue, looking for the entrance to the small public part of the park. A guard from the horse-racing stadium across the street waves to us.

"What are you looking for?"

"How can we get into the Horsh?"

"It's easiest if you go through that gap in the fence you see right there."

A security guard advising us to climb through a hole in a fence? It's not clear if there's a more official entrance or if, as we duck into the gap and climb in, we've just breached the private fence. But we seem to be the only ones in the Horsh today. We walk along a paved path, between pine tree groves and landscaped flower beds that look partly neglected. The air feels fresh here, and the sight of endless trees and no people is so un-Beirut and so

calming. If the city had more spaces like this and made them easier to access, it would be so much less claustrophobic. But despite
some rallies and efforts here and there to open up the entire Horsh
to the public, the government seems to have no plans to anytime
soon. We keep walking deeper into the park until we reach a gazebo with a few chairs, under an oasislike cluster of palm trees. An
old man is pruning a tree and appears to be the only other person
here. He nods at us, and we sit in the gazebo in the shade, look
around at the quiet forest, catch a half hour's complete silence.

For the rest of June, it's looking like every day and night will
be filled with beach plans, music shows, dinners, or drink outings.
My mind drifts back to when I first got here last August, and how
I spent weeks wondering if I'd ever have a life here, ever get to be
part of the whirl instead of looking in on it from the outside. And
wondering if my decision to move back here was dumb, doomed.
Now, a year later, I feel both surprised and grateful about the life
I've managed to build here. I have new friends I love, and I've
grown closer to my childhood friends, cousins, and older relatives,
and many of them live so near that I get to see them regularly. My
full calendar surprises me still when I look at it now.

I don't take any of the relationships I've created and strength-
ened this year for granted. I feel lucky to have these people in my
life—now and hopefully always. Also, having so many people I
care deeply about in Beirut makes me confident that, if I do return
to New York this summer, I can come back someday, not just to
visit but even to live here again.

I know there's one aspect of Beirut life I'll miss if I leave: how
easy and quick it is to get onto a beach. This month is still a little
nippy for June, but once it starts getting warm enough for me

to brave the water, I hit the beach as often as I can. Sometimes I walk to the Sporting, a private but casual beach club fifteen minutes from my apartment, near where Hamra Street slopes down to meet the Corniche. Visitors can pay a daily fee instead of the full annual membership to get in. It's a rocky beach, like most in Beirut. Sprawling on lounge chairs on the stone terrace overlooking the sea, I spot families with kids, groups of friends drinking beers or texting, and sunbathing women untying their tops and lying facedown to get a strapless tan.

One afternoon Shireen and I decide out of curiosity to visit La Plage, a more upscale beach club on the Corniche that attracts a crowd of fit, tan, flirty Beirutis in their twenties and thirties. I covet the white and gold designer bikinis I spy around me, expensive-looking but deliciously glam with their chain straps or 1940s-style tops—and a reminder of the chic bathing suits I used to envy at Beirut beach clubs as a child. We loll around and drink cocktails at the swim-up bar and look out over the Mediterranean, feeling fab and conspiratorial as we eavesdrop on groups gossiping about work and sex and drug-fueled club nights. Another day we go to Atlas, an unpretentious beach club on the sandy shore in Jiyeh, an hour south of Beirut, and I swim in the warm salty waves as Shireen sunbathes, and we devour melted-halloum sandwiches on sesame baguettes for lunch.

In summer, Beirut's music calendar fills up, and on the solstice night of June 21, known in Paris, Beirut, and other cities around the world (including New York sometimes) as Fête de la Musique, bands play on ad hoc stages all over the city, all night. This year's Beirut lineup has experimental rock, jazz, hip-hop, Arabic, and all kinds of music, starting in the early evening and going until almost dawn. After a birthday dinner with Hala at a new Moroccan-French downtown restaurant, I stop by a stage set up nearby and catch a midnight concert by a local punk-metal band, not the greatest I've heard but sounding forceful and vital as they thrash around under the stars on a brilliant Beirut night.

Anytime there's a cultural event happening in Beirut, especially in summer, posters appear all over town, along with a listing in the *Agenda Culturel*, a French-language-only but comprehensive rundown of what's going on around the city. There's usually a handful of events on any one night, and Beirut being relatively small, it's a sure bet you'll run into people you know wherever you end up, or at least see familiar faces. I know that if and when I leave, I'm going to miss this small-world routine in Beirut, as much as I also often crave the relative anonymity of New York. One night I go to an art opening at a gallery called the Beirut Art Center, to see a photo and film exhibit titled "Image in the Aftermath"; it includes videos from the Nakba Archive, the collection Diana is working on of interviews with Palestinian refugees. I spot a young filmmaker I'd met at Mona and Jia-Ching's wedding, a friend of theirs named Mary who grew up mostly in Boston but has recently moved back to Beirut. We'd chatted for a while at the wedding, and after the art opening tonight, we go out for drinks and talk for hours, comparing notes on our lives in Beirut and the States. We'd had similar experiences growing up, and I suddenly feel as if I've known her for years.

At a film fest in Achrafieh another balmy night, I run into May, the sister of my New York friend Hana, who was a Beirut classmate of mine before our families left Lebanon; happily Hana and I reconnected in New York after college. May lives in Beirut now, and I'd been meaning to get in touch with her. I'm thrilled when I spot her long wavy dark hair and bright eyes in the movie theater, after last seeing her a decade ago, and we make plans to go out for drinks this month as we laugh about the film we've just seen: a silent, subtly funny documentary about Lebanon's electric-company headquarters, Electricité du Liban. The building's neon sign never quite lights up properly, its letters flickering or burnt out. Electricité du Liban indeed.

One Sunday in mid-June I go on another solo adventure out of town: I head up to Hammana, a village in the mountains less than an hour from Beirut. Every June it's cherry season in Hammana, and on this day the town is throwing its annual cherry festival. On the way into town, I gaze at Hammana's bright green hillsides, its mountain and valley vistas and vast cherry orchards. When I arrive in its small downtown souk, I find it lined with stands manned by cherry vendors and local artisans selling terra-cotta cookware, and cooks serving platters of hot homemade dishes. I walk around, taste the Hammana cherries, and load up on a few bags of the juicy sweet-tart bombs. I buy a bowl of *zingol*, a soup-like dish I've heard of but never tried before, made of soft, golf-ball-size bulgur balls and chickpeas in a fragrant broth of lemon, olive oil, and garlic. When I go back to compliment the woman selling the zingol, she offers me another bowl gratis. I try to pay her but she refuses. I do love this about the Lebanese—the re-flexive hospitality, the generous instinct. Maybe I haven't been looking in the right places, but I haven't seen this quite as much anywhere else I've lived or traveled.

A while back Diana had offered to bring me with her sometime to meet the families she's friends with in the Palestinian camps in Beirut. I'm interested to get a feel for a part of Beirut that seems to exist unto itself, mostly neglected by the rest of the city, not to mention the world. I've also been wondering how the refugees, particularly the second generation who never lived in Palestine but were born and raised in the Lebanese camps, think of home. I've been thinking, too, about the word *refugee*—what it means, and how it's often associated with the destitute and abandoned, but doesn't it also refer to anyone who's had to leave home, seek refuge? Even to some of us who, thanks to luck and circumstance, had a softer landing? On a hot June Sunday—absolutely sweltering now, goodbye breezy early-summer days—Diana calls me up to join her, and we go visit her friend Rula, who lives in the Shatila camp with her husband and teenage kids.

Shatila, along with the nearby camp Sabra, was heavily bombed in 1982 under the command of the Lebanese right-wing Christian militias, working in cahoots with then–Israeli army chief Ariel Sharon; both parties had targeted the Palestinians, a mostly Muslim group rendered nationless post-1948, as an inconvenient element in Lebanon. Hundreds of refugees were killed, mowed down in a three-day-long massacre, most of them civilians. Thousands more were injured and maimed. Now, three decades later, the camp is a tightly packed cluster of concrete buildings, a few stories each, with narrow alleyways running between them. Some of the alleys are lined with tiny grocery stores, bread bakeries, the occasional mosque or school. We climb up five flights of stairs to Rula's apartment and find her sitting over Arabic coffee with her husband and neighbors.

Rula is a short, trim woman with salt-and-pepper hair held in a tight ponytail, and a pleasant laugh that lights up her eyes. Diana spent a few weeks living on the roof of Rula's building in Shatila last year while filming a documentary, and the two are now close: tall, soft-voiced British Diana, and diminutive, vivacious

Palestinian Rula. Diana and I have brought some pastries with us—zaatar-filled croissants and chocolate petit-four cookies—and we hang out in the living room snacking and chatting with Rula while Diana's blond one-year-old daughter runs merrily all over the sparsely furnished space. Rula's neighbor, a middle-aged Palestinian woman wearing a light-cotton dress and a head scarf, is there, too, and offers us cigarettes, and though I normally decline, this time I say yes. A plastic fan is blowing, the conversation flows—Rula's son is trying to get a visa to the United States to find work—and soon her husband, Ziad, brings in Arabic coffee on a tray for us. I feel welcomed here and comfortable even though I've only known these people for a few minutes. We all chat in Arabic, though everyone in the room can speak English, too. Ziad tells some stories—funny, and also poignant—about his frustrating work as a taxi driver in Beirut, the only job he's able to do since Lebanese laws prevent Palestinians from working in most professions.

Living in a concrete-slab building nearby are some other friends of Diana's, a couple with three sons and a daughter in their teens and early twenties. We pass by to bring them pastries and stay for a coffee. The couple is sitting with friends and with their teenage son, who is stretched out on his side on a mattress in the living room, nursing an injury. Turns out he was shot by Israeli soldiers during the Nakba Day protests in mid-May and has just come out of the hospital after several weeks.

As I sit here in front of a sweet-looking, dough-faced kid who, in his mind, was joining his friends in the camp to protest what he and Palestinians all over the Middle East continue to mourn as the loss of their country—and who was shot for being in the wrong place (in Israeli soldiers' view) at the wrong time—I'm suddenly aware of what someone who either doesn't understand or doesn't share this view of the Israel-Palestine struggle might think of this tableau. What if I just presented these bare facts: me in a Palestinian refugee camp, having coffee with a family whose son has just been shot by Israeli soldiers for venturing too close to the border? *So, having coffee with militants, then?* I imagine someone asking. How would this look or sound to someone who hasn't grown up here, hasn't been soaked in the realities of this conflict, and has only watched one-dimensional renderings on televisions oceans away? Even some Lebanese people I know would flinch at this kid's decision to protest, wondering, *Aren't we done with this struggle already? Why should we keep on carrying the Palestinians' burden along with our own?* Or, as I overheard an acquaintance at a party asking the night before crowds streamed to the Israeli border for Nakba Day, "Isn't it time to move on?"

But when Palestinians have so much difficulty getting visas so they can look for work opportunities overseas; when they can rarely find work in Lebanon, which still denies them their basic rights and outlaws their employment; and when, as Israel and the United States and various parties to the always-stalled peace talks tell them again and again, they cannot hope to return to Palestine in their lifetimes, how exactly can they—and the whole region—move on?

Walking me out of the camp to find a taxi back to Hamra, Walid, the twenty-four-year-old brother of the boy who was shot, gives me a brief tour of Shatila: the mosque his family goes to over here, his old high school over there (he's now enrolled in a master's program at a university in Lebanon), and the burial ground of the

Shatila massacre victims over there. I ask him whether, growing up in Lebanon and having never been to Palestine, he was raised to think of Lebanon as home.

Walid, stocky with curly brown hair, his smiling cheeks still showing signs of baby fat, comes off as a vibrant young man, eager to start his life. He tells me he and his siblings and friends in the camp grew up thinking of Lebanon as temporary, and thinking of Palestine as their real home. But it's strange to think of your home as a place you've never actually been, Walid adds after pausing for a minute. He tells me he was afraid to go down to the border to protest on Nakba Day because he suspected things might turn violent, and he wondered if he'd get too emotional catching a glimpse of the place he's been hearing about all his life and never seen. He'd tried to convince his brother it would be dangerous to go to the protest.

Walid seems undaunted by what's ahead for him in life, and I don't sense that he's downcast or embittered. Not yet anyway. He tells me he's one of only three Muslim students in his graduate program. At school he's become friends with some students who grew up in families loyal to the Phalange, the Christian right-wing militia that participated in the 1982 massacres of Palestinians in the Shatila and Sabra camps. He also befriended Jewish students he met on a recent trip to the United States, sponsored by a nonprofit that's trying to expose Palestinians to life outside the camps, and expose Americans to young Palestinians and their hopes for the future. Walid tells me: You don't have to agree completely about politics to be friends with someone. I tell him I, too, have friends from lots of different backgrounds, and we don't always agree politically. Walid nods: If there's friendship, he says, then pauses, trailing off.

JULY

It's getting too hot to walk much—the city is a bona-fide sauna now in early July—but I'm venturing out on foot as often as I can, and for as long as I can stand. I'm still mulling over whether I'm ready to leave Beirut, and walking, as always, helps me sort out the clamor in my head. On these walks, I'm also memorizing the city again, as many parts as I can, the way I did in those weeks when I first arrived and was trying to reconnect with the streets, carve out my paths through them. All these months later, as I contemplate leaving, walking around feels like a way to seal the city in, once and for all, to fuse the streets to my body.

On these sweltering July days, I stop often at Bliss House, a college-kids hangout at the edge of the AUB campus, to pick up one of their fruit cocktails, which aren't really cocktails (no alcohol) but instead some of the most thrilling fruit concoctions I've had. My favorite is the fresh-squeezed strawberry juice topped with a mountain of chopped pineapple, mango, kiwi, apple, banana, strawberries, grapes, almonds, and a dollop of sweet ashta cream. One of these fruit bombs in hand one morning, I stroll downtown to the Beirut Souks, the recently rebuilt downtown shopping area. The first few times I came here last summer and fall, I felt alienated from this spanking-new downtown, felt it was much too artificial and scrubbed and soulless. Now, on this sweatbath of a summer day, when I need some light-cotton tank tops and a couple of skirts and a new bathing suit, I figure I might be able to find what I'm looking for at one of the few discount shops in the Souks or, if I'm lucky, at a sale in one of the pricier designer stores.

Fans are blowing soft breezes through the Souk's tunnel ways, and window-shopping here feels not too unpleasant today, similar to what walking around Houston's malls felt like when we first moved there. Sterile and lacking any street life, sure, but conveniently laid out, the air-conditioning a lifeline on days this brutally hot. Beirut has plenty of street life everywhere else—too much, some might say. So an easy-to-navigate, architecturally stunning shopping center isn't too bad an option, is it? It depends on the weather, and on your mood, I suppose. And it depends on your willingness to overlook this area's past as a livelier, noisier, smellier, more diverse city center. With any luck, downtown will recover that dynamism again someday.

The other night I had a dream that I was trying to explain Beirut to a group of American friends who had all come to visit me at the same time, knowing I might be leaving soon and wanting to see this place while they had a handy guide. I heard myself spout the usual clichéd contrasts of the glossiness and the grime, and the east and the west, and so on. But in my dream I took them not just to the major sites but also to Dahieh, and to Dora, a part of Beirut where many of the city's Asian and African immigrant workers live and where some of them have opened food and spice shops, textile stores, and home-style restaurants. These businesses crowd along the dusty streets that spoke out from the enormous central Dora intersection, from which buses leave Beirut for points north and south. If you live in New York, Dora is Flushing, or Sunset Park, or Jackson Heights. A bustling ethnic enclave, and maybe you've seen something like it before. In Beirut, it's one of the necessary reality checks to a snazzy district like the new Souks, and a chance to dig deeper into a city that sometimes seems to worship only the tidiest, shiniest surfaces.

Shireen and I decide one July day to get to know Dora better, not just pass through it quickly en route to somewhere else, as I've only ever done before. We spend an afternoon strolling around and poking into the cluttered shops. I buy a spicy cashew curry sauce, to stir into rice and chicken I'll make some night; she buys a beautiful purple Sri Lankan fabric to sew into a handbag. As we're eyeing the samosas stacked up on a tray at the front of an Indian food and spice shop, the owner tells us his family runs a restaurant upstairs. We find the tiny stairway hidden in back and climb up, to find a few Indian men sitting around platters of what looks like *biryani*. That's today's lunch dish, we learn. The place doesn't look gleaming-clean at first glance, but two efficient women are working side by side in the kitchen—spotless when we take a closer look—and the customers are chatting with the cooks. Everyone here must be a regular. Soon we're served heaping plates of the warm rice, spiced with turmeric and cardamom and topped with pieces of roasted chicken on the bone, with a boiled egg and a cold yogurt-cucumber sauce on the side. I haven't had biryani this good in years. We linger over our plates—too much food, but we devour every last rice grain—and I marvel once again at the variety of people and communities this city manages to squeeze in. Incredibly, as relatively small as Beirut is, it never seems to run out of neighborhoods, alleyways, realities. Anyone eager to poke around will always find new places to stumble into.

I may be crazy enough to walk across the city on the most sweltering summer days, but when it comes to driving, I've been much less intrepid. It's bugging me that I keep making excuses about driving in Lebanon. Everyone I've talked to about driving here has advised me against it, saying gas is so expensive now, and I would be unnecessarily risking my life on these insane roads, and why drive when Beirut is crawling with service taxis and buses ready to take me anywhere for nearly nothing? So what—I still want to get over my fear.

And so one morning I force myself to try. My cousin Nada is in town from Paris for a few days, and we meet for coffee, then decide to spend the day doing a mini road trip so we can catch up more—and she's fearless enough to come along with me on a little driving experiment. We rent a car from an agency in Hamra and, since we'd both recently read about an odd-sounding place called the Mleeta Resistance Museum—a museum down south displaying war weapons and run by Hezbollah—we decide to try to find it. I'm mainly intrigued by the thought of a militia like Hezbollah running what's been described as a quiet, meticulously landscaped outdoor museum full of . . . well, weapons. The idea is infuriating to some, inspiring to others, and fascinating to me, for the novelty-show surrealness of it. So off we go.

Nada had been living in Lebanon until a few years ago, and drove all over the place here, so she takes the wheel of our rental car first and drives us out of Beirut, since I'm not quite ready to take that on cold turkey yet. I eventually take over from her in Sidon, and to my surprise, it takes all of sixty seconds before I feel normal driving on these roads. It's not the big deal I thought it would be. As everyone had already told me, you just have to be extra decisive, never go into autopilot, and always pay 100 percent attention to every vehicle and pedestrian and pet and obstacle and who knows what coming at you from all sides and directions, and remember that traffic lights and lanes don't necessarily count for much.

As Nada tells me about her university teaching job and her new boyfriend in Paris, and I catch her up on my life in Beirut so far, we get distracted by our own chatter and the hip-hop we're blasting on the car stereo. We keep missing turns from the directions we'd printed out, and as usual the roads have very few signs; the ones that do exist are often hidden behind billboards or trees. We end up having to stop and ask directions at a half dozen gas stations and grocery stores along the mountainous streets south of Sidon, until we eventually get on the right track and start winding up and up the hill that, at the very top, takes us into the driveway of the Mleeta museum. The mountains and valleys in the near distance lead to the Israeli border a few kilometers away. It's a ferociously hot day, and without hats the sun feels too close, on fire. After we park the car, we follow the pathways that lead through a forested, hilly area where tanks and Kalashnikovs and all manner of weapons are strewn around, each marked with the model number and the war it was used in. The other visitors on this day are a few European-looking tourists and a handful of families with kids. At one end of the park, a speaker built into the lawn pipes out the voice of Hezbollah leader Hassan Nasrallah making a speech about the necessity of resistance. It feels eerie being way up on this hill, in this remote part of Lebanon, surrounded by so much weaponry and, oddly, so many perfectly manicured flower beds and lawns and well-placed garbage receptacles.

"This might be the cleanest public park in Lebanon," Nada jokes as we head for the car, its leather seats baking in the sun. After the arduous drive here, we don't stay long; it's burning-hot outside and we're ready to hit the road again. I drive us all the way back, this time staying at the wheel through the Beirut streets, which at sundown today are less trafficky than they were hours earlier. After just a day, I feel used to the rhythm of driving here, merging and passing and hanging back when I need to, traffic lights or stop signs only occasionally popping up. I'm glad I don't have to do this daily but forcing myself to get comfortable with driving feels like a major hurdle cleared. Another way of feeling legit here in Lebanon, more fully at home.

Do I, then, feel truly at home here now? I haven't stopped asking myself this question since I arrived last summer. In the beginning the answer was mostly no. I felt, for those initial months, that I'd been gone for too many years, and that I couldn't just plop myself back down in Beirut and expect to slide right back into life here. I was also more self-conscious back then about my slightly American accent when I speak Arabic. In my walks around the city in those early months, and on the first few social nights out, I was still sensing myself an outsider, disconnected, just peering in but wishing I fit more comfortably into the scene around me. That feeling stung, especially since that's how I'd felt for so long in the States and still feel at times.

I was hoping that by moving to Beirut I'd feel an instant *ah, I'm home* and that those outsider twinges would just vanish. Still, I suspected it might not be so easy, and it wasn't.

But as I gradually started spending time with old friends, new friends, and cousins I could relate to, pieces of myself that I hadn't consciously realized I'd lost started coming back. My sense of outsiderness in the States had become vague over the years, persistent but mostly visceral in ways I couldn't always define. Here in Beirut, connecting with people who could reminisce about a similar childhood, and who had the same familiar reference points—for instance, how the city used to look, and places we remembered, and similar family dynamics and traditions, and even just memories of how we'd secretly gorge together on Choco Prince cookies or sip from those funny-looking triangular containers of Bonjus as kids—brought me closer to an elusive "belonging" than I've felt for as far back as I can remember.

Many of these people had felt the same kind of loss and experienced the shock of feeling suddenly foreign after they'd fled overseas during the war. They have the same scars, even if they don't often talk about them. Some of them could tell me about how their lives here felt during the war years, after my family left. Those memories, and sometimes even the trivial-sounding details, each added a piece to the puzzle, a more tangible answer to what I'd been missing all these years.

Many Lebanese people I've met in the States have had similar experiences, but reconnecting with parts of my Beirut past, on Lebanese soil this time, has felt different and more crucial.

Strangely, it's also had a demystifying effect: Painful memories don't seem to nag as hard anymore when they're so widely shared, and the more time I've spent this year around people who have a familiar background and have struggled internally in ways I recognize, the more those parts of my past seem commonplace, old news. It's a relief to feel this way.

Still, the sense of connectedness and belonging that I once took for granted, and that I lost when we fled Lebanon, may never fully come back, and I realize that more now. I'm not sure I'm prepared to call belonging "overrated," as Edward Said did—in his memoir of a life spent moving around and feeling out of place everywhere—but I may be more willing to let it go.

Moving back to Beirut has helped me shake the past in other ways, too. This year, by living and doing my work and building a social life here, and exploring much more of the country than I ever did before, I've felt more thrust into the Lebanon of right now, today—less so the Lebanon of years long gone. These adventures around the city and country have made me feel, as the months went by, that this little piece of the planet is mine.

But I also suspect I wouldn't be feeling quite as at home here now if this weren't such an ever-changing, dynamic place, with endless discoveries and adventures to be had—even if it's overwhelming in its own ways, too. Beirut, like New York, strikes plenty—most?—people as a "great place to visit but I wouldn't want to live there." Fair enough. But it turns out that I do like living in Beirut, and partly for the reasons that drive casual visitors nuts: the noise, the density, the unwieldiness. It's exhausting in heavy doses, to be sure, but still ultimately a sign, for me anyway, of life.

That said, the downsides of life in Lebanon are not trivial. Life here can be a constant grind. The government seems in no hurry to meet the basic needs of civilians, for instance by fixing the electricity and other infrastructural problems, instead of just making windy pronouncements about plans to repair them. The constant blackouts and water-supply problems, and the unreliable Internet, bring daily headaches.

The bigger picture gets depressing, too—the fact that the political situation never seems to fully stabilize, and there's always a looming threat of strife, if not all-out war. Some people are braver about it than others; I'm not one of the most blasé, in case that's not obvious by now. The ever-present possibility of violence here keeps reminding me of when I lived in Berkeley and realized I wasn't quite cut out for heavy-earthquake zones, as many Californians seem to be. I wonder if the fault lines of Lebanon's sectarian political system, and all the bigotry they reinforce, will ever fade away. Maybe things will very slowly, glacially, start to change soon, now that there have been more vocal movements for reform.

One July afternoon on a walk through downtown, I notice a roped-off area near the parliament building and the statue of Riad el Solh, the first prime minister of Lebanon after independence. A poster for the antisectarian movement, hanging near the statue, marks off the empty space near the Solh monument as "Midan al-Taghyir," meaning Change Square. In Arabic, the name rhymes with Midan al-Tahrir, the now-famous Liberty Square in Cairo. There's no one at Midan al-Taghyir when I walk by except two young guys sitting on a blanket next to the poster—in their solitude looking like caricatures of just how far Lebanon still is from bringing down the sectarian system. Could this change happen in our lifetimes? I want to be optimistic, but . . .

More than ever, I love Lebanon, dearly. And it breaks my heart. It's going to hurt to leave Beirut, but now I think I'm ready.

I've decided to move back to New York, at least for the time being. I'm also going to make frequent visits to Beirut, to keep my life here going as best I can, because who knows where I'll end up living in the future?

For now I'm going to try, once again, to love Lebanon from afar. A long-distance relationship. I've learned it can work—for two people anyway—against the odds. Maybe it will work for Beirut and me—and keep us close, somehow, through the seasons and the years.

EPILOGUE

It's early August and I'm back in New York. Crossing the tangled Flatbush and Atlantic intersection in downtown Brooklyn to get to the subway station, I could be in Hamra, navigating my way through the nonstop rivers of cars. For a second I'm confused about which city I'm in. The sensation lasts just for a moment, but long enough for me to notice: I like this feeling. New York. Beirut. Mad, maddening, magnificent cities. This is home. These are home. My homes, plural.

I have another home now, too: Richard's apartment, which I've just moved into in Brooklyn. We're four roommates in this giant loft: Richard, plus his friends Dan and Brien, plus me. I'm hoping this arrangement will feel like home for now. Neither Richard nor I, at this advanced point in our thirties, has ever lived with a boyfriend or girlfriend before. It's about time. And it's a little scary. But all the late-night e-mails of the past year, all the anxiety about whether we'll make it through my Beirut year, whether we're even supposed to make it, have been worth it so far. Shopping with him at the crowded, neon-lit Target store in Brooklyn for shelving units to hold all my stuff feels oddly romantic.

Living in this apartment with Richard and our roommates keeps reminding me of Beirut, of my building where relatives live upstairs and nearby, and always did when I was growing up. This past year was like this, too, with Shireen living down the block and various family members living in the building or just minutes away. In July, my aunt Maya came from North Carolina for her annual Beirut visit and stayed in her seventh-floor apartment with her longtime housekeeper Hanneh, who used to make the best French fries in the world when we all lived in Lebanon during the war. There's always someone around the building to chat with, someone to help lift the mood. I would've flinched at the thought of sharing a New York apartment with three other people at this point in my life. I like my privacy, and I'm also not the chit-chattiest person in the world. But this setup has felt easy, and also familiar deep down. It's going to be temporary—Richard and I are planning to move out into our own place soon—but so far it's made for a soft landing.

I understand now that it took going back to Beirut, finding my place there again, to feel more at peace in New York. Is it like those people who, when they meet The One, have to bust loose and sow their oats for a while to make sure they're ready to go full speed ahead into their future, with the person they sense deep down is right for them? The analogy isn't perfect. Cities aren't people, except in some ways. When it comes to cities, I realize now that I can't commit to New York or to Beirut fully. I need to keep a life going in both places somehow, even if most of my day-to-day life is in New York. They're both home, and I can't give up either.

My mother said to me on the phone the other day that she doesn't know of any people who talk as endlessly about their country as the Lebanese do: Lebanon this, Lebanon that. Oh, that beautiful country of ours, so warmly welcoming, such a rich culture, a close-knit family life, wonderful food, cosmopolitan people—don't get us started. Lebanese living abroad never seem to let go of Lebanon, don't shed their past quite as smoothly as some other immigrants do. So they keep going back to visit, once a year, every other year, twice a year. Often. And every time they go, what happens? Right—they can't wait to leave.

This doesn't apply to everyone, of course. I did get through a year in Beirut and could've stayed longer. Others I know have done the same, even moved back to Lebanon full-time after living in the States or elsewhere for years. But no doubt it can be an exhausting place—physically, emotionally.

Still, the tug is always there. In both directions.

Navigating my year in Beirut, easing my way from anxious to at-home in a challenging, feisty city, has put my New York life in perspective, too. In New York now, I'm less bothered by certain tiresome interactions, or annoyances like a subway-service disruption, or an Internet outage for an hour or two. Things are always worse somewhere else (in Beirut, for instance) and I can always escape to a happy place (well, Beirut again) even if just in daydreams or memories. Escaping the present moment, putting it in context, remembering that this minute and this square inch of space don't have to mean the world, helps, even if it's just a fleeting thought. It keeps me afloat in difficult places, tough times. And those will always come along, anywhere.

I remembered that over coffee one afternoon in Beirut last fall, my mom's cousin Afaf told me about her decision to return to Lebanon, after having moved to Washington, D.C., in her thirties, and spent three decades there. She still spends summers in D.C. teaching university art classes, as she does during the academic year in Beirut. She'd said to me, "The *tabkha*, the home-cooked dish, of life in Beirut plus life in the States is a good one—both places mixed in, a little of each."

I'm also remembering how in my first couple of months in Beirut last summer and fall, I felt very much like the new kid, the stranger, the foreigner in social settings even though I'm Lebanese. When you feel that way, it's hard to come across as intelligent, confident, in-the-know, the way you might on more familiar turf. Whatever confidence I thought I had gained in my New York life felt shaky in those early weeks, and I sensed all my shyness and self-consciousness bubbling back up, felt myself speeding back almost to square one. That feeling of being on unsure ground, having to find my footing all over again.

My New York friend Dave told me recently that he feels sorry for his co-worker's Italian husband, who was a tough and respected journalist back in Italy but, at social gatherings in New York, just seems "happy and simple." Dave doesn't speak Italian and can't interact with him on the same linguistic turf; nor can many New Yorkers the guy meets. The Italian stumbles along in broken English at parties his wife drags him to, in an environment he isn't yet used to. Instead of seeing the guy as the sharp, jaded journalist his friends and colleagues back home know him to be, Dave experiences him as a foreigner who doesn't speak English well, always seems out of his element, and is trying to project a positive attitude around his wife's New York friends, hence the "happy and simple" impression. At least Dave is self-aware enough to realize he's seeing the Italian in this surely deceptive way. But it's still hard for him to access the confident adult, the seasoned journalist behind the smiley, linguistically shut-out husband.

Switching from one setting to another, it takes a while to realign your insides with your outside, and sometimes it doesn't happen, or not for too long, and then it's time to leave. I was lucky that eventually it did happen for me in Beirut again—I had a hunch it might if I stuck it out—all these years after I'd had to adjust from my Beirut self to my new reality in the States.

I knew all along that I still loved Beirut. I just didn't know if I could live with it again.

Is it too simple to say home is love? Not necessarily romantic love. It could be love of a house or street or neighborhood, or self-love, or another kind—just a deep feeling of contentment and ease. For me, for years, New York has been the place where I've felt that the most, even when part of me always yearned for Beirut. Over the years, the Beirut of my imagination has been its own kind of home. But I learned that the real Beirut could be home, too: not just because it used to be home long ago, but because my feelings for it haven't died, and because Beirut, in all its craziness, is the type of city I like. I sense myself there, the way I felt when I first visited New York and still feel. New York and Beirut are, as I've discovered and rediscovered, my kind of cities: densely packed, mixed-up, crammed with nooks and crannies and, truth be told, some amount of chaos and unpredictability.

I guess home is where you are—not just physically. It's where you feel most yourself. I think to be really at home means having a relationship with that place, a relationship that isn't necessarily dependent on who else happens to be living there. But romantic love can make a place seem like home, at least for a time. Even more, friends can. Or one person, a handful of people, can start to build the foundations of home, if they welcome you in and help you ground yourself: the friendly and easygoing neighbor, the warm and smiling grocer, the funny and tough-love teacher.

I remember an unpleasant interaction with a snotty store clerk in Beirut one day not long after I'd arrived last summer, her frosty tone sending me into a low mood and sharpening my sense of awkwardness and alienation. I jotted this note to myself later:

In the world there are people who will ease your way and others who won't. And you'll ease the way for some and not for others. You'll eventually forget about the ones who froze you out, and they'll forget you. The world is for you and for the ones who roll out the carpet, even if it's tattered. They're scattered all over. And if you look carefully, they can help you find your way home, wherever you are.

That sounds too much like a self-help pep talk. Hide it from anyone peering over your shoulder. But I admit I've gone back to read this note: in Beirut, in New York, in other places, whenever I've needed to. Always secretly, as I've wound my way through the city, alone or uncertain. And on my way home.

Recipes

ZINGOL
TANGY CHICKPEA AND BULGUR SOUP

Zingol is one of those dishes you're unlikely to encounter in Lebanese restaurants or even in most homes; it turns up now and then in certain villages, and I still daydream about the fragrant, soul-warming bowl I tasted in the town of Hammana (actually it was two bowls, since the woman who cooked it insisted, in typical Lebanese fashion, that I have another). The presentation is especially appealing—the small chickpeas and bulgur spheres floating together in a lemony broth—although as with kibbeh balls, I had to practice rolling the bulgur mix into uniform, tight little marbles. But even if some balls fall apart into the broth, nothing is lost.

    1 cup whole wheat flour
    1 cup coarse bulgur
    2 small onions, minced and divided
    1 teaspoon dried marjoram
    1 teaspoon dried mint

(CONTINUES)

1 teaspoon salt, or more to taste
2 tablespoons olive oil
4 or 5 cloves garlic, finely chopped
1 cup boiled chickpeas (canned is fine; rinsed and drained)
juice of one lemon, plus 2 quartered lemons for serving
½ teaspoon sumac, or more to taste

1. Combine flour, bulgur, 1 minced onion, marjoram, mint, 1 teaspoon salt, and ½ cup water in a mixing bowl until well blended. Using palms, form mixture into small balls the size of grapes.
2. In a saucepan, heat the olive oil over medium heat and sauté the remaining onion until soft and translucent, then add the garlic. After 1 minute, add the chickpeas, then the bulgur balls. Add water to cover, and let boil until broth thickens. If some of the balls dissolve, that's fine; it will give the soup a more porridge-like texture. Stir in lemon juice, season with additional salt to taste, and sprinkle with sumac. Serve with lemon quarters on the side.

Serves 4

HRISSEH
CINNAMONY LAMB SOUP

❂

Hrisseh is often served for the Feast of the Assumption on August 15, commemorating the day when, according to the Eastern Orthodox church, the Virgin Mary ascended to heaven. It would be a shame if this lusciously meaty, rich soup were saved for just one annual holiday, and luckily some of my relatives like to indulge in it year-round. The exquisitely talented, dearly departed Fahimeh, who cooked for my mother's cousin Sami and his wife, Najwa, discovered I love hrisseh dearly, and so I'd be invited over when she made it. Prepare this on a day when you have lots of work to do at home, since the soup needs to simmer for several hours until the lamb falls apart into tender shreds.

6½ pounds cubed lamb meat from shoulder, plus 5 to 10
    pieces of chopped lamb bone (3 or 4 inches long each)
1½ cups barley, cleaned and rinsed
5 sticks cinnamon
1 tablespoon olive oil
3 cloves garlic, finely chopped
salt and pepper to taste
plain yogurt for serving

1. Place meat in a large pot with 5 quarts of water, and add as many bones as you can fit. Turn heat to medium-high, and when the water boils, skim greasy residue off the top, pour water out, and rinse meat and bones in cold water in a colander.
2. Set meat aside (preferably in the fridge), and put bones back in pot. Add 6 quarts water, and add additional bones if you have space. Bring to a boil, skim surface again, keep on medium heat for another 15 to 20 minutes, then add the barley and cinnamon sticks.
3. Raise the heat to high and boil for 15 minutes, then reduce heat to medium, and stir occasionally for another 15 minutes or so, until barley is puffy and soft.

(CONTINUES)

4. Meanwhile, heat olive oil on medium heat and sauté garlic for
   1 minute, being careful not to burn. Take pan off heat and set
   aside, leaving the olive oil in the pan with the garlic.

5. Add lamb meat back to the pot, along with the garlic and its
   oil, and raise heat until boiling; let boil for around 3 minutes.
   Then turn heat to low and simmer until the lamb meat falls
   apart into shreds and the barley has virtually disintegrated,
   creating a texture resembling a porridge; this will take approximately four hours. Add salt and pepper to taste and stir,
   leaving on low heat for another 10 minutes or so.

6. Take out bones, and ladle the remaining soup into bowls.
   Serve hot, and top each serving with a dollop of yogurt if
   you like.

Serves 6

FATTOUSH
TART TOMATO, MINT, AND BREAD SALAD

❂

*As much as I like tabbouleh, to me fattoush has more zing—plus it's
less time-consuming to make and more adaptable. Here's one version
of fattoush you'll encounter all over Lebanon, but in any home or restaurant you'll notice slight variations, depending on the season or the
cook's palate. You can either deep-fry or toast the pita croutons that
give the salad its special character; the fried bread will taste better, but
toasted is, obviously, healthier. When tomatoes are out of season, I like
to substitute cherry or grape tomatoes since they're likely to be juicier*

and more flavorful. If you can find purslane, use it (a cup or two, chopped); it adds authenticity and a nice peppery bite.

3 small pita breads
½ cup vegetable oil for frying (optional)
2 tomatoes, diced (or 1 pint cherry tomatoes, halved)
1 large or two small cucumbers, diced
1 cup scallions, chopped
1 cup green bell pepper, diced
3 radishes, thinly sliced in semicircles
1 romaine lettuce head, torn into small pieces
¾ cup parsley, chopped
1½ cups olive oil
1 cup freshly squeezed lemon juice
6 cloves garlic, crushed
½ cup sumac
1 cup fresh mint, chopped
salt and pepper to taste

1. Tear the bread into pieces (roughly 1-inch-square). Heat the vegetable oil over medium heat, and fry the bread bits until nicely browned and crisp, then set aside to drain on a plate lined with paper towels; or you can toast the pita instead of frying.
2. Combine vegetables, lettuce, parsley, and bread pieces in a large bowl, and toss well.
3. Whisk olive oil and lemon juice, and mix in garlic, sumac, mint, and salt and pepper to taste.
4. Pour dressing over salad and toss thoroughly.

Serves 4 to 6

BABA GHANOUSH
SMOKY EGGPLANT DIP

❈

Once you get the hang of baba ghanoush—we call it batanjan mtabbal in Lebanon, meaning "dressed eggplant"—it's one of the easiest dishes to make. Smoky, creamy, and fiercely addictive, it's handy to have in the fridge for snacking anytime, and guaranteed to vanish at parties. The key is to roast or grill the eggplants enough so they turn extremely soft on the inside; then you can just mash them with a fork. If after you cook the eggplants, you find that the insides are still a bit too stringy to mash properly, use a blender to finish pureeing them. Also, depending on your oven, you may need a higher temperature (500°F), or may need to cook them longer. Cooking them on the grill or stovetop burner instead of in the oven lends a smoky flavor I find crucial to a great baba ghanoush, but some prefer the less-messy oven method.

4 large eggplants
3 cloves garlic, peeled
½ teaspoon salt
4–5 tablespoons freshly squeezed lemon juice
4 tablespoons tahini (sesame paste)
olive oil and pita bread for serving
1 sprig Italian parsley for garnish

1. Pierce each eggplant a few times evenly all over using a fork. Do not peel the eggplants or cut off their stems. Then you can either roast the eggplants in an oven preheated to 450°F, for about 50 minutes, or grill them over high heat or on the flames of your stove burner for about 15 minutes. Turn the

eggplants over two or three times as they cook. They're ready when they're blackened and shrunken all over.

2. Set the eggplants aside for a minute or two, then peel off the charred skin with your fingers while they're still hot. Place the eggplants in a colander to drain. Meanwhile, using a mortar and pestle, crush the garlic cloves and mash the salt in to make a creamy paste. Sprinkle in a drizzle or two of the lemon juice, and keep mashing for a few minutes until you get a creamy texture. Then add 2 tablespoons of lemon juice, and stir, followed by 2 tablespoons of tahini, and stir again, then repeat with the remaining lemon juice and tahini.

3. Chop off the eggplant stems, discard, and mash the eggplants in a bowl until they form a creamy puree. (Finish with a blender if needed.)

4. Stir the tahini mixture in with the mashed eggplant, and keep mixing until the baba ghanoush is smooth throughout.

5. Place on a serving platter, drizzle with olive oil, garnish with chopped parsley, and serve at room temperature or chilled. Eat with pita bread.

Serves 4

HUMMUS
LEMONY CHICKPEA PUREE

✵

The proportions of garlic, lemon juice, and tahini vary in each hummus recipe. Some people will argue that certain versions are more authentic

(CONTINUES)

than others—a pointless battle if you ask me. Ultimately it's a matter of personal taste. In Lebanon I've had versions that are more lemony, more tahini-heavy, or more garlicky, and over the years I've figured out which I like best. I developed this recipe based on a hummus style I've loved most in certain homes and restaurants. It's extra lemony, and sometimes I use even more garlic; feel free to adjust it to your tastes.

> 1 cup boiled chickpeas (canned is fine; rinsed and drained)
> 3 garlic cloves, peeled and crushed, or more to taste
> juice of 1½ lemons
> 3 tablespoons tahini
> salt to taste
> pinch of paprika
> 1 tablespoon olive oil
> pita bread, for serving

1. Set aside a few whole chickpeas for garnish, then blend remaining chickpeas and garlic into a puree in a food processor.
2. Place puree in a bowl and gradually mix in lemon juice and tahini, adding 2 to 3 tablespoons of water to thin out the mixture if needed. Season with salt to taste.
3. To serve, put the hummus in a serving bowl, sprinkle paprika around the perimeter, place the whole chickpeas in the center, and drizzle olive oil between the chickpeas and paprika. Serve with pita bread.

Serves 4

Eggplant Fatteh

Baked Eggplant with Garlicky Yogurt

✺

Eggplants, chickpeas, yogurt, garlic, bread, and pine nuts. Six of my favorite ingredients, all starring in one easy-to-make, memorable dish. Lebanese and Syrian cuisines include lots of variations on this fatteh recipe—for instance, substituting chicken, spinach, or chickpeas (see the tiss'ye recipe below) as the main ingredient instead of eggplant. This eggplant version is especially robust tasting and filling, and a crowd-pleaser.

2 medium eggplants
3 teaspoons salt, divided
olive oil for drizzling
3 cups boiled chickpeas (canned is fine; rinsed and drained)
2 cloves garlic
2 teaspoons freshly squeezed lemon juice
3 cups plain yogurt
1 tablespoon tahini
2 small pita breads
½ cup vegetable oil for frying (optional)
2 tablespoons butter
½ cup pine nuts
pinch of paprika (optional)

1. Slice eggplant into ½-inch-thick rounds. Sprinkle with 2 teaspoons salt and set aside for 30 minutes. Rinse eggplant rounds and pat dry. Drizzle olive oil on a baking sheet and arrange eggplant rounds flat.

(CONTINUES)

2. Bake eggplant rounds at 425°F for 15 minutes, or until the tops are nicely browned. Turn over and bake until opposite sides brown.

3. Heat chickpeas in water (to cover) over medium heat, then lower heat to a simmer.

4. In a mortar and pestle, mash garlic with 1 teaspoon salt, and gradually drizzle in lemon juice until you have a creamy paste. Stir mixture into the yogurt, mix in the tahini, and stir well. Set aside.

5. Tear the pita bread into pieces (roughly 1-inch-square). Heat the vegetable oil over medium heat, and fry the bread pieces until nicely browned and crisp, then set aside to drain on a plate lined with paper towels; alternatively you can toast the pita halves instead of frying them, then break them into pieces.

6. A few minutes before you're ready to serve the dish, melt butter over medium heat, and sauté pine nuts until browned, being careful not to blacken.

7. In a deep-sided serving dish, set down one layer of eggplant rounds, alternating with the chickpeas and the pita bits. Continue layering until ingredients run out, then top with the yogurt mixture, followed with the pine nuts in their butter. Sprinkle with paprika (optional). This dish looks particularly appealing when assembled in individual portions for guests, layering the ingredients as above, but in small terracotta bowls instead of one large bowl.

Serves 2 as a main course; 4 as a side dish

TISS'YE
SPICED CHICKPEAS WITH YOGURT AND CRUNCHY PITA

❋

I love tiss'ye for many of the same reasons I'm fond of eggplant fatteh (above): It packs a variety of textures and bold flavors into one simple, comfort-food dish—which also happens to look elegant when served at dinner parties. My mother's friend Bushra often makes tiss'ye without frying or toasting the bread, preferring to let the soft pieces of pita absorb the sauces more fully. I like that version, too, but am partial to the crunch that comes from frying or toasting the pita. I've had this preparation more often at Beirut homes and restaurants, but experiment with both versions and see which you like more.

3 ½ cups boiled chickpeas (canned is fine; rinsed and drained)
2 cloves garlic
1 teaspoon salt, plus more to taste
2 teaspoons freshly squeezed lemon juice
3 cups plain yogurt
1 tablespoon tahini
2 small pita breads
½ cup vegetable oil for frying (optional)
1 teaspoon cumin
2 tablespoons butter
½ cup pine nuts
pinch of paprika

1. In a cooking pot, heat the chickpeas in water (to cover) over medium heat, then lower heat to a simmer.

(CONTINUES)

2. Meanwhile, mash garlic with 1 teaspoon salt in a mortar and pestle, then gradually drizzle in the lemon juice and keep mashing until you have a creamy paste. Stir mixture into yogurt, mix in the tahini, and set aside.

3. Tear the pita into roughly 1-inch pieces. Heat the vegetable oil over medium heat, and fry the bread pieces until browned and crisp, then set aside to drain on a plate lined with paper towels. Alternatively, toast the pita halves instead of frying, then break the bread into pieces.

4. Drain chickpeas, place them in a bowl, and sprinkle with cumin and salt to taste.

5. A few minutes before you're ready to serve the dish, heat butter over medium heat and sauté pine nuts until browned, being careful not to blacken them.

6. In a deep-sided serving dish, place one layer of the bread pieces, followed by a layer of the chickpeas, and alternate layers until you run out of ingredients (depending on the size of your dish, you may only have one layer of each). Ladle the yogurt over the top. Sprinkle the pine nuts in their butter over top, and add a pinch of paprika for color (optional). Serve immediately, while bread is crisp.

Serves 2 or 3 as a main course, or 6 as a side dish

HARRAK OSB'OO

LENTILS WITH POMEGRANATE MOLASSES AND CILANTRO

✦

I first tried harrak osb'oo at my mother's friend Bushra's house; the name of the dish means "burnt his fingers," but I haven't quite gotten to the bottom of why that is. I love the play of textures and of earthy, tangy, and sweet flavors. They sneak up on you in this deceptively humble-looking lentil dish. I've rarely encountered harrak osb'oo outside Beirut homes, except at Ashghalouna, a Muslim charity that helps widowed women and serves a legendary Friday lunch that attracts Lebanese society ladies and sells out well ahead. When I make this dish at home, I never quite come close to Bushra's rendition, but this recipe is adapted from hers—she uses tamarind paste instead of pomegranate molasses—and has become a favorite meatless main course or side dish.

> juice of 3 lemons .
> 1 teaspoon cumin
> 1 tablespoon pomegranate molasses (alternatively, you
>   can use 50g tamarind paste, sold in 500g squares at
>   some Middle Eastern or Asian markets)
> 1¼ cups all-purpose flour
> 1¼ teaspoons baking soda
> ½ teaspoon salt, plus more to taste
> ½ tablespoon vegetable oil, plus more for cooking
> 1 cup brown lentils
> 3 medium onions, slivered
> 4 cloves garlic, crushed
> 1 bunch cilantro, chopped

1. Mix lemon juice, cumin, and pomegranate molasses in a small bowl, and set aside. (If using tamarind paste instead, soak it in a bowl for at least 2 hours first; you'll use it in the last step of the recipe.)

(CONTINUES)

2. Make the dough strips: Mix flour with baking soda and ½ teaspoon salt, then stir in ½ cup water and ½ tablespoon vegetable oil. Blend until you reach a doughy consistency, then knead for 3 or 4 minutes, sprinkling with flour or water if needed as you go. Roll dough out into a thin sheet, and slice into strips the width of fettuccini strands, then cut into 1-inch-long pieces. If you like, you can sprinkle your palms with flour and roll each 1-inch piece between your palms for 2 or 3 seconds to form a cylindrical shape. (As a shortcut to making your own dough strips, use fettuccini instead: boil 6 ounces fettuccini according to package directions, and cut into 1-inch-long strips.) Set aside.

3. Pick stray bits out of the lentils, then rinse and drain them. Boil lentils in a pot with 7 cups water, then cook over medium heat for another 30 minutes, until they soften.

4. As the lentils are cooking, sauté the onions until browned. In a separate pan, sauté the garlic and cilantro.

5. Drop the dough strips (or fettuccini pieces) in with the lentils during the last 10 minutes of cooking, then lower heat to a simmer and stir in half of the browned onions and half of the garlic-cilantro mix. Let simmer for another 5 to 10 minutes.

6. When lentil mixture is done, remove from heat and stir in pomegranate molasses mixture. (If using tamarind instead, drain out the pulpy pieces that have been soaking, and stir the resulting tamarind juice in with the lentils.)

7. Place lentil mixture in a serving dish, and top with remaining onions and cilantro-garlic mix. Salt to taste.

Serves 4

Kibbeh 'Arass
Lamb Meatballs Stuffed with Pine Nuts and Onion

❉

Lebanese party hosts often buy kibbeh balls by the dozen from caterers or bakeries that turn out enviably smooth, uniform spheres; homemade versions often don't come out as perfect. Although it took me some time to hone my kibbeh-making technique—and I'm still practicing—I've been all too happy to eat the wobbly results along the way. Kibbeh is in some ways the quintessential comfort food, but it's also one of the proud national dishes, fit for feasts. You'll find it in many forms: as kibbeh 'arass, the meatballs here; or baked into large, round pies called kibbeh bil saynieh; or stewed in sauces in variations like kibbeh labniyeh (see below); or as kibbeh nayeh, a silky mound of raw lamb mixed with bulgur.

1½ cups bulgur, medium or fine grain

1½ pounds finely ground lean lamb (or beef), divided

2 medium onions, 1 coarsely chopped and 1 minced, divided

1½ teaspoons salt, divided

1½ teaspoons pepper, divided

2 teaspoons cinnamon, divided

2 teaspoons allspice, divided

6 tablespoons butter

⅓ cup pine nuts

2 tablespoons olive oil

vegetable oil for frying

(CONTINUES)

1. Soak bulgur for 30 minutes in cold water in a medium bowl. Drain, and get rid of excess water by squeezing bulgur through with a paper towel. In a bowl, combine bulgur with 1 pound meat, the coarsely chopped onion, 1 teaspoon salt, 1 teaspoon pepper, 1 teaspoon cinnamon, and 1 teaspoon allspice.

2. Place about a cup of the mixture in food processor and grind until the consistency is like dough; repeat with remaining mixture. Add one ice cube at a time while processing if needed to improve texture. Set mixture aside and cover. (If you'd like to use a mortar and pestle instead of a food processor, you'll need to grind for about an hour to reach the optimal texture.)

3. Melt butter in a large skillet, add pine nuts, and sauté until brown, being careful not to blacken. Remove from heat and set aside.

4. Sauté the minced onion in olive oil in a medium-size skillet. Add remaining ground meat, and season with remaining salt, pepper, cinnamon, and allspice. Once meat is lightly browned, take off the heat. Let cool for 15 minutes.

5. Set aside a small bowl of cold water, and a freezer-safe platter. Form the kibbeh balls by shaping golf-ball-size amounts of the meat and bulgur mixture, rolling it lightly in your hands. Then poke a hole in each ball with your fingers, stuff with the ·onion and pine nut mixture, and pinch to seal. You will need to dip your fingers in the water periodically so they don't get too sticky and hard to work with. Make sure the outsides of the kibbeh balls look as smooth as possible, with no visible onion or pine nut pieces sticking out. Mend any holes (with small amounts of the raw kibbeh), and slightly point the ends to form small football shapes. It will take a little practice to

get the kibbeh balls uniform and smoothly textured. Place the balls on the platter as you finish them.

6. Freeze the kibbeh balls for 10 minutes to firm up their shape, then fry them in vegetable oil in a pan or deep fryer—the oil should be at 350°F—for around 10 minutes or until golden brown. Drain on paper towels.

Makes 2 dozen

VARIATION

To make kibbeh labniyeh, or kibbeh balls in yogurt sauce, mix a whisked egg into a quart of yogurt and heat in a saucepan over medium-high heat, stirring constantly so the yogurt doesn't separate. Heat 2 tablespoons butter and sauté 4 cloves crushed garlic and a handful of chopped fresh cilantro or mint until wilted, and stir into the yogurt mixture. Place 8 to 10 kibbeh balls in the mixture, stir until the meatballs are heated through, and ladle into bowls. Makes enough for 2 servings.

SHISH TAOUK
SKEWERED CHICKEN KEBABS

❅

The smell of charbroiled chicken is one of the scents I've always as-sociated with Beirut, and these skewered kebabs, marinated in garlic, lemon, and sumac, are quintessentially Lebanese. Few main-course recipes are easier or yield more consistently thrilling results—just make

(CONTINUES)

sure to marinate the chicken long enough, so the flavors seal in before
you broil or grill the skewers. The juice-soaked pita and the garlic sauce
(toum) are key to a perfect shish taouk dinner, and if you happen to end
up with any leftover chicken kebabs (fat chance), wrap them up along
with the toum into a pita sandwich the next day.

3 tablespoons lemon juice
3 tablespoons olive oil
4 cloves garlic, finely chopped
¼ teaspoon pepper
⅛ teaspoon cayenne
2 pounds cubed chicken breast (skin and bones removed)
pita bread for serving

1. Whisk together all ingredients except chicken and bread in a medium bowl. Add chicken pieces, and marinate in the refrigerator, covered, for at least 3 hours (and up to 24 hours).
2. Preheat broiler or grill. Arrange chicken pieces on skewers, fitting about 6 pieces per skewer.
3. Broil or grill chicken, turning over a few times, for around 15 minutes or until cooked through and nicely browned all over. Remove skewers from heat and place over pita halves arranged on serving platter, allowing bread to absorb the juices. Serve with extra pita bread and toum (garlic sauce; recipe below), and encourage guests to pick up chicken with pieces of pita, and dip in the toum.

Serves 4

Toum
Garlic Sauce

❁

Toum is fiercely garlicky, and the Lebanese like it that way. This is my favorite method for making toum—easy and quick. If you find the sauce is coming on too strong, not to worry: dilute it with extra yogurt and olive oil.

8 cloves of garlic, crushed
¼ teaspoon salt
juice of ½ lemon
¼ cup olive oil
2 or 3 tablespoons Greek (or strained) yogurt

1. Pound the garlic with salt in a mortar and pestle, and gradually drizzle in lemon juice and olive oil, blending until you have a creamy paste. Alternatively, puree in a food processor.
2. Mix in yogurt. If you like, add more yogurt and olive oil to soften the garlic flavor. Keep in refrigerator until ready to use.

Serves 4

ATAYEF
SWEET DESSERT PANCAKES

❀

*These small stuffed pancakes come in various forms: filled with sug-
ared walnuts and deep-fried, or served soft and stuffed with walnuts
or a cream called ashta that's similar to English clotted cream. I prefer
the blini-like, non–deep-fried version, and I adore both fillings. Note:
Since ashta (made from the skin of long-simmered milk) is hard to find
outside the Middle East and rarely made at home even there, Lebanese home cooks often substitute a "fake" version. Below is a common
method for mimicking ashta that has been a hit when I've tried it, and
no one has been the wiser.*

¾ cup all-purpose flour
½ teaspoon active dry yeast
1¾ cup sugar, divided
1 cup finely chopped walnuts
2 tablespoons orange-blossom nectar, divided
4 pieces crustless white bread (optional)
2¾ cups half-and-half (optional)
½ teaspoon lemon juice
vegetable oil for frying
¼ cup candied rose petals or chopped pistachios (optional)

1. To prepare the pancake batter, combine flour and yeast in a
   mixing bowl. Gradually add ½ cup plus 2 tablespoons water
   and keep mixing, using a wooden spoon, until smooth and
   well blended. Cover bowl and set aside for one hour; batter
   should rise and the surface should show small bubbles.

2. Meanwhile, prepare the walnut stuffing, and the cream stuffing too if you'd like. For the walnut stuffing, mix ¼ cup sugar, chopped walnuts, and 1 tablespoon orange-blossom nectar. Combine well and set aside. For the cream stuffing, shred the white bread into bite-size pieces with your hands, and put them in a small saucepan. Add the half-and-half, stir with the bread pieces, and bring to a boil over medium heat, then lower heat and simmer for 10 to 15 minutes, stirring frequently, until you have a creamy consistency. Set aside to cool.

3. Make the ater (sugar syrup) by combining the remaining sugar with ½ cup plus 2 tablespoons water, along with the lemon juice, in a saucepan over medium heat. Boil, stirring occasionally. Keep on the heat, and after 3 minutes add the remaining orange-blossom nectar. Allow to boil for another several seconds. Set aside to cool.

4. Grease a skillet with vegetable oil and place over medium heat. When the oil is very hot, pour in a tablespoon of the pancake batter to create a thin circle of about 3 inches diameter. Use the back of your spoon to quickly coax the batter into a round shape, before it starts to cook on the bottom (which happens within seconds). Cook pancake for 1 to 2 minutes on one side only; bottom should be firm and lightly browned and the top dry and bubbly. Repeat until all batter is used up; set pancakes aside to cool for 15 minutes.

5. When cooled, top each pancake with 1 tablespoon of the walnut or cream filling; you can fill half the pancakes with one stuffing and the rest with the other, if you'd like to serve both

(CONTINUES)

varieties. Fold pancakes in half and pinch the bottom edges together, and leave the top open like a cone.

6. Arrange the filled pancakes on a platter, drizzle with the ater, and top with candied rose petals or chopped pistachios (optional). Serve at room temperature.

Serves 4

MOUFATTAKA
STICKY RICE AND PINE NUT CAKE

❂

Moufattaka is sold in certain Beirut pastry shops on urb'it Ayoub (Wednesday of Job), a now-obscure holiday in late April that commemorates the day when the prophet Job healed himself by jumping into the sea. The dessert is said to be appropriate for the holiday, since it takes the patience of Job to make it. That's a big exaggeration to my mind, because even though you do have to keep stirring the ingredients until they reach the desired texture, the process doesn't take all that long and is fairly simple. The result, a sticky-sweet rice pudding shaped into a cake, involves savory ingredients one rarely associates with dessert, namely turmeric and tahini. Unusual and beguiling, moufattaka is an ingenious little confection, and when I've had it at the occasional Beirut dinner party, its yellow color has made for a striking presentation.

1 cup rice, preferably long-grain
2 teaspoons turmeric
1 cup plus 2 tablespoons tahini

2 cups sugar

5 tablespoons pine nuts, divided

1. Boil the rice according to package directions. Set aside.
2. Stir the turmeric into 2 cups plus 2 tablespoons water, and bring to a boil.
3. As soon as the water-turmeric mixture starts to boil, add the cooked rice.
4. Reduce the heat to low and cook, uncovered, for approximately 10 minutes, stirring frequently. Take off heat and set aside. (Rice may still be a little wet, which is fine.)
5. In a bowl, mix tahini, sugar, and 4 tablespoons pine nuts. Stir well.
6. In a saucepan, combine the tahini mixture and the turmeric rice.
7. Stir frequently over medium heat for about 40 minutes. In the last 10 minutes, turn heat down to a simmer.
8. Remove from heat, and spread evenly on a round platter. Garnish with remaining pine nuts and leave to set in the refrigerator for a few hours or overnight. Serve at room temperature.

Serves 6

Acknowledgments

I'm deeply grateful to my extended family in Lebanon, the United States, England, and elsewhere. Listing them would take up an entire phone book, and I feel lucky to have such an enormous clan of generous, loving, cheerfully eccentric people who mostly get along well, certainly one for the record books. I owe eternal gratitude to Jamal, Mariana, and Samir Abdelnour, my beloved and endlessly supportive father, mother, and brother (respectively), and to the cousins, aunts, uncles, and their families (you know who you all are) who have made life in both Lebanon and the States sweeter. The same goes for my dear friends in New York, in Beirut, on the West Coast, and elsewhere, who have helped me get through this past year with a sense of humor and purpose. When I packed up and left my life in New York to move to Beirut, you all gently reassured me that I'd find everything pretty much the same when I came back to visit—yeah, right. Some of you had the nerve to have kids, change cities, find love, or make other big changes in your lives while I was away, and for that I'm grateful too. Your stubborn unpredictability—and your strength, loyalty, and love—are always an inspiration.

Speaking of the people in my life who made momentous changes while I was away: At the top of that list is my brother, Samir, who with his lovely wife, Laila, added the magical Marlena Josette Abdelnour to our family.

I owe deep gratitude to my agent, Jason Allen Ashlock, for having the vision to decide that my plan to move back to Beirut could turn into a book, even before I'd fully realized it myself. My editor at Broadway Books, Jenna Ciongoli, has been a pleasure to work with—enthusiastic and brilliantly incisive—and I thank her and the whole team at Broadway for their unwavering support during a difficult, madcap year.

For looking over early versions of my manuscript and giving invaluable comments, I owe huge thanks to my immediate family and to my friend and exquisitely insightful reader, Jennifer Paull.

For reading and commenting on the first draft of my manuscript, and not cringing (too much) at being in it, I thank Richard Gilman, who has given me more courage, calm, strength, and outrageous laughs than he knows.

About the Author

Salma Abdelnour is a writer and editor based in New York City. She has been the travel editor of *Food & Wine*, the food editor of *O, The Oprah Magazine*, and the restaurant editor of *Time Out New York*. Her writing has appeared in the *New York Times*, *Food & Wine*, *Travel + Leisure*, *Afar*, *ForbesLife*, and other publications, and has been anthologized in two volumes of *Best Food Writing*. She has taught writing courses for New York University's continuing-education department and for Gemini Ink, and has appeared in television segments about travel and food for CNN, CNBC, the Fine Living Network, and elsewhere. She divides her time, or aspires to, between Brooklyn and Beirut. Look for her online at Salmaland.com.